GOD'S BLUEPRINTS FOR CHURCH GROWTH

HOW TO GROW THE CHURCH, REGARDLESS OF ITS SIZE

JEREMY MYERS

GOD'S BLUEPRINTS FOR CHURCH GROWTH
How to Grow the Church, Regardless of Its Size
© 2020 by Jeremy Myers

Published by Redeeming Press
Dallas, OR 97338
RedeemingPress.com

ISBN: 978-1-939992-75-8 (Paperback)
ISBN: 978-1-939992-76-5 (Mobi)
ISBN: 978-1-939992-77-2 (ePub)

Learn more about Jeremy Myers by visiting RedeemingGod.com

Cover Design by Jeremy Myers
Cover Photo by Rachel French at Lightstock.com

All rights reserved. No part of this publication may be reproduced, stored in or introduced into a retrieval system, or transmitted, in any form, or by any means—electronic, mechanical, photocopying, recording, or otherwise—except for brief quotations, without the prior written permission of both the copyright owner and the publisher of this book.

Unless otherwise stated, all Scripture quotations are taken from the New King James Version˚. Copyright © 1982 by Thomas Nelson, Inc. Used by permission. All rights reserved.

JOIN JEREMY MYERS AND LEARN MORE
Take Bible and theology courses by joining Jeremy at
RedeemingGod.com/join/

Receive updates about free books, discounted books, and new books by joining Jeremy at
RedeemingGod.com/reader-group/

TAKE THE
SKELETON CHURCH
ONLINE COURSE

Join others at
RedeemingGod.com/join/
and take all my courses, including
"The Skeleton Church" online course:

**GET EBOOKS AND THEOLOGY COURSES AT
REDEEMINGGOD.COM/JOIN/**

Thanks for reading!

Books in the *Close Your Church for Good* Series
Preface: Skeleton Church
Vol. 1: The Death and Resurrection of the Church
Vol. 2: Put Service Back into the Church Service
Vol. 3: Church is More than Bodies, Bucks, & Bricks
Vol. 4: Dying to Religion and Empire
Vol. 5: Cruciform Pastoral Leadership
Get all six volumes in *Close Your Church for Good*

Books in the *Christian Questions* Series
What is Prayer?
What is Faith?
What are the Spiritual Gifts?
What is Hell?
How Can I Study the Bible? (Forthcoming)
Can I Be Forgiven? (Forthcoming)

Other Books by Jeremy Myers
Nothing but the Blood of Jesus
The Atonement of God
The Bible Mirror (Forthcoming)
The Re-Justification of God: A Study of Rom 9:10-24
Adventures in Fishing for Men
Christmas Redemption
Why You Have Not Committed the Unforgivable Sin
The Gospel According to Scripture (Forthcoming)
The Gospel Dictionary (Forthcoming)

Learn about each title at the end of this book

This book is dedicated to Dr. Earl Radmacher.

His books on the church were influential in my early thinking and development. He was also extremely encouraging to me when, as a young pastor, he visited my church for a conference and regularly disciple me through phone and email conversations.

It was also a thrill when he agreed to co-author this book with me, but, alas, it did not happen before he passed away on December 8, 2014. I look forward to discussing ecclesiology more with Dr. Radmacher in eternity, when we will finally know it all. Maybe.

AUTHOR'S NOTE

The first version of this book was written in the year 2000. (I guess that makes this the twenty-year anniversary edition!) It was the first book I ever wrote. I was straight out of Bible College and had just been hired as the pastor of a small church in Northwest Montana. I wrote this book as a personal manifesto on how I planned to lead the church. Since the town was rather small, I knew there was no chance of my church ever becoming a megachurch. But I didn't want that anyway. I wanted to love, serve, and minister in that church for the rest of my life. I wanted my "first church" to be my only church. And this book was my statement to myself of how I wanted to pastor and lead that church.

Sadly, it was not to be. The church had been struggling financially for quite some time, and had never had a pastor stay for more than three years. I stayed for three and a half years (a record!) before the church board said that they could not afford to pay my salary any longer. So I was faced with a choice. I could stay and pastor "for free" while getting a job in the local community, or I could resign and find another church which would hire me. I chose the second option. To this day, I wish I chosen the first option. I loved the town. I loved the people. I loved pastoring that small, rural church.

The reason I didn't stay, however, is because I didn't know then as much as I know now about the church. Back then, I thought that church buildings and professionally-paid pastors were *required* for the church to properly function. I thought that the church could not really exist if people didn't meet on Sunday mornings to sing songs and listen to a sermon. And since I believed it was my primary task as the pastor to diligently study the Scriptures so that I could provide these weekly sermons, I didn't think I could do this *and also* hold full-time job in the community.

I wish now that I had been able to read some of the books on the church I have published in the last 12 years. These books–the six volumes in the "Close Your Church for Good" series of books—go into great detail on what the church is, and how we can properly function as the church in our communities, even if we don't have a building or pay a pastor. In fact, I argue that Christians can *better* function as the church in our communities without such trappings. If I had read these books, I might have been able to stay in that community as their pastor.

This is not to say that I am no longer a pastor. I am. I will always be a pastor. In many ways, I am more of a pastor now than ever before. And I am so thankful for the patience of God in taking me down this path, and the truths He has taught me along the way. And while most of those truths are found in the six volumes of "Close Your Church for Good," this current volume now reflects some of those truths as well.

The first draft of this book twenty years ago was much different than it is now. In that span of time, much of my thinking about the church has changed. But thankfully, even though this present volume was the first book I ever wrote, it has never before been published. Remember, it was a *personal* manifesto on how I wanted to pastor. But I am putting it out now, so that others might benefit from it also. And best of all, I can now incorporate into this book some of the ideas I have learned over the past twenty years. I hope you find it encouraging and helpful whatever your role might be in the church.

I also hope that, although this is the first book I ever wrote, it is the last book I ever publish on the topic of the church. This is the seventh book I have written on the topic of the church, and I don't think I have much more to say. That could change, I suppose, but I have so many other topics and ideas I am itching to write about, they will likely hold my attention for the next twenty years (or more). Look for those books under my alternate pen name, J. D. Myers.

TABLE OF CONTENTS

Preface 17
    Where We are Headed 19
    My Hope for You 20

Part 1: Planning 21

1. Speaking to the Architect & Preparing the Site 23
    Defining "Church" 26
    Defining Growth 27
    It's Revolutionary 33
    It's Encouraging 34
    It's Applicable 35
    It's Liberating 37
    Discussion Questions 38

2. Building Resources 41
    The Riches of the Church (Ephesians 1–3) 44
    Every Spiritual Blessing 46

Praying for Riches 60

Conclusion 61

Discussion Questions 62

3. The Development Plan 65

The Responsibilities of the Church (Ephesians 4–6) 68

The Ultimate Goal (Eph 4:13; 5:27) 69

Step 1. Walk Worthy of Your Calling (Eph 4:1-16) 71

Step 2. Walk in Purity (Eph 4:17-32) 75

Step 3. Walk in Love (Eph 5:1-7) 78

Step 4. Walk in Light (Eph 5:8-14) 80

Step 5. Walk Carefully (Eph 5:14–6:9) 82

Conclusion 84

Discussion Questions 85

Part 2: Groundbreaking 87

4. Choosing a Contractor 89

1. Desire 91

2. Blameless 94

3. The Husband of One Wife 95

4. Temperate 97

5. Sober-Minded 99

6. Of Good Behavior 99

7. Hospitable 100

8. Able to Teach 101

    9. Not Given to Wine 102

    10. Not Violent 103

    11. Not Greedy 103

    12. Gentle 105

    13. Not Quarrelsome 105

    14. Not Covetous 106

    15. Rules His House Well 107

    16. Not a Novice 110

    17. A Good Testimony With Unbelievers 112

    Sub-Contractors 112

    Conclusion 114

    Discussion Questions 115

5. Pouring the Foundation 117

    The Foundation is Jesus Christ (1 Cor 3:11) 118

    Preach the Word! (2 Tim 3:15-4:4) 120

    Hear and Obey (Matt 7:24-27) 131

    Conclusion 136

    Discussion Questions 137

6. Following the Pattern 139

    Old Testament Patterns That Remain 142

    The Church's Form 145

    The Church's Function 149

    Conclusion 153

    Discussion Questions 154

Part 3: Constructing 157

7. The Foremen 159
    Apostles 161
    Prophets 167
    Evangelists 170
    Pastor-Teachers 173
    Conclusion 180
    Discussion Questions 181

8. The Crew 183
    The Task of the Foremen 187
    The Tasks of the Crew 189
    Discussion Questions 200

9. The Model 203
    Width: Unity 205
    Depth: Maturity 216
    Height: Christ-Likeness 218
    Conclusion 221
    Discussion Questions 222

10. The Program: Guarding Children 223
    No Longer Be Children 228

    Guarding Children 233

    Giving to Children 241

    Discussion Questions 246

11. The Program: Growing Adults 249

    What Church Growth Is 252

    How Church Growth Is Accomplished 254

    Personal Growth 266

    Church Growth 268

    The End is Love 271

    Discussion Questions 272

Part 4: Franchising 273

12. Grand Opening 275

    The Growth of the Early Church 276

    God Gives the Increase 282

    Discussion Questions 284

13. The Expansion of the Church 285

    Church Planting 285

    The Best Church Planter 289

    The Only Church Planter 293

    Expand the Church by Being the Church 294

    Conclusion 296

    Discussion Questions 297

Appendix: Spiritual Gifts 299

    What Are the Spiritual Gifts? 299

    How Can I Know My Spiritual Gifts? 311

    Spiritual Gifts Inventory 318

About the Author 359

PREFACE

When someone finds out I've written a book on church growth, the first question I nearly always receive is, "How big is your church?" Considering that nearly all of the books on church growth have been written by pastors of mega-churches, this is a valid question.

But the question comes from a mindset that has left thousands of pastors around the world feeling frustrated and inadequate because the church they pastor is not big enough or growing fast enough. I was once one of those pastors.

Yet despite what most pastors want for their church, statistics reveal that the majority of churches in North America have less than 200 in attendance, and the majority of people who attend church in North America go to one with less than 200 in attendance. This is something to be celebrated, for it has been frequently argued that smaller churches tend to be more effective than larger churches in changing the lives of the people who attend. Since this is true, why is it that a minority of the churches which minister to a minority of the people are held up as the ideal churches that everyone should copy?

The reason is because people have adopted the popular North American mindset that "bigger is better" and "numbers mean success." In our corporate economy, a business is not a good business unless it is growing year after year and has made more money this year than last. This same approach is applied to churches.

The mindset is that mega-churches must be doing things right because they have thousands in attendance and multi-million dollar budgets. Because they match the corporate model for success, they are held up as examples for other churches to follow.

Therefore, the impression is that if a church is small or shrinking in size, it must be a "bad" church. It must be doing something wrong. So these smaller churches try to conform to the mega-churches. The pastors read the mega-church books, attend the church growth seminars, and listen to the mega-pastor podcasts—all in the hopes of "growing" their church.

A friend of mine who is also a pastor read these books and attended these conferences and came away feeling he must not be cut out for the pastorate because he only has a church of 50 that used to be 200. Most people would look at that and think "failure." After reading these books and attending these seminars, he felt the same way and left pastoral ministry.

The truth, however, is that the decline in attendance at his church had nothing to do with him or the church. The church was in a dying community, which had three other churches as well. Even if the other three churches closed and every single person within a 15 mile radius attended his church, he would never be able to "grow" his church to more than 500 in attendance. In a community of 500 people, having 50 people on a Sunday morning is a smashing success! What mega-church can boast a 10% attendance rate of all people within a 15 mile radius?

But again, we've fallen into the trap of comparing numbers.

This is where the modern church growth movement has gone dismally wrong, and this is what *God's Blueprints for Church Growth* is all about. We will see that biblically, church growth has nothing to do with numbers. God measures church growth in a completely different way, and once we start measuring the church God's way, we no longer feel the pressure to keep up with the Johns. (No, that's not a typo. A while back I made a list of megachurch pastors that people tried to copy, and a large number of them were named "John." I have no idea why.)

When I first learned what I share in this book, it was incredibly liberating. I discovered that I could "grow" my church regardless of how many people attended, how big our budget, the population of our town, the size of our building, the numbers of our staff, or how many ministries we offered. Once I began to define "church growth" God's way, I came to realize that none of those traditional measures mattered anymore.

God made sure that when He created His church, every pastor and every local church could be a "success." The principles within this book have helped me understand this, and they can help you as well.

WHERE WE ARE HEADED

Chapters 1–3 of this book provide the Planning stages of church growth. In chapter 1, we discover who the Architect is, and what He thinks about the church and how to grow it. Chapter 2 reveals the resources available to build with. Chapter 3 talks about the development goal, and reminds us to build with the ultimate function in sight.

Chapters 4–6 are the Groundbreaking preparations. We learn

how to choose a contractor in chapter 4, find a foundation to build on in chapter 5, and then discover what the building should look like in chapter 6.

Chapters 7–11 are the actual Blueprints. There are five principles found primarily in Ephesians 4:11-16. These five principles will be explained in five chapters based on a detailed explanation of this passage. We will see that God has provided the Foremen (chapter 7), the Crew (chapter 8), a Model (chapter 9), and the Program (chapters 10 and 11).

The book closes with some Finishing touches in chapters 12–13. We will see the Grand Opening in chapter 12 and how to Franchise in chapter 13. This book is by no means comprehensive on what the Bible says about the church and its functions. It is nothing more than an introduction and a return to what the Bible says about church growth.

MY HOPE FOR YOU

My hope is that as you read this book, you will be liberated from the dominant approaches to "church growth." As you discover how God actually wants to grow the church, you will also discover your role within the church that Jesus is building and know how to define "success" as He defines it. You will be liberated from the church growth rat race and the pastoral ministry blues. After reading this book, I hope you will see that you can grow your church, regardless of its size.

PART 1: PLANNING

CHAPTER 1

SPEAKING TO THE ARCHITECT & PREPARING THE SITE

All pastors have a mega-church in their town that seems to always be in a perpetual building project. Such churches barely finish one expansion when they outgrow that one too and have to start another. When I was a pastor, there was such a church in our town. What made it worse for me, was that my brother was the architect for the frequent expansions of this church. While the small and struggling church I pastored tried to pay its electric bill, the big church down the road was paying my brother's firm thousands of dollars to draw up plans and construct miniature cardboard models. The cost of such plans were only a drop in the bucket of the actual cost of building the multi-million dollar addition.

My brother showed me the plans one day. They were impressive. Two hundred full size pages contained everything from capacity limits, weight loads, seating charts, roof plans, exterior and interior elevations, wall types, center line diagrams, code exiting plans, door and window schedules, and every detail necessary for constructing such a building.

After construction began, I visited him in his office one day and asked how the addition was going. "Fine," he said, "but let me show you something." He pulled out his copy of the blueprints, turned to one of the pages, and pointed to a couple of blue lines. "You see this wall here? I was down at the site today, and I noticed that this wall didn't look quite right, so I got out the blueprints and compared them with the wall. The blueprints show how thick the wall should be, what it should be made of—in this case it's a concrete wall—what texture the wall should have and so on." He showed me how the blueprints revealed all of this. Then he continued, "The wall they were building was not according to the blueprints. It was too thin, the design wasn't right, and the texture was wrong."

"Can they fix it?" I asked.

He looked at me with a small smile. "You bet they can. I told the contractor to knock it down and make a new one."

I was amazed that he had that much power. "Won't that slow things down and cost a lot of money?"

"Yes, it will, but that's the contractor's problem. If he had followed the blueprints as I had designed them, he wouldn't be in this mess. It's always frustrating when the contractor doesn't follow the architect's blueprints." He went on to explain why the wall needed to be the thickness it was and why it needed that certain design and texture, but I was still thinking about that last thing he had said. The frustration he was feeling is probably true of all professions. Doctors feel this way about the endless stream of patients that come through their doors because they didn't do "what the doctor ordered." Mechanics wonder how a person doesn't know to change their oil and check their fluids. Dentists are amazed at people's failure to regularly floss. Teachers wonder if the parents of their students even know what's going on in their children's lives.

But it got me wondering about the church God is building. I wonder if God ever gets frustrated at our failure to follow His blueprints? He gave us careful and detailed instructions about the design, operation, and growth of His church, but only after the church is in shambles do we consider reading the manual. Sometimes not even then. But if we do learn where we went wrong and try to fix it, the correction process is painful, slow, and costly. It involves some walls being knocked down. It causes a setback in our plans and schedule. But whether we correct a problem or start from scratch, if we want the church to be built, we need to follow the Architect's Plans as found within Scripture.

Most pastors agree that the truths of Scripture can be fully trusted. That is my conviction as well. I believe that if Scripture gives us principles for church growth (which it does), we should try to follow them. The scriptural principles about church will work in any country and at any time in history. Because they are God's universal principles for building His church, they will work in upper class suburban churches, ghetto housing project churches, rural churches, and inner city churches. These principles will work in rich countries and third-world countries. They will work in areas where there is a Western mindset and where there is an Eastern mindset. They will work in large churches and small churches. They will work in thriving communities and dying communities. They will work in mega churches and house churches. These principles will work in your church. But these principles must be followed as recorded in the Blueprints, or the project will not go as the Architect planned.

But before we can begin building, the ground must be cleared of all obstacles. We must define our terms.

DEFINING "CHURCH"

I took a class in my undergraduate studies called "Argumentation." It was an advanced debate class where we learned to argue logically. Every class period consisted of arguing with one another while the teacher and other students provided insights and suggestions on how to stay focused and make better arguments. Over the course of the class, we all learned to make our case and defend it well. In this class, the very first thing we learned, and the one truth the professor kept emphasizing over and over throughout the semester was the importance of defining our terms. She said that most arguments never begin properly because the terms being used are never defined properly. And when the terms are not defined, there is almost no way an argument can be resolved, because the two parties in the debate might be using the same words while talking about different things.

If you are married or have children, you already know this principle. When a dad says to his 16 year old daughter "Don't get home late," the difference between what he means by "late" and what the daughter understands as "late" is about six hours. Even in theological debate, what one person means by "justification" is completely different than what someone else might understand it to mean. Such differences in definitions lead to debates and arguments that never get resolved until we go back and define our terms. We can never truly argue and never truly agree until we carefully define our terms.[1]

---

[1] This is one reason I am currently writing a multi-volume work titled *The Gospel Dictionary*. It will look at 52 key words of the gospel so that we can have more fruitful discussions about the gospel. Learn more on my website Redeem-

So to avoid confusion, we must begin by defining what we mean by "church growth." Furthermore, to understand the phrase itself, we must first define the two words separately. Before we can understand what "church growth" is and how it occurs, we must first understand the words "church" and "growth."

When it comes to defining the word "church," I am not going to write much here. I have previously published a short book on how to define the church.[2] In that book, I define the church as *the people of God who follow Jesus into the world.* This definition states who makes up the church, how we are connected to Jesus, and what we are supposed to do.

But if this is the church, then what is "growth"?

DEFINING GROWTH

One problem with many of the church growth strategies available today is with how they define "growth." Ask almost any pastor how to grow a church and the response would consist of a variation of the following "P's": people skills, programs, preaching, paperwork, prayer, placement, presentation, politics, prominent location, prominent leadership, publicity, powerful Spirit manifestations, and psychology. They won't always use these exact words, but this is the general consensus.

Ask these same pastors what a growing church looks like, and the answer would be a variation of three "B's": bodies, bucks and

---

ingGod.com, where the Gospel Dictionary online course is already available.

[2] See my book *The Skeleton Church* (Dallas, OR: Redeeming Press, 2017) for a detailed explanation and defense of this definition.

bricks.[3] They would say that a church is growing when it obtains bigger membership rolls, bigger buildings, and a bigger budget. To put it another way, more people, more money, and more structures.

Inevitably, when someone hears I have written a book on church growth, I get the question, "Oh really? How big is your church?" I always say, "That's my point exactly!" Although increasing numbers may mean something positive in the business realm, the church is not a business, and so for the most part, numbers do not apply. Since the church is the people of God who follow Jesus into the world, different methods of measuring growth should be used.

I come from a family of ten children. I am the second eldest of ten kids. When people hear this, they say, "Wow! How did your parents manage it?" As a parent myself, I honestly don't know how they are still sane. But despite the amazement at the number of children in our family, I have yet to talk to someone who thinks that the family I came from was inherently better than their family because mine was larger. To judge the health of a family based on its size is ludicrous! Nobody says that large families are better off than small ones! Rather, the health of any family is measured by the spiritual, physical, relational and emotional qualities exhibited within that family. Many families choose to keep the number of their children low, just so that they can be healthy.

The church is just like that. If only churches that have grown

---

[3] See my book, *Church is More than Bodies, Bucks, & Bricks* (Dallas, OR: Redeeming Press, 2014).

to ten thousand in attendance are healthy, then the majority of churches in the world are sick. But church growth is not—and never should be—about numbers. This is because the church is not made up of numbers. The church consists of all those who believe in Jesus Christ for eternal life and follow Him into the world. The church is the Body of Christ, the family of God, and you cannot use numbers to measure the health of a body or a family.

How do you measure the health of a body, a family, or a group of people? You measure it by how they mature, what they do, and how well they get along. It is similar with church growth. Church growth happens, not when numbers increase, but when people mature in the faith, live productive Christian lives, and get along with each other. Church growth is not about growing numbers, but about growing people. *Church growth occurs when we teach and train the people who are the church to become what God wants them to be so they can do what God wants them to do.*

To put it more simply, church growth happens when Christians grow into spiritual maturity. The amazing thing about this kind of growth is that every pastor can accomplish this, no matter how large or small their church. This kind of growth is more than enough to keep any pastor busy. In the days of Charles Spurgeon, a young pastor came lamenting the fact of his small congregation. Spurgeon told the young man: "I imagine that on the day of judgment, when you stand before your Lord, it will be large enough."

Spurgeon was exactly right! Too often, pastors get caught up in thinking about those who are absent from church, rather than focusing on those that are present. Pastors should be focused on who is in front of them, no matter where they go or with whom they meet. Since the church is the people of God who follow Jesus into the world, church does not just occur on Sunday morning in a church building. Church is not in a place. Church is in a people, and the church goes wherever the people go. So wherever you go, there is the church. This means that you are always in church, and whoever is in front of you—right now—are people you can minister to. Church growth is not about adding numbers to the church, it is about helping whomever is in front of you right now become more like Jesus Christ.

Understandably, this kind of church growth is more elusive, relative, and subjective than numerical growth. But just as any kind of growth is measurable, we can measure this kind of growth as well. If church leaders really want to know if their church is growing, there are several diagnostic questions they can ask. In a pre-publication version of this book, I included the following questions:

- Do the people love God more today than they did last year (1 Cor 8:1; Php 1:9)?
- Are they growing in faith (2 Cor 10:15; 2 Thess 1:3)? Are they more faithful to God this year than last?
- Are they growing in love (Eph 4:16; 2 Thess 1:3) and grace toward each other (2 Pet 3:18)? Are they more willing to serve than ever before?
- Are they growing in the knowledge of God (Col 1:10; 2 Pet 3:18) and their salvation (2 Pet 2:2)? Have they learned more about God, His Word, and His ways?
- Are they more obedient to what they have learned (Jas 1:22-23)? Do they have an increasing desire to learn and apply God's Word (2 Tim 2:15)?
- Are they praying more and building each other up through prayer (Jude 20)?

- Are they growing in the power of the gospel (Col 1:6)? Are they bringing Christ into their homes and workplaces more?[4]

However, my wife, Wendy, read the pre-publication manuscript for this book and just about gagged on every one of these questions. She pointed out—rightly so—that most of these questions are meaningless clichés. After all, what *exactly* does it look like to "grow in the knowledge of God" or "grow in the power of the gospel"? With this observation, my wife put her finger on the exact problem with most "church growth" today. It is poorly defined and even when we try to move it away from the realm of getting more bodies, bucks, and bricks and into the realm of growth into spiritual maturity, we still have trouble defining what true church growth actually looks like.

So in counter-response to the questions above, below are the diagnostic questions proposed by my wife. I think they are much better, but I am definitely biased.

- Do the people truly understand how much God loves them … no matter what?
- Do they realize and accept God's full and complete forgiveness for everything they have done, are doing, or will do?
- Do they have more of relationship with God this year than they did last year? Do they know how they can know that their relationship with God is growing?

---

[4] These ideas were gleaned from: Kent and Barbara Hughes, *Liberating Ministry from the Success Syndrome* (Wheaton: Tyndale, 1987).

- As their faith is tested through life's daily trials, do they rely on God to bring them through these trials?
- Do they show more love and grace to each other? How about to the people they would rather hate?
- Are they excited to serve the people in the community who are overlooked, forgotten, unwanted, or neglected?
- Do they understand when to put further study of Scripture aside so they can practice what they have already learned from Scripture?
- Do they take practical steps to live out the love of God toward others? How?
- Are they seeking to become answers to their own prayer requests?
- Does the way they act at home and at work match what they teach and say when they are in the company of Christians?
- Does the overall conduct of their life look more like Jesus than it did last year?[5]

These questions can be applied to any church whether there are twenty or twenty thousand in attendance. Of course, the pastor must be quite involved with his congregation and know what is going on in their lives if he is going to answer these questions. The number of people who attend mega-churches make it impossible for the pastor to adequately answer these questions, so in such situations, it would be better for the small group leaders to answer the questions.

But whether these questions are answered for twenty or twen-

---

[5] These ideas were gleaned from Wendy Myers, my beautiful and intelligent wife of over twenty years.

ty thousand, even a church that is decreasing in attendance can "grow" under these guidelines. Regardless of who answers the questions, when a church grows in these ways, more and more people tend to show up and get involved. Sometimes the budget will increase. Occasionally, the number of programs will multiply. These things may very well happen when a church is growing, but they are not in any way indicators of biblical church growth or the lack thereof.

This is *real* church growth. When we understand church growth this way, it is revolutionary, encouraging, applicable, and liberating for the typical pastor and average local church.

IT'S REVOLUTIONARY

This conception of church growth is surprisingly revolutionary. Though all pastors know about the importance of discipleship and helping Christians grow in maturity, few equate such practices with church growth. This idea is mentioned by even fewer church growth books. Though many church leaders and writers criticize some of the aspects of the modern "church growth" movement, the criticisms are primarily aimed at some of the methods and messages of the church growth movement; not at how "church growth" is defined.

So when people think of "church growth" today, they think of increasing the number of people "in church" on Sunday morning. They want to fill the pews, the parking lot, and the offering plate. Yes, we see the church in Acts adding three thousand members in one day (Acts 2:41), but this was never the goal for why God sent His Spirit or why Peter preached. The goal was to make disciples who would go into all the world, showing the love of Jesus to others (Matt 28:19-20; John 13:35; Acts 1:8).

And disciples are not made simply by getting more people to hear the pastor preach. Sometimes, disciple-making is best when there are fewer who show up. Jesus took thousands of followers and narrowed them down to twelve. Among the twelve, He focused on three (cf. Matt 17:1). Jesus could have had a following of twenty thousand or more if He had wanted, but instead He focused on church growth. He knew it was better to fill a person's mind, heart, and soul with scriptural principles, spiritual desires, and loving actions, than to fill the hillsides with followers. He knew it was better to help a few fulfill their God-given purpose than try to get thousands to memorize and study a few Bible verses. Jesus knew it was more effective to model servant-leadership to twelve than to twelve thousand

I don't know if Jesus would have a large church today or not. If He did, we can be sure He would hand-pick a few individuals in which to invest His time. But even if He didn't have a large church, we can be sure He wouldn't be trying to get one. Jesus, if He were pastoring today, would do the same thing He did 2000 years ago. Wherever He was, He would use the God-given opportunities to invest in the lives of the few people who were in front of Him. This is true church growth—and in today's world, it is revolutionary.

IT'S ENCOURAGING

This understanding of church growth is also quite encouraging. Most pastors have had the frustrating experience of trying to implement some of the practices recommended by a church growth book or conference only to find that none of it works in their setting. Such pastors then assume that they did something wrong, or that there is something wrong with their church. This leads to great frustration and discouragement. It can also lead to feelings of guilt and inadequacy, which might even turn into blame and accusation. None of this is helpful for the life of the church.

But once we begin to see that church growth is not about getting more people in the pews, but about loving, serving, teaching, and training whomever is in front of us wherever we are, every day and every action can be a success. If the person in front of you is helped in any way to move closer to Jesus, gain a new experience of the love, acceptance, and forgiveness of God, or feels like they were heard or that someone knows their name, then church growth has occurred.

These little acts of love may not seem like much, but they add up over time. Even the ocean is filled with tiny drops of water. Slowly, but surely, as you sprinkle the love and grace of God upon everyone you meet, the church grows into an ocean of God's presence here on earth, and you can know that whether you ministered to one person each day or one thousand, you were successful in helping the church grow. When we look at church growth this way, it becomes extremely encouraging and exciting.

IT'S APPLICABLE

Probably the most frustrating things about most approaches to numerical church growth is that while they might have worked in one place with one church, they rarely work in all places with all churches. If a mega-church in Southern California provided the ten steps for how they grew from ten to ten thousand, it is quite unlikely that these same ten steps would yield the same results in Northern Europe ... or in Northern California for that matter. Most of the numerical church growth principles are simply not repeatable or applicable to other places and situations. Since every local church has different pastors, with different skills, ministering in different areas, to different people, in different cultures, with different education levels and socio-economic backgrounds, this means that the ten steps which worked in one place will most likely not work in any other.

I have also found that much of the numerical growth which mega-churches experience is not really numerical growth at all. That is, more people are not being added to the universal church. Instead, most of the numerical growth that happens in a mega-church is actually church cannibalism. The people from many local small churches leave their small fellowships and start attending the larger one down the street. This is not what happened in Acts 2. When three thousand people join a mega-church, it is not three thousand being added to the church; it is three thousand leaving many local churches to attend one large church. Much of the numerical church growth gains are not necessarily true numerical church growth at all, but is simply people transferring from one congregation to another.

So since most of the numerical church growth principles are not applicable to other situations, and since most numerical church growth is just church member migration, it is much better to focus on the true form of church growth described above, because when we grow the church God's way, it is applicable in all times to all people in all places. Anybody can grow the church when they focus on loving and serving others. Whether it is one person or one thousand, you can teach them about Scripture, show them how to pray, love them like Jesus, meet their needs for food and clothing, encourage them to follow God, and show them that they are forgiven and accepted. This type of church growth is practical and applicable.

IT'S LIBERATING

This idea of church growth is quite liberating. It is a relief to hear that we do not have to worry if attendance is up or down. We do not have to try to please all the people in order to keep them coming. The only Person we have to please is God, and if He sees the people under our care growing in wisdom, knowledge, love, and spiritual maturity, then we can expect to hear "Well done, good and faithful servant" when we stand before Him on judgment day. If we grow the church the way He wants it to grow, we will receive praise from the Master, even if our work was only among two or three people.

While men and women of this world may be impressed with size, God is not. God wants to see faithfulness and obedience. He wants to see us serve where He has placed us. God doesn't care about increasing size and growing numbers; what He cares about is spiritual growth and faithful progress.

Success is not indicated by numbers, but by faithful service and obedience to God which looks different with every Christian. As pastors, when we focus on the indicators of growth suggested previously, God is glorified, and we are encouraged and fulfilled. We no longer feel like we have to measure up to the church down the street and the pastor with a thousand people in the pews.

As lay people, we will be liberated from feeling the pressure to attend church every time the doors are open, memorize endless lists of verses, and read and study the Bible every day for years on end before we feel like we have spiritual conversations with other people. We will realize that we are not obligated to give ten percent of our income to the support the local church, but are freed up to spend our money on issues and needs that God brings to our attention, even if these needs don't have 501(c)(3) status. We do longer have to feel guilty about not volunteering for the nursery or Sunday school. We don't have to worry about whether our voice is good enough to sin in the choir, or whether or health can handle a trip to Mexico.

When we realize that church growth looks like us loving one another and enjoying whatever we are doing with God, then we will understand that true church growth is really just about looking like Jesus and loving others as He did. You can know the church is growing as individual people in the church love and look more like Jesus. This is what God the Architect of the church wants us to do, and He has given us the resources we need to do it. These resources are the subject of the next chapter.

DISCUSSION QUESTIONS

1. How do most church growth books define "growth"?

2. What is wrong with this traditional definition of church growth?

3. How do we measure health and growth in a human body or a family?

4. What sorts of things should we look for to *truly* measure church growth?

5. In John 13:35, what did Jesus say was a defining characteristic of one of His disciples?

6. Why is it not fair to say that if one pastor can numerically grow his church using certain strategies, that other pastor should be able to do the same thing in their communities?

7. What is the real cause of most numerical growth in megachurches of today?

8. How does this new way of looking at church growth help liberate you from various expectations and demands that have been placed on you from others?

CHAPTER 2

BUILDING RESOURCES

Money is a big issue in churches today, especially when a church is embarking on a new evangelism strategy or building project. Churches engage in all sorts of fundraising efforts, ranging from stewardship campaigns and budget meetings to bake sales and car washes. All of these are undertaken in the effort to get a few more bucks in the plate, to put a few more bricks on the building, in the hopes that a few more bodies will fill the pews.[1]

But when we define "church growth" not as bodies, bucks and bricks, but as Christians growing into Christlike maturity, our need for resources does not diminish, but exponentially multiplies. There is no price tag on sanctification. Just as raising one child into adulthood can cost hundreds of thousands of dollars, so also, turning only one sinner into a saint comes at great cost.

Yet the cost is not necessarily financial. While great resources are needed to turn a sinner into a saint, the required resources are already provided by God so that even the "poorest" group of Christians can successfully accomplish church growth God's way.

This is because God has not only provided His blueprints for

---

[1] See my book *Church is More than Bodies, Bucks, & Bricks* (Dallas, OR: Redeeming Press, 2014).

church growth, which will be considered later in this book, but He has also provided all the required "funding." He has made His limitless resources available to us so that we might accomplish His will in this world. As a result, we are rich beyond our wildest imagination. We may not have dollars and diamonds, but in Jesus Christ, we own possessions far more valuable. They are more valuable because these building resources which God has made available to His church are spiritual in nature, and will last longer than any worldly possession.

One of the best ways to judge the value of something is by how long it will last. A common saying today is: "They sure don't make things like they used to." This means that the things they made 30 or 40 years ago lasted longer than they do today, and so the cheap plastic parts of today are a waste of money and therefore not as valuable. There used to be a diamond commercial on television that said, "Diamonds are forever." The implication is that if you want to show someone how much you love them, you should give them a diamond, because, like your love, diamonds will last forever. Long after flowers fade and chocolates are eaten, the diamond will still be sparkling.

In reality, a diamond is not forever. Diamonds slowly degrade over billions of years. But for the purposes of loving relationships, diamonds always outlast their owners. Nevertheless, none of this really matters because nobody can take their diamonds with them when they die. The riches that we have as Christians, however, truly do last forever. Better yet, our spiritual riches can be taken with us when we die. This is one reason the riches God has made available to us are so valuable. These riches truly last forever. They are eternal riches. These riches belong to us now and throughout eternity.

This side of eternity, however, while we are on this earth, God wants us to use His riches in building His church, the body of believers. And the best part about these riches is that God doesn't need us to be careful with them. God doesn't put his church on a budget. Since He has made infinite riches available to us, we can be as "wasteful" in our spending of these riches as we want. All buildings have great cost, and so contractors and business owners want to keep their construction costs within a budget. If someone is not careful with their construction costs they will quickly drain their bank account and find themselves in bankruptcy.

But this is not so with God. While it is true that the church which God is building is extremely expensive, God tells us to not worry about the cost, because He's got it covered. God wants us to know right from the start that He will pay for it all. He will cover the cost. When God builds His church, money is no object because it is His spiritual bank account we are using, which has plenty of resources to build what God wants.

This is wonderfully liberating to remember if we ever get overwhelmed at developing the church according to God's blueprints. Whatever God asks the church to do, He has already provided the resources to do it. It all comes from Him. Along with the blueprints for how God wants His church to be built, God also hands us His credit card without a limit to cover all the costs of building it.[2] This is the main truths we learn in Ephesians 1–3.

---

[2] This is a truth that we not only need to remember for church growth, but also for discipleship. Most discipleship books begin with "What You Need to Do." But God never tells us what we need to do without first explaining what He has provided to do it. Only one discipleship manual that I am aware of begins with what we have from God before moving into what God wants us to do.

THE RICHES OF THE CHURCH (EPHESIANS 1–3)

The six chapters of Ephesians are all about the church.[3] The first three chapters explain the riches of the church, while the last three chapters detail the responsibilities of the church. If Ephesians 1–3 explains our bank account, Ephesians 4–6 contains the investment strategies with guaranteed results. The structure of Ephesians reveals that God does not invite us to do something with Him until He first inventories all the resources He has made available.

As we head toward a study of God's blueprints for church growth in Ephesians 4:11-16, it is important first of all to understand the riches God has provided for the work He has called the church to do. It is always wise before you set out to build anything to make sure your finances are in order and that you have enough money to finish the project. Jesus calls it counting the cost. You don't want to get half-way through building and then run out of money.

When I was growing up, there was a house just down from ours which took the owners about 17 years to build because they kept running out of money. It is not that they worked on it slow-

---

It is by Charles Bing and is called *Living in the Family of Grace* (Burleson, TX: GraceLife, 2003). More information can be found at www.gracelife.org.

[3] Throughout this book, whenever I write about the "church," I am *not* thinking about the brick building with the white steeple in your town, or even the events that take place there on Sunday morning. This is *not* the church. The church is the people of God who follow Jesus in to the world. The church is made of people, whether or not they sit in a pew on Sunday morning to sing songs and listen to a sermon. See my book *Skeleton Church* (Dallas, OR: Redeeming Press, 2014) for more.

ly for 17 years. No, they began to build this huge home, then ran out of money, and so just let the house sit for several years before they did anything else on it.

As the half-constructed house sat through the seasons, my brother and I used to go over there and walk around inside. Every time we went, we would notice more and more damage to the house. They didn't get it shingled or put siding on the exterior walls, so rain and snow started to warp and rot the wood. Squirrels found nooks and crannies in the house to make nests for their winter residence. One time, some neighborhood kids (not us) went in and broke some windows and spray-painted graffiti on the walls. So every time the owners started to build their house again, the first thing they had to do was repair everything that had been ruined. This cost so much money they never got very far with any new construction attempt, and they ran out of money again and again. I always wondered if things could have been different for these people if only they had counted the cost from the beginning, making sure they had enough money to see the project through to completion.

It would be wise if we Christians always made sure to count the cost as well, especially when we set out to get involved in the church that God is building. And this is exactly what Ephesians 1–3 provides. The church is a spiritual building, and is built with spiritual bucks and spiritual bricks. Ephesians is all about the church, and Paul devotes the first three chapters to explaining all the building resources which God has placed at our disposal. If we build properly, we will never run out of building materials, and will be able to complete what we have started. Let us look at some of the resources God has made available to the church as described by Paul in Ephesians 1–3.

EVERY SPIRITUAL BLESSING

Paul doesn't waste any time in getting to the point of his letter. Immediately after the greeting in chapter 1, he writes, "Blessed be the God and Father of our Lord Jesus Christ, who has blessed us with every spiritual blessing in the heavenly places in Christ" (Eph 1:3). This is the summary introduction to Ephesians 1–3. At the very beginning of his letter, Paul explains that God has blessed the church with every spiritual blessing.

There are some who teach that Christians need to pray for more blessings, second blessings, or greater blessings. But what other blessing can there be when God has already given to us *every* spiritual blessing? What more is there? You don't need someone to pray over you to receive another blessing or a second blessing. You already have all spiritual blessings. God has already given you everything you need for life and godliness (2 Pet 1:3).

When someone tells you that you are lacking some spiritual blessing, don't believe it. You already have *every* spiritual blessing. You don't have to go searching for more blessings; you just need to discover the blessings God has already given to you and then start using them. Life in the church is not about gaining more blessings, but about discovering and using the blessings God has already provided.

We must remember, of course, that these are *spiritual* blessings. While God does give physical blessings and meet material needs, we must not think that Paul is promising marble mansions on the coast and a Rolls-Royce in the garage. The riches and blessings of Ephesians 1–3 are entirely spiritual, which makes them exponentially more valuable. God's church is a spiritual building and He has given us spiritual riches to build it. The rest of Ephesians 1–3 lists some of these spiritual blessings.

He Chose Us

The first rich blessing is that He has chosen us. Ephesians 1:4 tells us that "He chose us in Him before the foundation of the world." This means that we are one of His choice servants. If you are part of God's church, you are chosen by God.

One of the things I always hated in grade school was picking teams. You know how it works. All the kids line up, two team captains are agreed upon, and then they take turns picking who they want to be on their team. If you have ever experienced this, you always hope that you get picked first or second. The feeling of getting picked last is the worst feeling in the world.

Well guess what? Ephesians 1:4 says that God chose you first. Before the foundations of the world, that's eons ago, God decided that every person who believed in Jesus for eternal life would be His chosen servant. Why? To accomplish His work and His will in this world. God has a game plan, and He picked you first to carry out that game plan. And while billions of others have also been chosen by God to carry out His game plan, only *you* can do what God has chosen you to do. There is not a single person in history who can do the things God wants you to do in the way that only you can do them. This makes His choice of you incredibly special, and completely unique. You are not just one of the chosen among billions of others; you are the only one chosen to do what no one else can do.

And note that I am not saying anything here about some choice of God from eternity past about who goes to heaven and who goes to hell. Although this is the common view of election and predestination, this common view is not taught in Scripture.

The Bible does not teach that election is to eternal life. Rather, election is to service.[4] When God chooses people, He chooses them to perform a specific task to accomplish a specific purpose in His plan for the world. Therefore, it is incredibly wonderful it is to be chosen as part of God's team. God is your team captain, and He picked you first. That is a wonderful blessing and a great feeling.

The fact that you are chosen by God means that you are a "starter" on God's team. You got picked first. You were a first-round draft pick. God knows that His team can only win if you are on it. This means, of course, that as a starting player on God's team, you need to figure out what position you play on God's team, and then practice and train for that position as much as you possibly can. We will look at this more later.

Adopted Into God's Family

Not only has God chosen us, but Ephesians 1:5 says that He has also adopted us. It is not just that we are chosen to be on His team; we are also adopted into His family. The biblical concept of adoption is quite different than the modern practice. When we think of adoption today, we think of a married couple who cannot have children (or a family who wants to adopt additional children) going to an orphanage or adoption agency to pick a child who has no parents to join their family. But this is not the way adoption worked in biblical times.

In ancient middle-eastern culture, the process of adoption was

---

[4] I deal with the issue of election in my books *The Re-Justification of God* (Dallas, OR: Redeeming Press, 2015), *The Gospel Dictionary* (Forthcoming), and *What is Election and Predestination?* (Forthcoming).

not about inviting a parentless child into your home, but was instead about a father making a child his heir. Typically, the firstborn son was the heir. But if the firstborn son died or displeased the father, the father could adopt someone else to become his official heir. If he had other sons, he might "adopt" one of his own children, thus making this child the heir. Occasionally, rich and powerful families would "adopt" the son of another rich and powerful family, thereby uniting the two families together.[5] Julius Caesar, for example, adopted Gaius Octavius as his son and heir, even though Gaius already had rich and powerful parents. But the adoption of Gaius by Julius Caesar united the two families together politically and financially. Once adopted, Gaius Octavius became the heir to Julius Caesar and eventually gained the throne of the Roman Empire. We now know him as Caesar Augustus.

So when Paul writes that we are adopted into God's family, He is not saying that we simply joined God's family. Don't think of yourself as an orphan that joined the family of God through adoption, and now you are just one of many millions of children in His family. No, to be adopted by God means you have become the heir of God. As an heir, all the spiritual wealth, riches, and power of God are available to you.

Can you think of any greater blessing than this? What would you think if Bill Gates adopted you as his heir? He is one of the richest men in the world. Or Donald Trump. He is not only rich, but now that he is President, he is also powerful. Whatever you think about Donald Trump, I am certain that if he called you up

---

[5] I discuss the concept of adoption more in my book *The Gospel Dictionary* (Forthcoming).

and asked if you wanted to become the heir to his fortune, you would not say no.

But we are the adopted heirs of God. We are heirs of the Creator of the universe. God didn't just create Microsoft Windows. He created wind. He created air. God didn't just build Trump Tower. He built the sun, the stars, and the moon. And you are the heir of God. He has made all of His powerful and creative resources available to you.

Redemption

If being chosen and adopted were not enough, God blesses us even more through redemption. Paul writes in Ephesians 1:7 that "in Him we have redemption through His blood, the forgiveness of sins, according to the riches of His grace." This is an incredibly rich blessing. Though our sin was an infinite offense against God that we can never repay, He freely forgives our sins. Though we were sold as slaves to sin, God redeemed us and bought us out of slavery so that we can live in freedom with Him.

Nobody—regardless how many years they are given, how many right decisions they make, or how many simple steps they follow—will ever be able to earn for themselves redemption from God or the forgiveness of sins. But thankfully, God redeemed us and forgives us, absolutely free of charge. Out of the riches of His grace, God gives us something of inestimable value.

When we let that truth get a hold of us, our lives will never be the same. We are redeemed. We were enslaved to sin, sold to the enemy, and in debt beyond our wildest imagination, but God picked us up, made us His own, bought us out of slavery, and paid our debt. These are great riches, but Paul is not even close to done.

An Inheritance

Beyond just being freed from slavery and having an infinite debt cancelled, Ephesians 1:11 says that we have also "obtained an inheritance." If you have ever dreamed of getting a letter in the mail saying that some rich relative you never knew just died and you inherited the entire fortune, consider that dream fulfilled. The balance of our ledgers used to be awash in red ink, but God went further than just zeroing out the debt; He also added an infinite inheritance to our account.

There are a lot of people today trying to get out of debt. For some, this just means paying off their credit cards. Others are trying to have no car payment or home mortgage. What would your reaction be if you were trying to get out of an overwhelming debt, and one day you received a call from a benefactor who not only paid your entire debt, but also deposited a million dollars into your bank account? You would be thrilled.

This is what God has done for us in Jesus Christ. In Him, we have been given an inheritance. This inheritance is more than just a million dollars. This inheritance makes us the heir of God and co-heirs with Jesus Christ. All that belongs to God also belongs to Jesus Christ, as well as to you and to me. And this isn't just a measly million. God owns everything. He owns the cattle on a thousand hills. He owns the universe. Everything is His. And He has given it to us, because through Jesus, we have obtained an inheritance.

Now a lot of people are a little skeptical of such wild promises, and so the next item that Paul writes about shows that God has made a down payment to us which guarantees our inheritance, and which allows us to start drawing on the riches we have in Jesus Christ. This is the seal of the Spirit.

A Spirit Seal

Paul writes in Ephesians 1:13 that we "were sealed with the Holy Spirit of promise." According to verse 14, this sealing is a proof, a promise, and a guarantee from God that He will give our inheritance to us in heaven, which will include the full and complete redemption of our bodies.

The word Paul uses for "sealed" was a term used in the lumber yards of the city of Ephesus to describe a stamp or signet ring that a merchant would put on items he wanted to purchase. He would go to the lumber yards, pick out the logs he wanted to purchase, put a down payment on the logs, mark them with his seal, and then come back later to pick them up and take them home.

In today's terminology, we might think of earnest money that is deposited when buying a house, or even an engagement ring when a man asks a woman to get married. People who want to buy a house put down earnest money as a way of promising that they are serious about buying the house. Similarly, an engagement ring is a promise from the man that he will marry the woman.

The problem with both of these pictures is that humans are not very reliable or trustworthy. People often go back on their word, even when they stand to lose some money or a loving partner. But God is not human. He does not lie or go back on His Word. God never breaks His promises, and He has given us the seal of the Holy Spirit. He has given us His signet ring saying that we are His, and He will return to pick us up to spend eternity with Him. This is a wonderful blessing from God.

But the blessing is more than just a promise that God will ultimately and finally take us to heaven to be with Him. While we are waiting, the Holy Spirit, the "signet ring" of God, doesn't just sit on the shelf looking pretty. This is no ordinary engagement ring. More than just a constant reminder of the promise of God, the Spirit of God is what allows us to access the power and riches of God right now. The Spirit of God is the access card, the gate pass, or the safety deposit box key which allows us to begin using and enjoying the riches of God in this life.

Some of the ways we see this is that the Spirit of God begins to conform our life to the image and likeness of Jesus Christ. The Spirit teaches us about God. He illumines our minds to understand God's Word. He helps us walk in God's will. He produces in us Christlikeness and Godly characteristics. God not only gives His riches to us, but through His Holy Spirit, He guarantees that they will be ours, and He gives us access to them right now. One of the riches we are able to access right now is salvation.

Salvation

Salvation is a spectacular blessing from God. Paul goes into great detail in Ephesians 2:1-10 explaining this amazing gift. Twice in these verses, Paul tells us that it is by grace we have been saved (2:5, 10). Grace, of course, is a synonym for "free gift." Paul wants his readers to know that this salvation is by grace, through faith, not of works.

It is important to understand, however, that when Paul writes about salvation here, he is not writing about escaping hell so we can go to heaven when we die. When most Christians talk and think about salvation, they think about going to heaven when they die. But this is not how the Bible uses the term salvation, and this is not what Paul is referring to here in Ephesians 2. Any time you see the word "salvation" (or save, saved, saving, Savior, etc.) in the Bible, you should do two things. First, to help you avoid thinking that the word is talking about going to heaven when you die, substitute in the word "deliverance" (or deliver, delivered, delivering, Deliverer, etc.). This word is a perfectly fine translation from the Greek. Once you have done this, the second step is to study the context for what kind of deliverance is in view. Following these two steps will help you better understand dozens of tricky passages in the Bible.[6]

When we follow these two steps in Ephesians 2, we discover that Paul begins the chapter by talking about the problem that has plagued humanity since the beginning of the world. This is the problem of sin (Eph 2:1), which Paul defines as living according to our fleshly desires so that we engage in angry violence toward one another (Eph 2:3). We know that this is what Paul means because in the second half of Ephesians 2, Paul writes about how we should be living now in light of what Jesus accomplished for us. He writes that there is now peace between Jews and Gentiles (Eph 2:11-13), that the enmity created by the law has been abolished (Eph 2:14-17), and that we can now work together in unity and harmony to become the spiritual temple that God wants us to be (Eph 2:18-22).

Based on this context then, the "salvation" in Ephesians 2 is not about going to heaven when we die, but is instead about turning away from violence and enmity and following Jesus into a life of peace and unity on this earth. Ephesians 2 follows a "Problem, Solution, Application" outline, and we only see how all three fit together when we recognize that salvation in Ephesians 2 concerns the issue of human divisions and violence rather than the issue of escaping hell and going to heaven.

---

[6] See my book, *The Gospel Dictionary* (Forthcoming) for more on this topic.

Yes, eternal life is one of the great riches that God gives to anyone and everyone who believes in Jesus for it (cf. John 3:16; 5:24; 6:47), but this is not what Paul is writing about in Ephesians 2. Instead, Paul is writing about the new way of living that Jesus revealed to us through His own life, death, and resurrection. We have been raised with Jesus to this new way of life (Eph 2:4-6). He revealed it to us by His grace, and we follow Him into the new way of life by faith (Eph 2:7-8). This new way of living in peace and unity with others is not something we humans could have figured out on our own, which is why Jesus came and revealed it to us and showed us how to live, which is the way God intended us to live since the very beginning (Eph 2:9-10).

When we live this way, we live according to the riches of God's grace, and we truly reign with Jesus Christ in this world. We show that Jesus is living and reigning through us by how we live in peace and unity with one another.

Peace

In eternity, we will live in perfect peace with one another. But God does not want us to wait for eternity to experience this peace. Through the riches of God's grace, by the sealing power of the Holy Spirit, and following the perfect example of Jesus, we begin to make our future reality an actual presence here on earth. This is what Paul writes about in Ephesians 2:11-17. By following Jesus, the church brings heaven down to earth. We are to begin living with each other now in the way that we will live with each other in eternity. When we do this in the church, the world takes notice, because it recognizes in us the one thing it longs for. Peace is the greatest longing of this world. Sadly, most people believe that peace is achieved through war. Or that peace will be gained through one powerful country exerting its will on less powerful countries. But Jesus showed a different way to peace, and the church is called to reveal this to the world.

We think that it is impossible to live in unity with other people, especially those who are from different cultures and classes, religions and races, or political persuasions. But Paul writes that in Jesus, the dividing wall of hostility between Jews and Gentiles has been broken down. If you took every division we struggle with today and wrapped them all together, you would have the division between Jews and Gentiles in Paul's day. It was cultural, racial, political, religious, and financial. They despised each other, hated each other, scorned each other, and frequently tried to kill each other. But Paul writes that these two groups can now live in peace with each other in the church because of what Jesus accomplished.

This also is how the church should be functioning today. The peace this world longs for is attainable and available, but it does not come through technology, medicine, education, money, political dialogue, or war. It only comes through Jesus Christ as we follow Him into self-sacrificial service and consider others more important than ourselves. As the church is built upon the cornerstone of Jesus, the church reveals to the world the way God intended humanity to function. We live this way, however, because we are no longer citizens of this world, but citizens of heaven.

Heavenly Citizenship

Most U.S. citizens are proud to be American. We sing songs about our country. We cheer when our athletes win gold at the Olympics. When we travel overseas, we say "It's good to be back in the USA" when we get home. One of the reasons we are proud to be an American is because by most worldly standards, the Unites States is one of the best countries in the world. We are a major superpower. We are one of the richest nations in the world. We are culturally and ethnically diverse. We are creative. We are on the cutting edge in most technological fields. Overall, our governmental structure is sound. America truly is a great nation, when compared to all the others.

But America is by no means ideal. Crime, suicide, drug abuse, and abortion are all on the rise. There are millions of Americans without jobs, good health insurance, or the basic necessities of life. Our educational system is crumbling. Social Security is failing. Welfare is a mess. Our national debt is skyrocketing. Though America is one of the best nations in the world, it is near the bottom of the barrel when we compare it to the ideal.

Of course, nobody can agree on what the ideal nation would be. When people try, they come up with names for it. Plato called it The Republic. Thomas More called it Utopia. The Bible calls it the Kingdom of Heaven.

Though heaven is radically different than The Republic or Utopia, it nevertheless is the ideal society. It is governed by God. There is perfect peace and harmony. Nobody is in need. Nobody gets injured. There is no crime. Though America is great, it is a far cry from God's kingdom. And so when we read in Ephesians 2:19 that we have been given citizenship in heaven, it should make us intensely proud to be a citizen of such a great place. Anyone who is proud to be an American can be even prouder to be a citizen of heaven.

In Paul's day, people were proud to be citizens of Rome. Paul himself was a citizen, and was proud to be a citizen, and even used his citizenship to his advantage when necessary so that he could better share the gospel with others. Of course, there were different classes of Roman citizenship. It was best to be born a citizen, as Paul had been. But people could also buy their citizenship if they had enough money. However, since this path to citizenship was so expensive, the multitudes of slaves and servants usually had no hope of ever becoming a Roman citizen in this way. And even when they were able to scrape together enough money to buy their citizenship in this way, they were still viewed as second-class citizens.

This is what makes Paul's statement in Ephesians 2:19 so shocking. Citizenship in heaven is free, and it is available to all. We did not have to buy it. When we are born again in Jesus Christ, we are born into heavenly citizenship. And heavenly citizenship is not open to just the rich or the elite, but to all.

Roman citizenship also provided different rights and privileges which the average person did not have. Citizens could not be punished without a trial. If they thought the trial went poorly, they could appeal to Caesar. They were taxed differently and treated differently. It was a special honor to be a Roman citizen. Similarly, as a citizen of heaven, we receive special treatment and honor as well. We have constant access to the throne room of God so that we can bring our prayers and petitions before Him. God views us as His children and heirs rather than as His servants. In the age to come, as citizens of heaven, we will rule over the universe and even over angels. There are great privileges to being a citizen of heaven. This is yet another of our great, rich blessings God has given to us in Jesus Christ.

But most importantly, the greatest thing about being a citizen of heaven is that we are called by God to live now, on this earth, as a citizen of heaven, so that we can show this world how God wants us to live and how true and lasting peace can be achieved. God is building His church in this world, and Jesus Christ is the chief cornerstone of this church, and we, as members of the church, follow the example and teachings of Jesus so that we can lead this world in the way of peace.

The Hidden Mystery

This talk of Jesus Christ as the chief cornerstone causes Paul to turn to the final blessing he wants to discuss in Ephesians 1–3. This final blessing is what Paul hinted at in the end of chapter 2, and which he spends all of chapter 3 explaining. It is the mystery that was hidden for ages and generations, but has now been revealed. What is the mystery? It is the church.

Though most Christians fail to recognize it, the church is one of the greatest blessings God has given. In fact, there are many blessings which Paul does not mention in Ephesians, but which come to us as we get involved in the church. Many of the riches of divine grace God has given to us can only be used and experienced in and through the church.

Some people say that they do not need to be involved with other Christians, that they do not need to meet regularly with other believers for encouragement and edification. Technically, they are correct. But this is like saying that you don't need any friends in life. Or that you can go through life all alone. Technically, you can. But it will be a dull, boring, and difficult life. So also with life in the church. You can try to live your life as a Christian all alone. But why would you want to? You will miss out on so many of the blessings and riches that God has made available to you, and which you can only receive and experience as an active member of the church.

This is why the church and finding your place in the church should be such a priority. It is important to God. It is important to Jesus. It is important to Paul. And it should be important to us as well. Paul spends chapter 3 talking about the riches of the church, and about his own role as an apostle to the Gentiles. As Paul writes about this, he writes about the revelation, understanding, blessings, promises, fellowship, wisdom, power, and purposes that are only made available to people who participate in God's church. There are so many blessings to be gained within the church, you are primarily hurting yourself when you refuse to participate. The church itself is one of the riches God has given to us in order to help us get involved in growing His church. It is a mutually beneficial relationship. As you get involved in the church, there are benefit for both the church and for yourself.

Paul writes more about all of this in Ephesians 4–6, where he goes into great detail about what you can do in the church so that you can experience the blessings of the church. But before he moves on to our responsibilities, Paul closes out the first section of his letter with a prayer. Paul prays for his readers that they would not only know about the riches God has made available to them, but that they would experience these riches as well.

PRAYING FOR RICHES

Paul closes chapter 3 with a prayer. He prays that God will do amazing and incredible things in the church through the lives of the believers who use these riches for God's glory (Eph 3:14-21). God wants you to be part of a growing church, and He has given you everything you need to make that happen.

When we make use of the riches God has given to us, He will do things beyond our imagination. Paul piles on terms here to make his point. God will do exceedingly abundantly above all that we ask or think. God will do more than we can even imagine. When it comes to making use of God's riches to carry out our God-given responsibilities, there is literally no limit to what God will do in and through us. The sky is not the limit.

CONCLUSION

Have you ever had your credit cards stolen? I have. When Wendy and I moved to Denver, our first day there my wallet and my laptop computer was stolen out of our moving van while it was parked in the church parking lot. By the time I found out that I was missing my wallet, whoever stole it had already charged $2000 on my credit cards. This person had tried to get access to riches that were not his.

In order to access divine riches, you don't have to steal God's credit card. He has already given His credit card to you, and invited you to use it. Best of all, His card has no limit, for it is connected to the limitless supply of God's spiritual wealth. He freely hands this card to you, and says, "Go ahead. I want to build my church, and I am giving all of my infinite resources to you for that purpose." When you are doing God's work and there is something you need, He will make sure you get it.

The church, being a spiritual building, is built with spiritual bucks. In the book of Ephesians, which is a book about the church, we learn that we have the infinite resources of God at our disposal. When it comes to church growth, money is not an issue. We've got the divine credit card at our disposal. We don't need to go around asking, begging, and pleading with God to give us the resources needed to help grow His church. Instead, we just need to access and make use of the infinite resources He has already provided to us. The church is not a pauper; we are princes in the family of God. Ephesians 1–3 clearly gives an account of the incredible riches that belong to us as part of the church.

In this chapter, we have surveyed these riches, and will turn in the next chapter to consider how God wants us to spend these riches.

DISCUSSION QUESTIONS

1. Ephesians is a book about the church. It is divided into two sections. What are these two sections, and what is the theme of each?

2. When talking about the church in this book, I am not referring to buildings that people gather in on Sunday morning. To what am I referring?

3. What is it that God freely gives His church? What are the limits on these gifts?

4. What does it mean for God to have chosen you before the foundation of the world?

5. What does it mean to be adopted into God's family? Does this mean that you become His child? If not, what does it mean?

6. What is redemption? How is it a gift to us from God's riches?

7. What blessing grants us access right now to all the power and riches of God? What does it mean to be conformed to the likeness of Jesus Christ?

8. Since the blessing of salvation is not about going to heaven when we die, what is the blessing of salvation?

9. How is peace actually obtained, and what role does the church have in leading the world into peace?

10. Though our final blessing is citizenship in heaven, what are we called to do with this citizenship right now?

CHAPTER 3

THE DEVELOPMENT PLAN

When it comes to setting goals for ourselves, the greatest danger is not that our aim is too high and we miss it, but rather, our aim is too low and we reach it. Then there are those who don't really have any goals at all. And of course, when you don't have any goals to aim for, you hit them every time.

The same is true for the church. Some people don't have any goals or expectations for the church they attend. Their idea of "church" is to show up in a building every Sunday morning, sit through some prayers, songs, and a sermon before going home. When it comes to their own lives or to what the church is doing in the world, their number one priority is to make sure that everything stays the same. They don't have any goals for the church beyond what the church is already doing.

Others do have goals for the church, but they set them way too low. They base their ideas for what the church should be and do on their own opinions and experiences. But any manmade goal, any manmade opinion always falls far short of God's goals for His church. God's opinion of the church is the only one that matters.

So what does the perfect church look like? If you could come up with a list of the things which the perfect church had, what would you put on that list? If you could paint a mental picture of what your dream church would be like, what do you imagine? If you were to take this mental image and compare it with others who also created mental images of the perfect church, I doubt that you would ever find someone whose idea of the ideal church perfectly matched yours.

This is one reason for all the church hopping today. People are continually trying to find the "perfect" church. They have a mental picture of what the perfect church does, what happens on a Sunday morning, what kind of music the church plays, what sort of ministries and outreaches the church is involved in, what the pastor is like, what his sermons are like, how many people attend the church, how long the service is, and a host of other items.

In one church I pastored, a visitor who attended one Sunday morning told me afterwards that he couldn't come back to our church because we had orange carpet. He said that the color was so shockingly bad, it distracted from his ability to worship God. Personally, I didn't like the orange carpet either, but that wasn't on my list of what makes or breaks a church. But apparently, it was on his.

So what is on your list? What mental checklist do you have that determines what a church should look like and how a church should function? Can I say something bold? It is quite likely that many of the items on your list are manmade items and are not at all biblical. This doesn't mean these items are necessarily wrong; it just means they are not required. Church buildings, for example, while frequently helpful, are not necessary for the church to exist and function. The same goes for pulpits, paid pastors, worship bands, children's programs, ushers, bulletins, communion trays, offering plates, pews or padded chairs, and parking lots. In fact, pretty much everything about the Sunday morning service is completely optional for the church to exist and function in the world. Except for the people. Only people are necessary for the church to exist. People who are willing and ready to follow Jesus into the world. I cover all of this in my *Close Your Church for Good* book series.

Again, the fact that pretty much everything we think is necessary for church is not biblically required does not mean that such things are wrong or sinful. If they help us function as the people of God who follow Jesus into the world, then they can be used and enjoyed. But if not, then they should be abandoned. God wants us to be the church in the world, and gives us great freedom and flexibility in how we do this.

So how can we know whether or not the way we "do church" and the "accessories" we add to our church functions are helping us "be the church" in the world? The answer is to ask God what is on His list for the "ideal church." Just like the rest of us, God also has a picture of the "perfect church" in mind, but since the church is God's church, it is His picture we should seek to learn and emulate. And when we take a look at God's idea of the perfect church, we discover that He does not include anything about outward appearances, but only about inward realities. God is not nearly as concerned with the form of church as He is with how it functions.

Throughout the New Testament, God provides several descriptions of what the church is supposed to be and do, and none of these divinely-inspired lists contain the types of things that exist on most people's lists. Instead, God wants the church to look like Jesus. He wants the church to love all, forgive all, accept all, and serve all. He wants the church to work toward unity and peace. He wants the church to champion the cause of kindness, and to live righteously and faithfully in this world.

One of the premier descriptions of the church that God envisions is found in Ephesians 4–6. Though other lists of God's ideal church can be found elsewhere in Scripture, these three chapters contain the most comprehensive picture of what God wants the church to be and do. Ephesians 4–6 contains the responsibilities of the church as given by God.

THE RESPONSIBILITIES OF THE CHURCH (EPHESIANS 4–6)

In the previous chapter we learned about the riches which God has made available to the church. These riches were outlined in Ephesians 1–3. But God does not provide riches to the church so that we can hoard them. He wants us to take the infinite resources He has made available to us so that we can use them to do His work in this world. He provided the riches so we can perform our responsibilities well. If Ephesians 1–3 tells us what we have been given, Ephesians 4–6 tells us what we are supposed to do.

One of the key words throughout Ephesians 4–6 is the word "walk." Everybody knows what it is to go on a walk. We know how to walk and why we walk. We walk to get from one place to another by putting one foot in front of the other. A walk happens one step at a time. The same is true when we walk with God to become the church of God. When we seek to become the church that God wants, it does not happen all at once. It happens step by step as we go on a walk with Jesus, as we follow Jesus into the world.

It is important to keep this image of walking in mind as we

look at what God wants His church to do with His riches. Ephesians 4–6 lists five steps in the walk to becoming God's ideal church, and each one takes time, energy, discipline, and devotion to accomplish. Furthermore, I believe that each subsequent step builds on the previous one. If you are on a five-mile walk to a beautiful mountain lake, you cannot simply jump to mile five. You first have to walk through miles one through four. It is the same as the church. God has something beautiful in mind for the church, and Paul lays out five steps to getting there, but in order to arrive at God's ideal church, we must go on a walk with Him through five steps. These five steps provide God's development plan for the church so that we can arrive at His ultimate goal for the church.

Before we consider the five steps, let us look at the ultimate goal God has for His church.

THE ULTIMATE GOAL (EPH 4:13; 5:27)

When an architectural firm sets out to design a grand building, they very often create a wood model of the building. This not only helps people visualize what the finished project will look like, but also serves the purpose of maintaining excitement and passion for the project as it drags on for months and years. When fundraising or investment efforts are involved in the building project, the model helps people see what they are giving their money to build.

It is the same with the church that God is building, except that in this case, He has provided all the funding. But so that we can get excited about what He is building, He has provided us with a model to stare at in wonder and amazement. This model keeps us motivated as the process drags on. What is this model? It is Jesus Christ. Jesus Christ is the model for the church. He is the ultimate goal for the church. When the church truly becomes what God wants, the church will look, act, and function like Jesus. But then end.

Paul points this out in two places in his development plan for the church: near the beginning (Eph 4:13) and near the end (Eph 5:27). Paul writes that God wants a perfect man (Eph 4:13) and a glorious church (Eph 5:27), and that both will be holy and blameless like the measure and stature of Jesus Christ. The word *perfect* (Gk., *telos*) that Paul uses in Ephesians 4:13 not only includes moral perfection (for Jesus was sinless), but rather to the *end* or *purpose* that God has planned for us. Paul specifies what this end or purpose is when he writes that we will be conformed to the measure and stature and fullness of Christ. Similarly, when Paul writes about the glorious church in Ephesians 5:27, he defines glory as being holy and without blemish. This theme is also how Paul began his letter (cf. Eph 1:4), which shows that the goal of the church becoming glorious is what Paul's letter is primarily about.

This ultimate goal of perfection and glory will not be fully achieved until after the resurrection when God glorifies us in eternity, but Paul writes Ephesians 4–6 to show the church how to live now in light of that future reality. By following the five steps Paul lays out, the church can bring heaven down to earth and that future reality into the present. God wants His church to be perfect and holy, without spot or blemish, to be formed according to the measure and stature of Jesus Christ. The five steps He put in place helps this happen as we walk through them one at a time. So let's put our shoes on and take the first step in becoming what God wants the church to be.

STEP 1. WALK WORTHY OF YOUR CALLING (EPH 4:1-16)

The first step in walking toward God's development goal is found in Ephesians 4:1-16. In 4:1, Paul invites us, in light of everything he has written in the first half of Ephesians, to walk worthy of the calling with which we were called. This idea of calling is very similar to the idea of God choosing us in Ephesians 1:4. Paul begins the second half of his letter in the same way he began the first half.

Back in Ephesians 1:4, Paul wrote that God chose us in Jesus Christ to be holy and blameless. The text does not say that God chose us *to be* in Christ, but that He chose us in Christ. This means that from eternity past, God chose Jesus Christ, and by default, also chose all who were in Christ. When we believe in Jesus for eternal life, we are placed in Christ, and since Jesus Christ is the Chosen One, we too become chosen in Him.

This makes more sense when we recognize that the choosing, or election, of God, is not to eternal life, but to service. God doesn't choose who will get eternal life and who will not. He chooses people and nations to serve a purpose in His divine plan. He chooses people and groups to help Him carry out His will on this earth. In Ephesians 1:4, Paul wrote that God chose us to be holy and blameless, and here in Ephesians 4:1, Paul writes that God chose us so that we can fulfill our calling. In other words, God has chosen us for a reason. This means that the first step in becoming the church that God wants is for each Christian to discover their God-given purpose and start living in light of that purpose.

Every year the NFL has a football draft. The football draft is a time when the various teams try to strengthen their team by picking players to fill the holes in the team. If they need a quarterback, they draft one. If they need a linebacker, they draft one. Those who are drafted have very specific skills or abilities which that specific team needs in order to become stronger. No NFL team will ever draft someone who will be of no benefit to the team.

At the same time, once a player is chosen to fill a team position, they are expected to play that position to the best of their ability. They are expected to train and practice, and to eat and live in a way that allows them to stay healthy and strong. If a wide receiver is picked for his speed, but he decides to eat Doritos and Twinkies all day long so that he gains fifty pounds, he will probably be quickly dropped from the team or at least be benched until he brings his weight down. Similarly, if a drafted quarterback decides he would rather play linebacker, the team will suffer, and the coach will likely have some strong words to say to the quarterback. Each player is chosen for a specific role and task, and is expected to fill that role.

It is the same with you. God chose you, called you, picked you, drafted you onto His team because you have a specific strength, ability, or skill which He wants you to use in His church. Of course, the special gifts and abilities you have were actually given to you by God as well (cf. Eph. 4:7-10), which we will discuss in future chapters. But the reason He gave these gifts and abilities to you, and then chose and called you to play a part on His team is that God wants you to fulfill a very specific purpose.

Of course, God's team is not exactly like a professional sports team. When players on a professional team age, get injured, or fail to measure up to expectations, they get cut from the team. Not so with God's church. You have been drafted onto the team, but if you fail to play your role, God will not dump you. He might bench you until you get your act together, but you will always remain on the team. Yet when you fail to fulfill your role, the team is weaker because of it. You alone can do what God wants you to do the way God wants you to do it. If you don't do it, it doesn't get done. If you don't do it, the church will be weaker because it is lacking what only you can do.

You are like a completely unique piece of a giant jigsaw puzzle. If you refuse to participate with the pieces around you, God cannot simply jam another piece in your place. No other piece fits as perfectly into your place as you do. This is one reason why many Christians feel empty in life. They are trying to be a piece of the puzzle or play a role on the team that God did not call them to fill. If you don't do what God gifted and called you to do, you will always feel like you are missing something in your spiritual life. When you do not know what God has called you to do, and when you do not walk worthy of that calling, life will seem empty and drab.

So the first step in walking toward the development goal is to live up to the purpose for which you were called by God. Do you know what your God-given purpose is? If you know what it is and you are living it out, great. Keep it up. If not, there are multiple ways to discover it. Many have found Rick Warren's bestselling book, *The Purpose Driven Life*, to be helpful. Others have found it best to just pray for God to reveal His purpose to you, and then step out in faith by experimenting with various forms of service in the church. As you experiment with service, God naturally leads you to your purpose and role in the church. But however you find your purpose and calling, make living it your top priority.

Paul gives some further instructions on this in Ephesians 4:2-16. For example, in verses 2-6, Paul teaches that although we all have different callings, we must remember to live out our individual callings with unity, love, patience, and humility. Your purpose is not somebody else's purpose. While there are similarities, God has given a different purpose to each Christian, a different calling to everyone. So don't think everybody has to live like you and do the same things you do.

Similarly, your purpose is not better than their purpose. You may have more prominence, but you need them just as much as they need you. So don't start getting proud and arrogant and looking down on others. God made us all different, with different gifts, abilities and callings. But though we are all different, we need to work together as one. Paul likens the church in verse 4 to a body. This is one of his favorite pictures of the church. Just as your body is made up of different members that do different things, it all works together for the good of all the other members, so too, the church is a body made up of many members, all of which are important. And if our ultimate goal is to become like Jesus Christ, to achieve the fullness of the image and stature of Jesus, then we must begin by learning what our specific responsibility is within the Body of Christ.

In verses 7-10, Paul tells us that spiritual gifts are intimately tied with our calling. Part of your calling is to use your spiritual gifts in and through the local church. Paul gets very specific about all of this in verses 11-16. These verses contain the actual Blueprints for Church Growth which we will look at in great detail later in this book. So Step 1 in your walk is to discover your calling and live it out. The first thing God wants each person in the church to do is to discover their calling and fulfill it.

STEP 2. WALK IN PURITY (EPH 4:17-32)

Only after completing Step 1 can we go on to Step 2 in God's development goal. This is the step of purity. God wants His church to walk in purity (Eph 4:17-32). Paul writes in these verses about living a pure life. He says we should not live the way the world does, in ignorance and lewdness, with uncleanness and greed. Instead, he says we need to be renewed in the spirit of our minds, and live in purity and holiness.

It is critical to recognize that this is the second step out of five. While there are many reasons that we sin so frequently, one of the reasons we so often fail to walk in purity is because we have not accomplished Step 1 of discovering and living out our calling. The most thrilling thing a person can do in life is to follow Jesus wherever He leads. But when we do not know where Jesus is leading, or what role we are to play in this journey of faith, then we miss out on all the excitement and thrill of following Jesus. Without this excitement, we go looking elsewhere. When life seems empty and devoid of meaning, we start searching for something to fill the emptiness. We think that sin will provide it for us. Sin is sometimes an attempt to find satisfaction, pleasure, and enjoyment in life, because we are failing to find such things in our life with Jesus.

We look around at the world and they seem to be enjoying themselves, so we try to fill our lives with the things they use, such as sex, drugs, money, power, food, entertainment, and recreation. But such pursuits never satisfy in the long run. While they may fulfill us in the short term, they soon lose their glamour and thrill, and we have to turn to something else or up the ante so that we feel alive once again. But the only reason we do not feel alive in the first place is because we have not discovered our calling. Once we discover the reason God has us on his team, and work to live in light of that calling, life will never be dull again.

There is fulfillment and satisfaction in fulfilling your calling. When we live in light of our calling, sin does not have the pull it once did. And when life is not dull, we don't go looking for thrills in sin, and hence, we walk in purity as Paul instructs. When we are doing what we know we were made to do, life just feels right. Everything fits into place. Life feels exciting and full. When we have taken the first step of living out our calling, it is much easier to take the second step of living in purity, because the lure of sin is not as attractive as it once was.

In verses 25-32, one of the main ways to walk in purity is to guard what comes out of our mouth, to watch what comes off our lips. Every word we speak, Paul says in verse 29, should edify others rather than tear them down. Tearing others down with the words that come out of our mouth is a sin that grieves the Holy Spirit. The Spirit exists only to point us to Jesus as we edify one another and build one another up, but the Holy Spirit is saddened when we use our words to tear each other down. We grieve the Holy Spirit whenever unedifying words pass our lips.

Although free speech is a primary value of many modern civilizations, the Christian who truly follows Jesus does not have free speech. We are not permitted to say whatever we want, but only what will build others up and introduce them to the love, grace, and forgiveness of God. When we tear others down with our words, whether it is through gossip, slander, blame, accusation, name-calling, or unjust criticism, such words deeply sadden the Holy Spirit. When we speak with bitterness, anger, wrath, or malice, we grieve the Holy Spirit. When we rejoice with our words at the downfall of others, the Holy Spirit does not rejoice with us.

Paul focuses so much on the words that come out of our mouths because words reveal what is in our heart. Jesus instructed His disciples to be pure in heart (Matt 5:8), and Paul wants the church to walk in purity. The best way to discern whether or not you are pure in heart and whether you are walking in purity is to listen to the words that come out of your mouth (Matt 12:34; Luke 6:45). There is no better litmus test about the condition of your heart.

Lewd and crude jokes and licentious humor indicate a heart filled with lust and perversion. Gossip, slander, bitterness and anger reveal a heart filled with hate and spite. It doesn't matter how sweetly a person smiles, a pure heart is revealed by pure words. Jesus even teaches in Matthew 7 that "by their fruit you will know them." Do you know what the fruit of Matthew 7 is? It is not their works, but their words (cf. Matt. 12:33-37). And James 3 says that the one who is able to control his tongue is a perfect man. One way to judge your own personal purity is to watch what words come out of your mouth. Pure hearts lead to pure lips. Such purity is desirable because purity is the second step to becoming the church that God wants us to be.

As we live in light of our calling and walk in purity, we will look more and more like Jesus Christ. Only when we live this way will we then be ready to take the third step in becoming like Jesus, which is to walk in love.

STEP 3. WALK IN LOVE (EPH 5:1-7)

The third step to becoming God's ideal church is found in Ephesians 5:1-7. This step is to walk in love (5:2). Do you ever have trouble loving other people? Oh sure, you might *say* that you love them, and in your heart, you logically know that you really do love them, but when it comes to actually showing them love, you find great difficulty in it. You cannot stand to be with them. You hate talking to them. You have trouble finding anything good to say about them.

If that is where you are at, very likely you need to make sure you have gone through Steps 1 and 2 of your walk. Often, our disdain for other people is due in large part to sin in our own lives. I have found personally that the areas in other people's lives about which I am most critical, are often areas that I struggle with the most in my own life. It may not be the exact same struggle, but if you struggle with self-control in the area of eating, you may find yourself judging somebody else who struggles with self-control in the area of television watching.

The sins listed in verses 3-4 are the ones which are the most damaging to the church. As you read through such a list, the tendency is to think of other people who struggle with those particular sins. But oftentimes the sins we are most critical about in others are often the same sins we have hidden in our own heart. This is why it is helpful to carefully listen to what you say and think about other people. Quite often, such judgmental words and thoughts about others are actually a mirror into the condition of our own heart.

Once we begin to recognize this, we discover that we are no better than anyone else. We learn that we are sinners, just as much as they are, and that just as God loves and forgives our sins, He loves and forgives them for theirs. Once we see that God loves and forgives all of us for all our sin, we are then in the position to start loving others the way God loves them.

So do you want to walk in love toward these people? You may need to go back and repeat step two about walking in purity. Ask God to search your heart and see if there is any wicked way in you (Ps 139:23-24). Ask yourself what about that person annoys you, and then see if that same sin might not be in your own life. Jesus says "Take the log out of your own eye before you can help your brother remove the speck from his" (Matt 7:1-5).

God wants you to help others overcome their sin, but only after you have taken care of your own sin. And even if that other person never does gain victory over their sin, you can love them anyway because you know the struggle they are facing. In fact, in Ephesians 5:2, Paul writes that we are to love others the way Jesus Christ has loved us. We walk in love by seeing how Jesus loves us. And how is that? While we were still sinners (Rom 5:8). He did not wait for us to become lovable, but loved us despite our sin and rebellion. So too, Jesus is leading us into similar love for others.

As you live according to your calling and learn to walk in purity, this hopefully does not lead you to live judgmental lives toward others, but rather to love and forgive others unconditionally, just as God in Jesus Christ loves and forgives you. It is only when we live this way that the fourth step toward Christlikeness is accomplished.

STEP 4. WALK IN LIGHT (EPH 5:8-14)

Once we have mastered walking in love, the next step in God's development goal is that we walk in light (5:8-14). Ephesians 5:8 tells us to walk as children of light. While it is true that all Christians are to be lights in this world (Matt 5:14), many Christians have their lights covered with scum and grime so that barely a twinkle escapes into the dark night. But as we live in purity (Step 2) and reveal the love of God toward all (Step 3) the grime is washed away and the light of God within each one of us will shine forth (Isa 58:8).

Walking as children of light is closely related to the idea of walking in the light. Walking in the light is a biblical term for deep, intimate fellowship with God and other Christians (cf. Eph 5:11, 1 John 1:6-7; 2:9-11). In Revelation 21, where the new heavens and the new earth are described, we read that it is then that we will forever walk in the light (Rev 21:23-24).

Does it ever seem like God is distant from you? Does it seem like God is silent and is not at work in your life? When you come to the place in your Christian development where you are walking in the light, you will experience fellowship, intimacy and communion with God that you never imagined nor thought possible. When you come to this fourth step, it will be as Paul says in 5:14: "Awake, you who sleep, arise from the dead, and Christ will give you light." When you begin to walk in the light, it will seem to you as though you have been asleep your whole life. It will seem to you like you have been locked away in prison without ever seeing the sun. It will seem like your whole life has been night and now the day has dawned.

These are the kind of Christians God wants His church filled with. He wants people who are in deep, intimate fellowship with Him. He wants people who want Him. And it is these people who God reveals Himself to in all of His light and glory (Matt. 5:8). God's fourth goal for every person in the church is that they will walk as children of light. In this way there will be constant communion and fellowship.

This constant communion and fellowship will only be accomplished as we take the steps in order. Many Christians seem to believe that walking in the light means pointing out the sin in everyone else. Such Christians make it their goal in life to quote Bible verses at every person behaving badly, and to condemn and accuse those who disobey God's instructions. Such Christians only behave this way because they have taken the steps out of order. They are trying to live as lights in the world without love. But just as there cannot be truth without love, so also there cannot be light without love. Only by taking the steps in order as Paul lays them out here can you learn to walk in the light and be a light to this world.

Besides, if there is no more condemnation (Rom 8:1), why do we condemn? If Satan (not God) is the accuser, why do we accuse? If Jesus has forgiven all, why do we refuse to forgive? If you consider yourself to be a guide to the blind or a light in the darkness, make sure you are a light in the same way God is, calling people to Him through love, grace, and mercy, rather than through judgment, blame, and accusation. Learn who you are in Jesus Christ and what He has called you to do (Step 1), so that you will not be tempted by the thrills of this world but will instead be addicted to the adventure of following Jesus (Step 2) as He shows you how to love others as He has loved you (Step 3). Only then will your light shine before men, and lead you to the fifth and final step.

STEP 5. WALK CAREFULLY (EPH 5:14–6:9)

The fifth step in accomplishing God's development goal is to walk carefully. Paul says in Ephesians 5:15 to see then that you walk *circumspectly*. To walk circumspectly means to be careful what you do. Now really, this is not actually a fifth step, but more of a practical application of how it will look when we are walking in the other four. In Ephesians 5:14-6:9, Paul provides some concrete examples of what it will look like when you are fulfilling your calling, living purely, loving others, and spreading God's light.

In 5:18, Paul talks about being filled with the Spirit, which means to be controlled by the Spirit. This does not mean you act like a lunatic, for Paul writes elsewhere that one of the fruits of the Spirit is self-control. When you are filled with the Spirit, you do not lose control, but actually gain self-control for the first time in your life. Being filled with the Spirit also leads to the other fruits of the Spirit in Galatians 5, as well as singing, giving thanks in all situations, and submitting to one another (Eph 5:19-21).

Singing and having a thankful heart in all situations is definitely something that comes only through the Spirit. Where the world sees only defeat and darkness, the Spirit-filled person sees God's hand at work. The Spirit-filled person even sees God at work in terrorist attacks, the death of loved ones, or even in war and violence. This does not mean that God caused such things, or that we must thank God for such things happening. No, to be thankful *in* such events means that you are able to see how God is working to bring good from them.

Submitting to one another is also a great sign of the Spirit-filled life. The Holy Spirit leads to mutual submission. Mutual submission is so important that Paul goes on to give some clear examples of how it looks in real life. He explains mutual submission in the marriage in verses 22-33, while in chapter 6 he explains mutual submission in the family and in the workplace. When we are controlled by the Spirit, He affects all of our relationships in all areas of our life.[1]

Does any of this sound like the typical description you have heard of someone who "has the Spirit"? What most people say it looks like to be filled with the Spirit is not at all similar to what Paul says it looks like. If a Spirit-filled person is as Paul describes, we must reassess what a "Spirit-filled church" looks like too. It is not necessarily where people are rolling in the aisles, speaking in otherworldly languages, and having their fillings changed to gold. Rather, a Spirit-filled church is one where the people sing joyfully, give thanks in all situations, and willingly submit to one another. This is the kind of church God is trying to develop.

This fifth and final step in our walk toward God's development goal is vitally important, because it actually takes us back to Step 1. The first step in becoming the church that God wants us to be was to discover our calling and walk in light of it. And when Paul discusses some concrete examples of what we can do and where we can serve, he writes about the "mundane" aspects of

---

[1] Ephesians 6:10-20 is not about our spiritual walk but about spiritual warfare. The key verb is no longer "walk" but "stand." Since warfare is not part of God's development goal, a discussion of it will not be included here.

family and work. This means that when you discover where God wants you to serve, do not be surprised to learn that it is not up on stage or in front of an audience, but in your home with your wife and children and with your boss (or employees) at work. Your primary calling is not in the limelight, but in how you live your day-to-day life with the people God has placed around you. That is where real *church* takes place.

So Step 5 takes us right back to Step 1, and starts the cycle all over again. In other words, in this life we will never arrive at the end of what God wants for us. No person, group, or church will ever fully achieve the ultimate goal for which we have been called. But this is no reason to stop striving for it, because only as we follow Jesus wherever He leads will He make progress in redeeming our lives and rescuing this world. So do you want to see where Jesus goes next? Follow Him over the horizon to see what adventure awaits!

CONCLUSION

It has often been said that the best way to start a project is to begin with the end in mind. In Ephesians 4, 5 and 6, Paul has painted a picture for us of God's ultimate goal for His church, and has given us the 5 steps in His development plan. Where are you in accomplishing this plan? Have you discovered why God called you? If so, are you being purified day by day? As you become more and more pure, are you loving others more and living in the light of God more? And in all of this, are you learning day by day to be filled with and controlled by the Holy Spirit so that you serve and submit to those around you? Only as you do these things will you be conformed to the image and likeness of Jesus Christ and become the glorious church that He wants in this world.

DISCUSSION QUESTIONS

1. What would your ideal church look like? Describe it.

2. What is the word "walk" such an important word regarding our responsibilities listed in Ephesians 4–6?

3. What is God's "model" for His church? How does this model help us know what the church should look like? How well does this model fit your description of the ideal church above?

4. What does God "choose" us for?

5. What does it mean to walk worthy of our calling?

6. What is the best way to discern if you are pure in heart?

7. What is the first thing we must take care of before we can walk in love? Why?

8. What does it mean to walk in light? What does it not mean?

9. What does it look like to be filled with the Holy Spirit?

PART 2: GROUNDBREAKING

CHAPTER 4

CHOOSING A CONTRACTOR

All boys dream of becoming "men." They play at going off to war. They try to act "manly" around girls. They experiment with shaving. Oftentimes, the father is the role-model for the young boy and the father's behavior determines what kind of a man that boy will grow up to be. Most boys will also develop other role models though, such as movie stars and football quarterbacks. Boys desire to emulate such men because of certain qualities these men exhibit.

The interesting thing is that different boys will have different heroes in different cultures. What is valued by men differs from one culture to another. Bravery, courage, confidence, and strength are the traits most valued in a competitive or warlike culture. In an intellectual society, men value wisdom, honesty, and truthfulness. Where business is prominent, a man is judged by what position he has, and what kind of car, house, and clothes he owns. In mountainous forest settings, it is a man's skill at hunting and fishing that matter most, as well as the quality of his truck or fishing boat.

On a construction site, the one who is most esteemed and valued is the contractor. The contractor provides direction and leadership over the entire building project. He determines who gets hired and who gets fired. He makes the hard decisions and sets project priorities for the crew. Though some crews do not like their contractor, most crew members would like to become a contractor themselves. He has the blueprints in mind, and he knows what needs to be done, who needs to do it, and in what order. He guides and directs the overall construction process so that the building goes up quickly and safely.

The construction site that is God's church also has contractors. Under headship of Jesus Christ, the contractors are the leaders and authority figures in the church. We often call them elders, or overseers, but when it comes to the role of providing direction and leadership for the spiritual construction of God's church, they also serve in the role of contractor. They oversee, guide, and shepherd the church. They are the ones who help the rest of the crew figure out what to do, when to do it, and how to do it as a unified team.

But who gets to be a contractor in God's church? Well, just as with any job position, there are very specific job qualifications a man must meet before he can become a contractor in God's church. And while many in the church look for qualities about age, charisma, leadership skills, or how many initials they have after their name, such items are not all that important to God. God has His own list of qualifications for those who would be a contractor in the church. There are seventeen qualifications on God's list, which are found in 1 Timothy 3:1-7.

No person, of course, will fulfill all seventeen qualifications perfectly. But any person who desires to lead the church should have all seventeen items to one degree or another. The seventeen items can be thought of as a chain. Chains are used to perform all sorts of work, but a chain is only as strong as its weakest link. So also with God's contractors. A person who would be a contractor in God's church will have all seventeen links, but some will be weaker than others, and it is these weak links that should be focused on first. This work of strengthening various links will be a life-long process. No person can ever say that they have "arrived" and is exactly what God wants them to be. If someone *does* say such a thing, they are arrogant and thus have disqualified themselves from being a leader in the church.

Having said this, there is one perfect example of all seventeen items. That person is Jesus. I will not point it out with each item in this list, but if you ever wonder what it looks like to perfectly achieve the type of person that God wants His contractors to be, all you have to do is look at Jesus. He is the perfect example of God's leader. As such, He is the Chief Cornerstone, the Head Architect, and Lead Contractor on the church that God is building. When we follow Jesus, He will show us how better to become like Him and become the leaders He wants us to be.

1. DESIRE

Paul begins by saying that "If a man desires the position of a bishop, he desires a good work." The phrase "If *a* man" could also be translated, "If *any* man." This means that what Paul writes applies to all men.[1] If you are a man, this applies to you. It

---

[1] Could Paul's description apply to women also? No. And Yes. Paul is clearly only thinking about men, for he says a bit later that an elder should be the husband of one wife (a one-woman man). Nevertheless, this does not mean that Paul thought that women could not be elders, or that women could not serve as spiritual leaders and directors in the church. In various other contexts, Paul

doesn't matter who you are. It doesn't matter what is in your past. It doesn't matter how old you are, or how young you are. It doesn't even matter what your current spiritual maturity level is. If you are a man, Paul says that you can become a contractor in the church God is building.

Paul's term for the church contractor is "bishop," but some translations might have elder or overseer. The word is *episkopē* in Greek, and is made up of two words, *epi* which means "upon" or "over," and *skopē*, which means "to watch, to observe, or to see." It is from *skopē* that we get our English word scope. *Episkopē*

---

seems to be fine with female spiritual leaders, teachers, and directors of church life (cf. Rom 16:7). Paul's overall outlook on church ministry allowed for complete equality between men and women in all roles and functions (Gal 3:28). Therefore, while the description for elders in 1 Timothy 3:1-7 cannot be *exegetically* applied to women, it can be *theologically* applied.

Nevertheless, for the sake of consistency and expediency, I will maintain the masculine nouns and pronouns that were used by Paul in this text, but please know that in so doing, I am not trying to restrict the role of spiritual overseer in the church to men only. I think that women are the much-needed and far-too-often missing voices in church leadership and direction today. The church in general would be much healthier if women had more of a voice in the direction, care, leadership, and emphasis of the church.

Also, it is important to note in passing that the issue of women leadership in the church fades away into an inconsequential issue when we move away from the hierarchical structures of organized, traditional Christianity. When church is viewed more as a people of God who follow Jesus into the world, or as a family of God who live and work together throughout life, then we see that female leadership is absolutely essential if we are going to survive and thrive. It is ludicrous to think that any group of people or any family could ever survive without the active involvement, insightful wisdom, tender teaching, and natural leadership abilities of women. The starting place for any discussion about the role of women in church must begin by discussing the role of women in a family. Since church is the family of God, anything that you say about women's roles in the family must also be said about women's roles in the church.

then, means to watch over, or to oversee. Therefore, since the term bishop brings to mind Catholic clergy, and the term elder make people think of those who are old, the best way to translate the term is also the most literal way. An *episkopē* is an overseer. Therefore, this chapter will use the term "overseer" to describe those who serve as contractors on the construction site of God's church.

Paul goes on to say that if any man desires this position, he desires a good work. Paul actually uses two different words for desire. The first is *oregomai* and means "to stretch oneself out in order to touch or to do something, to reach after or desire something."[2] The second word is *epithumei*, and it speaks of a passionate, inner compulsion to be used in service to the Lord. In other words, it is a good thing to want to be an overseer. It is not covetousness to seek the role of overseer in the church. If you desire it, you desire a good work. Some people seem to think that all desire is wrong, but there is nothing wrong with desiring the things which God desires for us. Accomplishing God's will for our lives often begins with a desire to do so.

If a man desires to be an overseer, he has begun at the right place. But desire, all by itself, is not enough. A contractor on a construction site must have the right qualifications, training, knowledge, skills, and character. Many men desire to become a contractor, but few achieve it. Desire is only the beginning point, the springboard, the catalyst to gaining these necessary qualifications, but any man can become an overseer if he is willing to do

---

[2] J.H. Thayer, *Thayer's Greek-English Lexicon of the New Testament* (Grand Rapids: Baker, 1977), 452.

what it takes.

But the calling is high. Most of the literature on 1 Timothy 3 today says that these qualifications are the goal, the pinnacle, the target to aim for. Most men, we are told, will not achieve this. If they are making progress in the right direction, that is good enough. However, if we go back and look at the literature from the past, even from only fifty years ago, the list of qualifications in 1 Timothy 3 was the starting point, the bottom rung. This list was the bare minimum a man had to have in order to qualify for the position of overseer. Though there will always be room for improvement in all of the qualifications, a man must at least have them all in seminal form before he can be considered for the office of overseer.

2. BLAMELESS

Paul then writes that the overseer "must be blameless." The word "must" communicates something that is essential and mandatory, not suggested or optional. Whenever a business or company outlines the necessary job qualifications for an opening, they are looking for someone who at least fits that description. If someone applies who only has half the qualifications, their application will not even be considered, but will be quickly discarded instead.

It should be the same with God's church. Many of the problems associated with leadership in the church today could be avoided if God's list of qualifications were resolutely followed. It is better to have no leaders than to have unqualified leaders. The damage that unqualified leaders can cause is much greater than the damage that might result from having no leaders at all.

So this second qualification eliminates quite a few. For who among us is blameless? It is the overarching, all-encompassing qualification in the list. All of the other qualifications are to be understood in light of this one. However, though being blameless seems overwhelming, is not quite as impossible as it seems. "Blameless" does not mean perfect. Obviously, it cannot mean that a candidate has never sinned or never will sin. What it means is to be above reproach. Literally, the Greek word means "not able to be held. To provide no handles."

The man who is blameless has nothing in his life for which he can be arrested or accused of. He is not involved in any illegal practices. His life is not marred by any obvious sinful defect. He is a model for the other members of the congregation to follow. He is an example of godliness in his marriage (v 2), his personal life (v 3), and his home (vs 4-5). He may not be perfect, but his character is such that when people who know him hear that he is a leader in the church, they do not raise their eyebrows in surprise, but instead nod their heads in agreement. Rather than saying, "Really? Him?!" they say, "Yes, I can see that."

It brings terrible shame to the church in general and to the name of Christ when church leaders are involved in shady or immoral practices. If a man desires to be an overseer, he must first of all be blameless. Nobody can dig up any dirt on him, or blackmail him. There are no skeletons in his closet, for he is blameless.

3. THE HUSBAND OF ONE WIFE

The third qualification is that an overseer must be the husband of one wife. Many believe that this second qualification automatically disqualifies men who are unmarried or who have been divorced. But this is not what the phrase implies. Literally, the Greek reads, "a one-woman man." It means that a man is completely devoted to his wife. This second qualification goes a lot deeper than whether or not a man is married or divorced.

If a man is unmarried, it means that he does not have a wandering eye. He does not let himself view movies, magazines, and pictures that bring lustful thoughts into his mind. Even though he may not have met the woman who will be his wife, his thoughts are only for her. He protects his mind and thoughts for the woman who will one day be his wife. And even if, like Paul, he never gets married, he is fully devoted to his first love, Jesus Christ.

If a man is married, to be a "one-woman man" means that all of his thoughts and energy go toward loving and caring for his wife. He does not flirt with other women. He does not look lustfully at other women. A man who has a wondering eye cannot be described as a one-woman man, even if he has never been divorced. This is why this third qualification is not about divorce. It is not about the past, but has everything to do with loyalty and faithfulness to the woman who is his wife now.

This leads us to recognize that the position of overseer in the church is also open to men who have been divorced. If a man has a divorce in his past, this second qualification means that he is completely devoted to his present wife and that divorce is not an option with her. If his past divorce is fairly recent, it would be wise to proceed with caution before installing him as an overseer in the church, for only time can tell if the causes for the previous divorce have been corrected. If a man has two or three divorces, this may indicate a deeply entrenched habit of unfaithfulness that may require years of observation to see if he has learned to love his wife like Christ loves the church.

A one-woman man is a man who is completely devoted in his heart, mind, strength, and energy to the woman who is his wife. He loves, desires and thinks only of her. He maintains sexual purity both in thought life and conduct. This is a one-woman man.

You might wonder how Jesus can be a one-woman man when He never got married, and never intended to. The answer is to remember that the church is the Bride of Christ. Jesus always and only thinks about us, the church, and how He can protect and provide for us. He is always faithful and caring, and never lets His eyes or mind wander to some other object of attention. For the overseer who is married, Jesus is the perfect example of how to love your wife (cf. Eph 5:22-33).

4. TEMPERATE

The fourth qualification for the overseer is that he must be "temperate." The Greek word literally means "wineless," but Paul is not talking about alcohol. He mentions drinking in verse 3, so here it refers to something else. The term "wineless" or "temperate," was used of drinking water that was unmixed with wine.

To understand what Paul means, it is important to know that they made their wine a bit different than today. They pressed the grapes in such a way that some of the pulp remained in the wine. They were not able to filter and purify it as we are today. This made the wine cloudy. When this cloudy wine was mixed with water, it also clouded the water, like when we accidentally mix a little orange juice or milk in with water. When Paul says temperate, or "wineless," what he means is "clear, unclouded" drinking water.

But why would someone mix wine in with their drinking water? At that time, people often got sick from drinking the water, but they discovered that if they added some wine to the water, they would not get sick as often. They didn't understand the science of bacteria and germs, but the alcohol in the wine helped sanitize the water. So they would make bad water somewhat more drinkable by mixing it with wine. This would, of course, make the water quite cloudy.

It was very rare then, to find clean and clear water that was safe to drink. Such unclouded drinking water was very precious and sought after. Pure water was very valuable. Only those who were rich could afford to buy pure, clean, clear water. It was called "wineless" water. Today, we get such water out of our taps, but such water was extremely valuable in Paul's day.

Paul then takes this kind of water, and applies it to the type of man who can lead the church. He is thinking about a person's temperament. On overseer, Paul writes, is to be temperate, wineless. This is a man who is alert, watchful, vigilant, clear-headed. Nothing clouds his judgment. He doesn't allow emotions, people, events, popular opinion, culture, or anything else, affect his decisions. If a man makes rash judgements in the heat of the moment, he is not temperate. If his decisions are formed by times of anger or stress, he is not "wineless." If he allows prominent people to whisper in his ear, he has become clouded. If he only makes decision to quiet the clamoring masses, he is not fit to be a leader of the church. Such men must purify their minds with the washing of the water of the Word (Eph 5:26; Rom 12:1-2). Then he will become temperate.

5. SOBER-MINDED

The next qualification is that overseers are to be "sober-minded." This could also be translated as "self-controlled." When some see the word *sober*, they again think of drinking. But what Paul is referring to is seriousness. He doesn't mean someone who is without humor, who is cold and never laughs, but someone who is able to view the world through God's eyes. A sober-minded man knows there is a time for laughter and a time for crying, a time for jokes and a time for seriousness.

To some men, everything is a joke. They always want to be the funny guy who makes everybody laugh. They always want to be the life of the party, even if there is no party. We have all known men who try to make jokes at a funeral just to break the tension. That is not being sober-minded. A sober-minded man knows that spiritual matters are a grave concern and there is not much time for frivolous living. There are important decision to make and important priorities to set. He should be able to have fun and to joke and laugh in proper situations, but he should also be able to buckle down and focus on the task at hand in leading the church and serving the people of God.

6. OF GOOD BEHAVIOR

Sixth, the man who wants to be an overseer in God's church must be of "good behavior." This could also be translated as "respectable." The Greek word here is *kosmios* and is a derivative of *kosmos*. We speak of the universe as the cosmos, which in English also means orderly, or structured. It means the same in Greek. *Kosmios* is the opposite of chaos. When something is *kosmios*, it is organized so that everything is in its proper place and performing its proper function.

When used to describe a person, the word has in view a man who is orderly and organized. He is well-disciplined in mind and life.[3] He is not surrounded by chaos or disorder. He has good behavior at work, at home, and at play. Others respect him for his upright conduct in all areas of life. He knows what to do, when to do it, and how best to do it. Orderliness is important for spiritual leaders because of the high demands upon them for their time and energy. If a man is going to balance ministry with his personal and family life, he must be orderly and organized.

7. HOSPITABLE

The seventh characteristic of an overseer is that he must be "hospitable." The word literally means "to love strangers." This not only refers to how he welcomes people into his home, but also to the manner in which he interacts with strangers away from home. Whether in his study or in his home, his door ought always to be open to those who are needy. And when he is shopping at the grocery store, sitting in traffic on his commute, or being served by a waitress at a restaurant, he treats people with dignity and respect. He is kind, thoughtful, and generous toward strangers.

Spiritual leaders should not be elevated to a place where they are unapproachable or think that they are better than everyone else. They are to be available.[4] They are not to be like a figure in

---

[3] John MacArthur, *1 Timothy* (Chicago: Moody, 1995), 107.
[4] Ibid, 108.

an ivory tower, so far above everyone else that they are not accessible and cannot relate to others. He welcomes people into his home, and when he is out, he makes people feel at home.

8. ABLE TO TEACH

Overseers should also be "able to teach." This is a somewhat debatable term. The general consensus is that Paul probably has a double meaning in mind. He not only means that this sort of man has the ability and knowledge to teach others, but also that he is able to accept teaching from others. He is both able to teach, and he is teachable. In fact, it could easily be argued that someone who is not teachable should not themselves be teaching others.

Most men are one of two extremes. Some only want to teach, but not to be taught. Such men love to be heard. They always want to be right, to get the last word in and have their opinions expressed. On the opposite extreme, there are those who have wonderful understanding, knowledge, and insights of God's Word, but when they try to explain these things to others, it is like listening to a scientist talk about quantum physics in another language. This second type of person may be very teachable, but is not really able to teach others. God wants the men who lead His church to be balanced in both. The things that they learn must be passed on to others (2 Tim 2:2; Titus 1:9).

The best place for a man to practice this eighth qualification is in the home. God wants all men to be Bible teachers at home. Scripture contains instructions about this in Deuteronomy 6 and the book of Proverbs. There are also negative examples in Scripture with a father like Eli in 1 Samuel 1–2, and positive examples with a father like Abraham. Men who leave the spiritual training and instruction of their children up to others are not acting according to God's standard.

Isn't it interesting that the Bible does not say that to be a truly great man, you need to be an expert hunter or fisherman? The Bible does not care how great a man is at sports (In fact, sports aren't even mentioned in the Bible). Nowhere do we read that truly great men make six-figure incomes. Truly great men are not described as having large houses and nice cars. Instead, everywhere in the Bible we read that God wants men to be teaching their wives and children at home through their words and by their example. When a man learns to teach at home and is faithful in this, God may give him further opportunities to teach in the church.

9. NOT GIVEN TO WINE

Paul finally mentions something having to do with alcohol in verse 3. He says that a man who desires to be an overseer is "not given to wine." This has in mind excessive drinking or drunkenness. Biblically, drinking a glass of wine or having a beer is not sin. Getting drunk is sinful, especially when we become enslaved or addicted to strong drink. A man who wants to be God's kind of man must not allow himself to be controlled by alcohol. He can have a drink, just as Jesus sometimes did, but he must not allow himself to be controlled by drink.

Although Paul only mentions wine, there are other controlling substances which can also be abused. Drugs, tobacco, caffeine, and excessive food may be some things which the man who would be an overseer must refrain from. Though some of these things may not be sinful in and of themselves, the damage that can be done to the body and the control they can exert on behavior when used in excess make them dangerous to the man of God. The man of God must not be controlled by any outside substance. There must be no substance which controls a man who would be a spiritual leader in the church.

10. NOT VIOLENT

Tenth, the man who would be an overseer is "not violent" or pugnacious. The Greek literally reads "not a giver of blows," or "not a striker." There are some men who try to settle everything with their fists. When a disagreement breaks out, they seem to think they've got five good points in each hand. Such a man is not fit for spiritual leadership within the church. A man who desires to be an overseer does not resort to blows, but to the Bible. With a calm head and cool words, he reasons things out with his adversaries. He is not violent. He does not engage in violence, nor does he call for violence against others. He is a peacemaker and wants all people to live in peace.

11. NOT GREEDY

The man who wants to be an overseer should be careful about why he wants such a position. The eleventh necessary qualification demands that the motivation not be greed. Paul says that an overseer is "not greedy for money."[5] The phrase actually includes

---

[5] This item is not in the NIV or the NAS because a different Greek manu-

more than just money. It also includes greed for material gain. While money is one manifestation of greed, it is not the only thing we can be greedy for. Greed can also include houses, cars, possessions, or recreational toys. We've all seen the bumper sticker which says "He who dies with the most toys wins." The person who wrote that bumper sticker was greedy for material gain.

In 21st century North America, this hits most men right at home. Most men want more money and few think they have enough. Christian men would almost never say they want a lot of money, just a little bit more than they have now. And the money they do have, they think is theirs to use the way they want. They think, "It's my money. I worked for it. I earned it. I get to keep it. Besides, I have all those bills to pay and a family to feed." Biblically, however, it is not their money. Even though they did work for it, the only reason they have the job they do and the ability and health to perform the job is because God gave these to them.

Such an attitude often reveals a heart of greed. So if you want to be an overseer, you must work to defeat greed. The simplest way to defeat greed and the love of money is to give it away.[6] John Wesley said that if when he died, there was found more than $10 in his pocket, you could consider him to be a thief. Malachi 3 says that the man who does not give back to God is robbing God. That is a serious statement to consider. Robbing

---

script family is used.

[6] Note that I am not saying that you must tithe to the church. I am not at all convinced that "giving money" or "giving to God" or even "tithing your money" means "putting money in the offering plate at church." I write more about this in *Church is More than Bodies, Bucks, & Bricks* (Dallas, OR: Redeeming Press, 2015).

God is what the greedy man is doing. And nobody who is robbing God can be serving Him as an overseer.

12. GENTLE

An overseer must also be "gentle." A gentle man is one who is considerate, forbearing, and gracious. He frequently overlooks the wrongs of others and pardons human failure. He does not return insults for criticism. He remembers good, but not evil. He does not keep a record of wrongs done to him. He does not hold a grudge. He treats everyone with respect in his words and actions. Being a gentleman is a lost art today, but it is a requirement for the contractor in God's building program.

13. NOT QUARRELSOME

Somewhat related to being gentle, one who is an overseer is "not quarrelsome." Previously, we learned that an overseer must not be violent; he must not be one who settles everything with his fists. A quarrelsome man is one who tries to settle everything with argumentative words. We all know men who love to argue. It doesn't really matter what the topic of discussion is, or what the various viewpoints are, men who love to argue will find out where you stand on an issue and then take the opposing viewpoint and argue it. Such men often become lawyers.

Now a good debate can be quite enjoyable, but there are men who always try to pick a fight. Whatever comes out of their mouth is meant to offend, insult, or challenge. The man who is going to become an overseer avoids a fight. He does argue and debate, but will stand up for the cause of someone who cannot defend themselves.

As with all of these qualities, Jesus is the perfect example. He never defended himself, never quarreled. When people insulted Him, struck Him, and spit on Him, He never fought back. He was very argumentative, though, when He stood up for orphans and widows, the poor and the needy, and when He stood up against the Pharisees and Sadducees who had perverted the gospel. Like Jesus, the man who would be an overseer in God's church must only fight God's battles.

14. NOT COVETOUS

The fourteenth requirement is that an overseer be "not covetous." Since the eleventh was "not greedy for money," this character qualification is somewhat different. While greed is wanting more of what you already have, coveting is wanting something that you don't have. Coveting is wanting what someone else has. Just as greed is a big problem in our society, so also is coveting. Most of the advertising strategies on television and in print media are based on encouraging greed and getting people to covet.

Covetous desires cause people to want what their neighbor has, whether it be a ski boat, a top-of-the-line computer, a big-screen TV, a riding lawn mower, a fancy vacation, name brand clothes, a richer husband, a sexier wife, or anything that you don't have but which you think will make your life better once you get it. As a result of always thinking about what else they need, people who are covetous are rarely happy with what they have or thankful for what they get. Therefore, the man who is training to become an overseer must learn to be content with the things he has and not try to keep up with the Jones'.

15. RULES HIS HOUSE WELL

One of the most important qualifications for being an overseer is the fifteenth. While Paul only writes a few words about all of the other qualifications, he takes two full verses on the requirement that an overseer must take care of his household. Paul writes that an overseer "must be one who rules his own house well, having his children in submission with all reverence (for if a man does not know how to rule his own house, how will he take care of the church of God?)."

It is shocking how neglected this requirement has become today. Many pastors take pride in never being at home with their family. They talk, almost boastfully, about how they love the ministry so much they spend 80 or 90 hours a week at work. Most never spend an evening playing games with their children, taking their families on vacations, or even eating supper with this families around the table. I fell into this problem as well when I was a pastor, and am thankful for the second chance my wife and family gave me. Now I spend more of my free-time with my family.

I recently had a conversation with a prominent pastor of a larger church who used to be a district leader in an internationally recognized denomination. He said that God's primary avenue for caring for people was not the family, but the church. In other words, he believed it was okay for a man to not provide for his family at home mentally, emotionally, spiritually, and physically, because this was the task of the church. He took Hillary Clinton's idea that "It takes a village to raise a child" and applied it to the church. It would have been better if this pastor had followed the Bible instead.

Paul is very clear who is primarily responsible for the family. The man is. The husband. The father. He must be one who rules his own house well. This does not mean that he rules with an iron fist and forces his family members into subjection under him. The word for "rules" carries the idea of "presiding over, providing or caring for, assisting, to be concerned about." Jesus is the perfect example. Jesus rules the church, but He never forces us to do anything, but only loves, cares, guides, protects, and sacrifices Himself for our sake. This also is how a man should care for his wife and children at home.

He is to be the leader, the bread-winner, and the soul-tender. This means that he cares for his family and provides for their mental, emotional, physical, and spiritual needs. He knows that his wife and children are the most valuable possession he has been given, and will make sure he is involved in their lives as much as possible.

Paul speaks primarily in verse 4 of the father's relationship to his children. He says that he must have his children in submission with all reverence. This does not mean that his children always obey and never get into trouble. Nobody's home is perfect all the time. Just as there is no perfect church, there is no perfect family. Instead, Paul means that the general tenor of the home is one of submission, respect, and obedience. The children, though they may disobey, do not have a reputation for rebellion.

The reason this is so important is because if a man cannot manage or rule well over his own household, he will not be able to manage or rule well in the church either. Every man should view his home a mini church in which he is the overseer. And if he is not overseeing his home well, he cannot be an overseer in the church. If he is unable to build up the people in his home, how he will be able to build up the people in the church?

> A man may be a successful businessman, a capable public official, a brilliant office manager, or a top military leader, but a terrible church elder. In the family of God, a man's ability to lead his family is the test that qualifies or disqualifies a man to be an elder. An elder's relationship with his children will manifest itself in his relationship with the congregation. If he is too harsh with his children - rigid, impatient, insensitive, permissive, inconsistent, or passive - that is how he will respond to the congregation. If one wants to know what an elder will be like, observe how he manages his children.[7]

The following diagnostic questions are helpful for determining what a man's home life is like:

- Are the kids usually respectful and is the home normally well-ordered?

- Are the mother and father in good relations with one another? As parents, are they attentive, involved and supportive of each other and of their children?

- How is the communication? Do they talk or does every conversation degenerate into yelling and name-calling and slamming of doors?

---

[7] Alexander Strauch, *Biblical Eldership* (Littleton, CO: Lewis and Roth, 1988), 202.

- Is there an atmosphere of spiritual development being fostered? Is Jesus Christ openly discussed? Is the Word of God studied? Does the father teach his children to pray and to read the Bible and to become Christ-like?

This is part of what it means for an overseer to rule his own household well. In John Bunyan's *Pilgrim's Progress,* there is a character named Talkative, who is described as being a saint on the road but a devil at home. Many men would never behave in public, let alone at church, the way they behave at home. But the man who desires to be an overseer needs to rule his own household well.

16. NOT A NOVICE

The sixteenth qualification is that a prospective overseer must not be a new Christian. He is "not a novice, lest being puffed up with pride he fall into the same condemnation as the devil." The role of overseer in the church calls for spiritual roots. It requires perception, experience, and wisdom that comes only through time as a Christian.

A brand new Christian, however old they are, may have a lot of enthusiasm. Many people will look at him and say "Wow, is he ever on fire for God. Let's get him on the elder board. That'll fire them up." A new Christian may learn a lot about the Bible in a very short period of time. He may even turn his life around and get rid of many old habits, while revealing many new Godly traits. Nevertheless, he cannot be an overseer. Paul says that placing a new Christian into leadership too soon may result in pride and arrogance, which is the same sin the devil fell into. Therefore, however great a new Christian may be, and whatever spiritual strides they may have made, it is the duty of the church to protect such Christians from pride by not giving them a position of overseer too quickly.

When pride sets in to spiritual leaders, they tend to think they know better than everyone else what to do. When New Christians are placed too quickly into leadership positions in the church, they have a tendency to judge and condemn those who are stuck in sin or who do not seem to be progressing in their Christian walk as fast as the new Christian might have done. Such attitudes can quickly lead to many people getting hurt and offended.

So how new is too new? How can a church know when a person has matured to the point that they are no longer a new convert? It is relative to the congregation. In places where there are no churches, and a missionary has planted a new church, the men who show the most godliness and spiritual maturity after a year or two can no longer be considered a new believer. Such men might make good candidates for overseers.

But in a church that has been in existence for a long time, there are undoubtedly many mature men of God, and so it may take a long time for a new Christian to mature to the point where they are no longer a novice. The respectable thing for a Christian to do in this situation is be patient and learn, rather than get impatient and go off to start a ministry of their own. When they do this, it only reveals the type of pride Paul was worried about here.

17. A GOOD TESTIMONY WITH UNBELIEVERS

Finally, from verse 7, a potential overseer must have a good reputation with unbelievers. Paul writes that he must have "a good testimony among those who are outside, lest he fall into reproach and the snare of the devil." In other words, the question here concerns how the person is viewed by people who are not part of the church. What do the people in his neighborhood think of him? What do his coworkers have to say? Do they even know he is a Christian? Does he uphold Christian standards among them or does he try to fit in and not rock the boat? A man who desires to be an overseer must let people know and see that he is a Christian by his words and actions.

At the same time, a person who wants to have a good reputation with those outside the church must not be seen as an arrogant, self-righteous, judgmental religious fanatic who is always quoting Bible verses and condemning the sins he sees in others. This is not ever what Jesus did, and so should also not be what we do. People of all types loved to be in the presence of Jesus, and so if the church is looking for those who would make good overseers, it might be wise to look at those who have lots of non-Christian friends.

SUB-CONTRACTORS

Before we end this chapter, something should also be added about sub-contractors. Overseers are not the only leaders in the church. Overseers, since they are the contractors, will oversee the work of sub-contractors. These sub-contractors need to be examined as well. The qualifications are less stringent because the requirements are ministry specific rather than general as with an overseer. Paul mentions specifically the requirements for Deacons, or Servants, in 1 Timothy 3:8-13. Many of the qualification are very similar to that of the overseers, with the main difference being that overseers are involved in *spiritual* oversight, while deacons are involved with *physical* oversight. While overseers take charge of the spiritual needs of the church body, the deacons are primarily in charge of taking care of the physical needs.

But beyond the overseers and deacons there are many other possible positions of leadership in the church. For example, in some times of gatherings, there are needs for music leaders, children's teachers, and people to clean the building where the church meets. Even here, there should be some sort of minimum qualifications necessary for such positions to be filled. Sometimes musicians are allowed to lead the music simply because they can play the guitar. Sometimes Sunday school teachers are chosen simply because they are willing to do it when no one else is. Sometimes people are asked to serve on a board just because they have a lot of money or hold prominent political positions in the community. While this is understandable, it is not advisable from a biblical perspective.

Biblically, for any leadership position in any church, there are three basic requirements: they must have a heart for God, be filled with the Holy Spirit, and have humility with people. Ability, experience, and education are nice, but are not quite as important. It is better to have somebody who loves God, loves His Word, and loves His people than to have someone with a Ph. D. and 37 years of experience. A person who loves God and wants to serve God will make sure they develop the abilities and skills they need to serve Him better. But a person who is proud of his or her position, experience and titles will never try to develop love for God, a knowledge of His Word, or humility with people.

Spiritual leadership is vitally important for the health and longevity of any church. A church who needs leaders can pray for God to send them, and pray for God to raise them up from within the church. The leaders who are already there should be making sure they are doing what they can to train leaders for the next generation. Leadership is vitally important for every church. Paul has revealed that God's desire is for the leaders of the church to be a group of overseers who fit certain character qualifications. When such Godly leaders are in place, God will work through them to build His church according to His divine Blueprints.

CONCLUSION

We have looked at the seventeen characteristics of the man who desires to become a contractor, an overseer in God's church. This is God's description of His ideal man. All men should desire to become like the man listed here. He is not only a man's man, but also God's man. On God's Construction Site, these are His contractors. Once the contractors are in place, we are ready to begin construction. And all construction begins with something quite boring: digging a hole and pouring a good foundation. It is to this idea we turn next.

DISCUSSION QUESTIONS

1. Can women be leaders in the church? Can they be overseers? (See the footnotes for my view on this topic.)

2. How does viewing the church as a family help see that women must have an integral part in leading the church?

3. If a person wants (or desires) to be an overseer in the church, is that enough to qualify him? What else must they have?

4. What does it mean to be blameless? Does this mean that the person never sins?

5. Is it possible to be divorced and still be a "one-woman man"? Is it possible to have never been divorced and fail at being a "one-woman man"? Why?

6. How does Paul apply the term "wineless" to overseers? Does it mean that such leaders never drink alcohol? What does it mean?

7. Since both "sober-minded" and "good behavior" have to do with a person's actions, how are they different?

8. Does being hospitable mean that the overseer has to have the spiritual gift of hospitality?

9. What is the double meaning of "able to teach"?

10. What does it mean to be "not given to wine"? Does it apply only to wine? What else could it apply to?

11. What is the difference between the three terms "not violent," "not quarrelsome," and "gentle"?

12. What is the difference between "not greedy" and "not covetous"?

13. What qualification is the most important of them all, and why?

14. Why most an overseer not be a novice?

15. What kind of testimony must an overseer have among non-Christians? Why is this important?

CHAPTER 5

POURING THE FOUNDATION

Many of the large cities in the world are known for their skyscrapers. New York has the Empire State Building. Washington D. C. has national monuments. Chicago is known for the John Hancock Building and the Sears Tower. As beautiful as these buildings are, underneath each is an incredibly strong and solid foundation. Nobody in the construction world ever thinks about skimping on the foundation. No matter how creative the building, no matter how many cost-cutting corners a construction company takes, nobody cuts corners on the foundation.

Ravi Zacharias tells of a Newsweek which hailed the completion of the "first deconstructionist building.

> Its white scaffolding, red brick turrets, and Colorado grass pods evoke a double take. But puzzlement only intensifies when you enter the building, for inside you encounter stairways that go nowhere, pillars that hang from the ceiling without purpose, and angled surfaces configured to create a sense of vertigo.
>
> The architect, we are duly informed designed this building to reflect life itself—senseless and incoherent—and the 'capriciousness of the rules that organize the built world.' When the rationale was

explained to me, I had just one question: 'Did he do the same with the foundation?'[1]

All buildings, including the spiritual building of God's church, must be constructed on a firm and solid foundation. But what is this foundation?

Far too many churches seem to be building on a shaky foundation. When churches rely on such things as corporate philosophies, marketing strategies, business principles, worldly philosophy, human wisdom, political activism, opinion surveys, or the latest church growth fad to hit the bookshelves, it is just a matter of time before those churches come crashing to the ground. If a church is going to do God's work, it must stand on God's foundation.

THE FOUNDATION IS JESUS CHRIST (1 COR 3:11)

A pastor in Kansas City, Missouri was asked one Sunday by some visitors if they could see the church constitution. He noticed they were carrying their Bibles, so he told them, "You have it in your hands. Our church is governed by the Word of God."[2]

This pastor was correct, and yet a careful distinction must be made. While I have no issue with calling the Bible "the Word of God," we must remember that the Bible is the Word of God only when we use it to teach others about Jesus Christ. Jesus Himself

---

[1] Ravi Zacharias, *Can Man Live Without God* (Dallas: Word, 1994), 21.

[2] This was Chester McCalley as related in a sermon titled "The Centrality of the Bible."

chided the Bible experts of His day for diligently studying the Scriptures while not seeing that the Scriptures pointed to Him (John 5:39). If we learn, study, and teach Scripture just so we can learn more about Scripture, we have lost our way, and are not actually studying the Word of God. If you are studying the Bible and it is not pointing you to Jesus, then you are not truly studying the Word of God. The Bible is only the Word of God when our study of it points us to Jesus, who is the Word of God.

With this in mind, it is important to read and study Scripture, for it can show the church what the foundation of Jesus Christ looks like and how we are to build our lives and ministries upon Him. If God's church is going to be built with God's riches toward God's goal, then it must be built on God's Word, which is Jesus Christ as found within the pages of Scripture. This is the only sure foundation there is. This is exactly what Paul writes to the Corinthian church.

The church in Corinth was a troubled church. It had fallen prey to numerous heresies and moral failures. So when Paul writes to both correct and encourage them, one of the first things he does is call them back to remember the foundation on which their church was planted and built. Paul begins at the very beginning. He knows that it does no good to focus on crooked walls and broken windows if the foundation is shaky and unstable.

So in reminding the Corinthian Christians of the proper foundation for their church, he first asks them to recall what he preached when he was among them, which was nothing but Jesus Christ and Him crucified (1 Cor 2:2). The suffering Savior was the source for all of Paul's sermons. He preached Christ, pointed people to Christ, and called people to imitate Christ, not just in His life, but also in His crucifixion and death. The reason for

Paul's emphasis on the crucifixion is that it is in the crucified Christ we see the clearest portrait of God in Scripture, and also where we see the clearest revelation of the wisdom and power of God.

Paul then goes on to call the Corinthian church to follow his example and build their lives and their church on the only foundation there is, Jesus Christ. He writes in 1 Corinthians 3:11 that no other foundation can be laid than the one that is laid, which is Jesus Christ. This means that no church or ministry should ever try to build their foundation on anything other than Jesus Christ. Trying to build a church on worldly principles will be like trying to construct a building with wood, hay, and straw.

So if Jesus Christ is the foundation, how do we build upon it? How does the church make sure it is founded upon Jesus Christ and Him crucified. Paul writes about how to do this in numerous places, but one of the clearest is in 2 Timothy 3:14–4:4 where Paul instructs timothy to preach the Word.

PREACH THE WORD! (2 TIM 3:15-4:4)

God reveals in numerous places in the Old Testament and in the New Testament that the foundation of Jesus Christ as the Word of God is poured through the preaching and teaching of Scripture (Hos 4:6; Neh 8; Amos 8:11; Luke 4:43-44; Acts 2:42; 6:1-7; Rom 10:8-14; 1 Cor 1:17-23; Col 1:25; 1 Tim 5:17; 2 Tim 3:15-4:4; 1 Pet 5:1-4). We see this most clearly in 2 Timothy 3–4. Paul wrote this letter to Timothy, the young pastor of the church in Ephesus to tell him what he should focus and what his priorities should be in the church. Second Timothy 3:15–4:4 explains how Timothy is supposed to tell others about Jesus as the Word of God. But first he reminds Timothy that this is where the power for wise ministry comes from.

Power of the Word (2 Tim 3:15)

> ... and that from childhood you have known the Holy Scriptures, which are able to make you wise for salvation through faith which is in Christ Jesus.

Scripture has the ability, or power, to make a person wise. As Matthew 7 revealed, it is the wise man who built his house upon the teachings of Jesus. Paul says the same thing here. Those who learn the Scriptures, and how they point to Jesus Christ, will become wise. Those who neglect Jesus and His teachings in Scriptures will continue to be ignorant and foolish. If a Christian wants to become wise, and if a Christian leader wants to wisely lead other people in ministry, then a high degree of attention to the Scriptures is a requirement. This is not only true in knowing the Scriptures, but in living them in love toward others, just like Jesus. The power of the Word is not just in knowing the Scriptures, but in living the Scriptures toward others.

Provider of the Word (2 Tim 3:16a)

> All Scripture is given by inspiration of God ...

Based on how most Christians use the Bible, it seems they think of it as just another book with a collection of stories and sayings—some of them interesting, some of them boring. But what most Christians seem to not realize is that the Bible is completely different than any other book ever written. The Bible is a divine revelation from God. All other books are the ideas of men.

When this is understood, how could anybody prefer to listen to the words of men rather than listen to the Word of God? The Bible comes from God, and as such, should be given priority and prominence in churches. Yet sometimes it is given minimal attention. Some churches seem to focus on everything but Scripture. But God has provided Scripture to the church for the purpose of leading us into Christlike living. We therefore ignore Scripture at our own peril.

When we focus on Scripture, however, and how it inspires us to follow Jesus, it is then that we discover how profitable Scripture can be.

Profit of the Word (2 Tim 3:16b)

> ... and is profitable for doctrine, for reproof, for correction, for instruction in righteousness ...

The reason churches should focus so much time and energy on the Word is because it alone is profitable. There is a huge movement in churches today away from doctrine, correction, and instruction. A lot of churches say, "Don't talk about sin. Don't talk about theology. Don't make your services a time of instruction. Instead, make them entertaining and enjoyable."

But this movement away from doctrine, correction, and instruction is a movement away from God, for verse 16 indicates that it is for these reasons that God provided Scripture. If we refuse to teach theology, correct people about sin, instruct others in the faith, and encourage others to follow Jesus, then we might as well not even have the Bible. If The Bible was given to us for such purposes, but we do not use it for these purposes, then it is nothing more than just another book of ancient stories and sayings. The church that fails to use Scripture for doctrine, reproof, correction, and instruction in righteousness is failing to use the Bible as God intended, and should therefore not even bother using it at all.

Note as well that Scripture is not just about doctrine, or theology, but also about correction from sin and instruction in righteousness. Scripture does not simply contain what we must believe, but also how we must behave. This is similar to what Jesus said in Matthew 28:19-20, when He wanted His disciples to go and teach others to obey everything He had commanded. He did not stop with teaching, but also included obedience to His teaching. Scripture is not given for doctrine only, but also for daily living.

Purpose of the Word (2 Tim 3:17)

> ... that the man of God may be complete, thoroughly equipped for every good work.

The reason Scripture teaches us what to believe and how to behave is so that we might become who God wants us to be. Second Timothy 3:17 says that when Scripture is properly taught, it causes Christians to mature. They become complete, equipped, and enabled to live Godly lives. When Scripture gets into their lives, they are able to live according to God's will rather than continue to live in sin. They are able to follow Jesus into the world and do what Jesus wants them to do, rather than continue to follow the ways of this world into darkness and destruction.

One reason so many Christians live in failure and defeat is because their church leaders fail to give them clear teaching from

Scripture and instruction on how to follow Jesus as the Word of God. When Scripture is not taught, Christians do not mature, and are therefore not able to walk in good works, but instead continue to walk in darkness and sin. A church that does not teach Scripture is a church that is starving its members. This is why Paul says what he says in 2 Timothy 4:1-2.

Preach the Word! (2 Tim 4:1-2)

> I charge you therefore before God and the Lord Jesus Christ, who will judge the living and the dead at His appearing and His kingdom: Preach the Word!

Paul could not have emphasized this any stronger. He tells Timothy to preach the Word. The "Word," of course, is Jesus Christ (John 1:1-14). But we preach Jesus as the Word by teaching people about how all Scripture points to Jesus and how we must do so as well with our lives. Since it is Jesus who is the Word of God, we can preach the Word by preaching and teaching Scripture in a way that points people to Jesus, the living Word of God.

It is important that we do this, because Paul tells Timothy he will stand before the judgement seat of Christ to answer for how well he taught Scripture to others so that they might better follow Jesus, this means that all pastors and church leaders will similarly stand before Jesus Christ on that day. Knowing this, Paul exhorts Timothy to make preaching the Word his priority. He says, "Timothy, you want to know what you should do as a pastor? I charge you, I command you, I urge you—preach the Word!"

The times that Timothy lived in were much like ours, so possibly, when Timothy read these words, he thought, "But people don't want to hear me preach the Word. People get bored with the Word. It takes a lot of time to preach the Word. Some people won't understand the Word. It's not very exciting to preach the Word." Paul, anticipating, these sorts of objections, tells Timothy in the rest of verse 2 that it doesn't really matter what people say, or what people think. Timothy is to continue to preach the Word.

> Be ready in season and out of season. Convince, rebuke, exhort, with all longsuffering and teaching.

The practice of preaching should be a pastor's priority when it is popular and when it is not. When people want to learn Scripture and when they do not.

Thankfully, there are many ways to preach the Word. My personal preference is to preach through books of the Bible verse-by-verse. It appears that the prophets of God taught Scripture this way (Neh 8:8; Isa 28:10-13; Hos 4:6; Amos 8:11), as did Jesus Himself when He preached in the Synagogues on the Sabbath (e.g. Luke 4:43-44), and the apostles when they ministered to the churches (Acts 2:42; 6:1-7; Rom 10:8-14; 1 Cor 1:17-23; Col 1:25; 1 Tim 5:17; 2 Tim 3:15-4:4; 1 Pet 5:1-4).

But I am not as concerned with the form that the preaching takes as I am with how the preaching calls those who hear it to participate in what God is doing in the world. No preaching is truly biblical preaching unless it leads the hearer to apply what was preached, which is how Paul concludes this instruction to Timothy.

Practical Application of the Word (2 Tim 4:3-4)

> For the time will come when they will not endure sound doctrine,

but according to their own desires, because they have itching ears, they will heap up for themselves teachers; and they will turn their ears away from the truth, and be turned aside to fables.

This is the overall point of Paul's instruction to Timothy about preaching. Paul wants Timothy to preach the Word, not because people want it, but because they need it. Of course, just like healthy eating and exercise, after people receive healthy teaching for a while, they develop a taste for it and come to want it as much as the need it.

Sadly, however, Paul's actual point in these verses has been widely misunderstood and misapplied by modern churches and pastors. Every church you will ever encounter thinks that they believe and teach "sound doctrine." You will never encounter a group of Christians who says to themselves "Oh yes, we teach false doctrine here. We love our fables and our lies! So we expect our pastor to give to us what our itching ears want to hear."

No, you will always hear the exact opposite. You will always hear pastors and Christians say, "Oh yes, we teach sound doctrine here. Those churches down the street? Not so much. And while we do our best to preach and teach what is correct, some people don't want that, and so they leave us and go down the street to that other church where they will receive what their itching ears want to hear."

So since every church thinks they teach sound doctrine, and since every Christian believes they receive sound doctrine from their church, how are we to tell the difference between sound doctrine and unsound doctrine? What is the determining factor?

In many circles, it seems that determining sound doctrine from unsound doctrine boils down to a popularity contest. People tend to decide which teaching is correct by which church is the largest, or which pastor sells the most books, or which particular doctrine has been in vogue for the most number of years so that it becomes "the traditional teaching of the church."

And yet such a way of determining "sound doctrine" has led to widespread division within the church, as each group thinks they themselves are the keepers of the truth, while everyone else has been led into some kind of error or heresy. This emphasis on "sound doctrine" has led to the creation of over 33,000 Christian denominations, which cannot be what Jesus had in mind when He prayed that we would be one as God is one (John 17:21), or what Paul envisioned when he wrote about unity in the truth (Eph 4:1-16).[3]

So it appears that a large part of the problem lies in a widespread misunderstanding of what Paul means by "sound doctrine." The words which are often translated "sound doctrine" might better be translated as "sound teaching" or better yet, "healthy teaching" (Gk., *hugianousa didaskalia*), which is the opposite of unhealthy teaching. So what is the difference between healthy teaching and what is unhealthy? It is not that one form proclaims the gospel every week and invites people to "come forward" while another form of preaching does not. Nor is it that one form digs deep into the Hebrew and Greek words of the text, quotes Augustine and Calvin, and uses big theological words, while another form does not. It is not that one church hands out

---

[3] David Barrett, George Kurian, Todd Johnson, *World Christian Encyclopedia: A Comparative Survey of Churches and Religions in the Modern World* (Oxford: New York, 2001), I:16-18.

bulletin inserts for note-taking, while the other does not. It is not even necessarily that one form preaches through books of the Bible verse-by-verse while the other does not.

No, in the immediate and wider context of Scripture, sound doctrine, or "healthy teaching," is that which encourages a person to enter into the world, and live like Jesus among the people of the world. Healthy teaching is teaching that leads us to love. This form of teaching is how one lives out the message of the gospel and the Kingdom of God.

Unhealthy teaching is the kind of teaching that causes people to withdraw from the world, while seeking greater, deeper, and more speculative teaching. Healthy teaching sees love, service, and action in the world as the goal. Unhealthy teaching sees knowledge and more learning as the goal. While healthy teaching invites people to not only learn Scripture, but to apply it through loving actions toward others. Health Christian teachings leads to healthy Christians lives. If Christian teaching and preaching does not lead to Christian love and service, then it is not healthy Christian teaching, no matter how theologically correct it may be.

Unhealthy teaching is that which leads to nothing but more teaching. It is heaping up for yourself more and more teachers, more and more sermons, more and more Bible studies, more and more conferences. It is being so excited about what you heard, that you cannot wait to hear more. And after you hear more, your primary response is an excited expectation to hear even more.

Unhealthy teaching is the teaching that only results in more teaching. As great as Scripture study can be, it can also become addictive. Bible study is like a drug that pulls us away from God. The more we study the Bible, and the more we learn about God, the less we end up obeying the Bible or following God. Sometimes you have to give up your commentaries and word studies so that you can actually hear what God is saying and follow him, not deeper into the text, but deeper into the sin and darkness of this world, to be a light to those who dwell there.

Healthy teaching, on the other hand, while it does provide information from Scripture, follows up on this teaching by leading people into the world to put into practice what was learned. Healthy preaching does not simply invite people to more preaching and teaching, thus pulling people away from the world where they are to apply what they have learned, but pushes people back out into the world to face the issues, problems, and questions of life.

Healthy teaching does not deal with the lofty ideas, theoretical explanations, or the speculative theology which so many pastors and Christians are fond of providing. No, healthy teaching takes seriously the gospel announcement that the Kingdom of God is at hand. Healthy teaching gets our noses out of the Bible and into the streets and stores of our cities. Healthy teaching is the teaching that results in loving and serving others.

Therefore, who are the Christians who follow teachers that give them what their itching ears want to hear? They are the Christians who only want to gather more and more teachers, listen to more and more sermons, and gain more and more Bible knowledge, without ever putting any of it into practice. They are the Christians who are so busy with Bible study that they never get around to applying it to their lives or practicing it in the world. Though they have perfect doctrine and completely correct theology, it is unhealthy and unsound if they don't practice love toward others.

This is the point of Paul in 2 Timothy 4. Paul wants Timothy to lead his church away from simply wanting to get more and more teaching, and instead, take them out into the world, where they can proclaim the gospel, and put it into practice by loving and serving others, just as Jesus has done for us. Listening to "sound doctrine" is not a matter of who is right and who is wrong, but rather, who puts into practice what they have heard. Sound doctrine is not about hearing more truth, but living the truth we already have.

While the ears of some people do itch for funny stories, jokes, and encouraging insights based on psychology and current events, the ears of other people itch to hear the latest insight on a difficult Bible passage, or the newest scholarly explanation of a particular word in Scripture. This second group attends Bible studies, listens to expositional preaching, buys commentaries, does word studies, learns Greek and Hebrew, and all the while, looks down their noses at people who don't listen to such things.

According to Paul, neither group is better than the other. What God wants is that we go and make disciples, which does not mean teaching people everything there is to know about Bible and theology, but leading people to live like Jesus within the world. Making disciples means much more than filling people's heads with expert knowledge of Scripture. It means more than teaching, preaching, and Bible Study. Making disciples means encouraging people to put into practice what they learn by giving them the freedom to follow Jesus into the world.

This is also what Jesus said at the conclusion of His most famous sermon.

HEAR AND OBEY (MATT 7:24-27)

Matthew 7:24-27 is found at the very end of Jesus' Sermon on the Mount. After providing great teaching to His disciples, He concluded the sermon by telling them what to do with everything they had just heard. This final element of the sermon contains the story about the wise and foolish builders. This story is told at the conclusion of Jesus' Sermon on the Mount, and it shows what His disciples are supposed to do with everything they just heard Him teach. Jesus says this:

> Therefore whoever hears these sayings of Mine, and does them, I will liken him to a wise man who built his house on the rock: and the rain descended, the floods came, and the winds blew and beat on that house; and it did not fall, for it was founded on the rock.

> But everyone who hears these sayings of Mine, and does not do them, will be like a foolish man who built his house on the sand: and the rain descended, the floods came, and the winds blew and beat on that house; and it fell. And great was its fall.

The story contains two different builders. Both build homes, and both homes go through a terrible storm. The first builder builds his home on a solid rock foundation. Because his foundation is good, when the storm comes, his house stands firm. The second builder builds his home on sand. Sand is not a good foundation at all. Thus, when the same storm comes against him, his house is crushed by the storm.

This story, just like all the stories of Jesus, contains great spiritual truth. Most people automatically assume that they are a wise builder because they have a Bible. The average Christian thinks, "I have a better foundation than that heathen neighbor of mine who goes to the bars all the time and watches television instead of coming to church. I have the Bible, and better yet, I read the Bible, and I go to church where I hear good Bible teaching, so I have a better foundation for life than he does."

But notice in the story that both builders have the words and sayings of Jesus. Both builders have heard the teachings of Jesus. So the difference between the two is not that one knows the teachings of Jesus and one doesn't. We could even say that the difference between the two is not that one has Bible knowledge and one doesn't. The difference between the two is that one obeys the teachings of Jesus while the other one does not.

When it comes to individual Christians or local bodies of believers, the one who builds on the solid foundation is not determined by which one knows the Bible better, but by which one follows the instructions of Jesus more completely. And to follow Jesus doesn't mean "not sin." Love and grace are needed. To follow Jesus is to obey Jesus, which means we are to love God and love each other. The emphasis is always on love. To follow Jesus means to look like Jesus in how He loves other people. To do otherwise is to build on shifting sand.

James, the half-brother of Jesus, wrote similarly in James 1:23 that the one who reads the Bible and doesn't do what it says is like one who looks in a mirror, but doesn't do anything about the messy hair, the facial blemishes, or any of the other problems he sees, but goes away and forgets what he looks like.

So the church does not build on the foundation of Jesus Christ by possessing lots of Bibles, or even by promoting lots of Bible study. No, the only way to build upon Jesus Christ is to hear what He says, *and then do it.* Only obeying Christians will pass the divine building inspection to be useful for ministry in

God's Kingdom.[4] Only those who build on obedience to the words of Jesus will stand the test of time and weather the storms of life.

Think again of the imagery of the church as a building. A physical building with a faulty foundation will crumble and be destroyed within a few short years. A bad foundation will result in cracked windows, jammed doors, creaky floors and essentially, a building that quickly falls apart. Sadly, this is the way we could describe many Christians and church ministries today. They are falling apart. Though the physical buildings themselves might be brand new and beautiful, the individual Christians are worn down by strife, ragged with dissention, cracking from the strain of arguments, and crumbling from petty disagreements. We have all heard of Christians splitting from one another over the color of the carpet in their church building and whether or not to have coffee in the foyer. These sorts of disagreements point to a failure to build on the good foundation of Jesus Christ. But when we build on Jesus Christ by following the teachings He provided, then we build on Him as the foundation, and our life and ministry will stand strong and true through the worst of life's storms.

We run into problems when we try to build the church on anything else, whether it is entertainment, quality music, numerous programs, or nice buildings. All of these are nice trappings for a church to have, but without the proper foundation, all such things are worthless.

---

[4] This doesn't mean that only obedient Christians go to heaven or receive eternal life. I am not saying anything of the sort. I am talking about being useful for ministry.

The first and foremost concern of any Christian or church gathering is to focus on teaching and training one another about the words and works of Jesus Christ so that we can follow His instructions and do what He wants in this world. A Christian or a church which is not founded on studying Scripture so that we can see and follow Jesus is building on a faulty foundation. Such ministries and missions may gain much worldly wealth, popular power, praise, and recognition from man, but it will not be a mission or ministry that is pleasing to God. Only a church that hears and obeys Jesus Christ will be pleasing to Him.

One writer came up with the following fictional board-meeting scenario based on how things might have gone if some of today's church leaders had been apostles of Jesus:

> Pete calls the meeting to order. "This meeting has been called at the request of Matt, John, Tom, and Little Jim. Bart, will you please open with prayer?"
>
> "Certainly," Bart says. "Almighty God, we ask your blessing on all we do and say and earnestly pray that you will see our side as your side. Amen."
>
> "Let's get right to business," begins Pete. "Jesus, we have been following you for some time now, and we are getting a little concerned about the attendance figures. Tom, how many were on the hill yesterday?"
>
> "Thirty-seven," Tom answered.
>
> "Yes," Pete continues. "It's getting to be ridiculous, Jesus. You're going to have to pep things up to keep the people interested. We expect things to start happening. Isn't that right John?"

John nods his head. "Yeah! I'd like to suggest you pull off more miracles, Jesus. That walking on water bit was the most exciting thing I have ever seen, but only a few of us saw it. If a thousand or more had a chance to witness it, and if we could televise it, we would have more than we could handle on the hill."

There is excitement in Little Jim's voice as he agrees. "The healing miracles are terrific, but only a limited number really get to see what has happened. Let's have more water to wine, more fish and chips (it never hurts to fill people's stomachs), calm more storms, give more signs. All the opinion surveys say that this is what people want."

"Right," says Pete. "And another thing. Publicity is essential, but you tell half the people you cure to keep it quiet. Let the word get around. Maybe we should advertise a bit. We could say, 'Miracles and healings performed weekly.' That'll bring them in."

"That's a great idea," Matt exclaims. "And along with the miracles, Jesus, you should tell more stories. People don't have the attention spans to listen to long sermons and explanations of boring Old Testament texts. I know you do tell some stories, but nobody ever understands them! You have to make it simple and clear in order for anybody to take anything home with them. You know what they say, "Put the cookies on the bottom shelf.'"

"Here is the order of service we have all agreed on, Jesus," Big Jim booms in his heavy voice. "First, a story. Then a big miracle, followed by the offering. It's been proven that people will give more money after a miracle. You could maybe throw in a wise saying or two after the offering, but keep it short and sweet. After this, do another smaller miracle to bring them back next time. And then close with a prayer. This will really help keep our attendance."

"That's right," adds Judas. "And we should probably think about improving the appearance of the upper room. That carpet color is just atrocious."[5]

And the meeting continues with more of the same.

Can you imagine Jesus putting up with a meeting like that? Of course not. Yet these are the kind of actions and attitudes that guide many prominent Christian ministries around the world. They are trying to build on a faulty foundation. Jesus stated that the proper foundation is hearing and obeying His teachings as found in Scripture. Teaching others is important, but we are called to do more than just teach. We are called to "teach them to obey" (Matt 28:19-20). The healthy church which is built on the foundation of Jesus Christ not only learns the truth, but learns to love others in the truth, just as we see in Jesus Christ.

CONCLUSION

Several years ago, I went on a missions deep into Mexico to help construct a church. When we arrived one of the things they needed done was to pour the foundation of the church. This part of Mexico was very mountainous and they had no way of getting a cement truck up there, and nobody owned a cement mixer. They didn't have hoses or running water either. There was a small mountain stream running through town about 200 yards away from the church.

---

[5] This idea was taken from Charles Swindoll, *Tale of Tardy Oxcart* (Dallas: Word, 1998), 93-94. Minor edits were made for readability.

The first step was to unload all the unmixed bags of concrete from the truck. Then we emptied them all out onto a big concrete slab that had been pre-poured. Next, several men were given shovels, and the rest of us were handed five-gallon buckets. We had to carry water up the hill from the stream in five gallon buckets to the mixing slab. After it was well mixed, we then had to carry the concrete in the buckets and pour it into the molds for the foundation. It took a long time, but we got it done.

This is the same way to pour the spiritual foundation for the church. Preach Jesus Christ from Scripture one bucket at a time. One shovel at a time. One verse at a time. And it is not just teaching the same thing Jesus taught, but also showing them how to obey all that He commanded. Only in this way will the church be built upon the foundation of Jesus Christ.

DISCUSSION QUESTIONS

1. What does a building foundation provide?

2. Who is God's foundation for the church? Why is it important to recognize this?

3. If you study the Bible, what should it point you to know, be, and do?

4. What did Paul preach? What did he call people to do?

5. What are some things we can do to build upon God's foundation?

6. What is Paul's overall point to Timothy in 2 Timothy 3:15–4:4?

7. What is the difference between healthy and unhealthy teaching? How can you recognize the difference?

8. Who are the two groups of Christians that gather about themselves teachers to give them what their itching ears want to hear? Is one group better than the other?

9. Is obeying God only about not sinning? What does it mean to obey God?

10. To properly learn the Scriptures, what is needed beyond just studying the Scriptures? Why is this an essential part of learning?

CHAPTER 6

FOLLOWING THE PATTERN

The modern church is confused. Ask someone how a church should be structured, and you will get answers ranging from cell churches to program churches, from house churches to mega churches. If you ask how to evangelize, some will tell you that crusades and revivals are the best way, while others argue for a social gospel friendship evangelism approach. When the issue is raised on what kind of music a church should have, some champion traditional hymns while others argue for an upbeat, contemporary style.

Yet almost without fail, as you talk to people about what church is and how church should function, you will find someone who is looking for the "New Testament church." They say they want a church that is patterned after what is seen in the New Testament. Whenever I hear this, I always wonder if they are reading the same New Testament that I am. Right from the beginning, the church had problems. People were lying to God and to one another (Acts 5), there was racial discrimination (Acts 6), and simony (Acts 8).

Furthermore, almost every one of the Epistles was written to correct some error or false teaching in one church or another. Paul's two letters to the Corinthians deal with sectarianism, self-glorification, sexual immorality, Christians suing one another, wrong ideas about marriage and divorce, idolatry, improper forms of worship, abuse of the Lord's supper, arrogance about spiritual gifts, false gospels, misunderstandings about the end times, and a failure to be generous with their money. I thank God that I am not part of this ideal "New Testament church."

In fact, I'm not sure people who talk about a "New Testament" ideal know what they are talking about. Nowhere in Scripture do we find a blanket approval of all actions of the early church. On the contrary, many of the early churches were far from "model" churches. Division, heresy, immorality and immaturity were frequently more visible than the grace of God. When we try to live up to the ideal "New Testament church" we will always fail because no such church ever existed.

Or maybe we could say that if the New Testament church truly was ideal, then this means that all our churches today are also ideal, for just like every church today, the New Testament church was full of problems. As long as the church is made up of sinful people, it will have problems. That's the way God made it. Until God creates a new heaven and a new earth, the ideal church is the church with many problems.

This is not to say that there is no room for improvement. We must not say "Well, all churches have problems, including the New Testament church, so we shouldn't even try to get better." To the contrary, one of the main reasons God gave us the Bible is so that we, as the people of God, can strive to become better. The Bible reveals our faults and failures to us so that we can work to improve them and better reflect God to a watching world. Since this is the case, it is worth asking what the church is supposed to be and do.

There are many places in Scripture we can go for guidance and instruction on this issue, but surprisingly, the best place to start is the Old Testament. Although the church does not officially begin until Pentecost in Acts 2, all New Testament theology and practice has its basis in the Old Testament. This is even true of ecclesiology, the study of the church.

Failure to understand what the Old Testament teaches about the church as the people of God has led to many harmful ideas and practices within the church. Most of these are half-truths about the nature of the church, or an overemphasis on a certain aspect of the church. One church will go off on one extreme, while another goes off the deep end in the opposite direction. Both sides generally have New Testament Scriptures which seem to support their views, but in reality, both are wrong, because neither has considered the Old Testament pattern. Both are unbalanced because they have not been balanced by all of Scripture.

One of the reasons there is so much confusion about church today is because of the neglect of Old Testament ecclesiology principles. When we focus on just the New Testament we get a warped view. It may be that one of the reasons the New Testament is so vague on the divisive issues of our day is because there was no need to give instructions when the New Testament was being written. It is not that they struggled with different issues, but that they already knew the answers from the Old Testament.

For example, how did Paul know what to write in his Pastoral Epistles? How did he know what instructions to give to the churches in Corinth, Ephesus, and Philippi? When his letters are read, it becomes clear that he used the Old Testament as a basis for nearly everything he said. As an expert student of the Law and the Prophets, he was both answering questions Jews had about how to live as Christians and also questions that Gentiles had because they didn't know the Old Testament. Paul was using an Old Testament model, and incorporated Christ into what was already set up.

This is not to say that the New Testament church is an exact replica of Old Testament worship patterns. It obviously is not, and Jesus Himself clearly set aside and superseded many of the practices and traditions that were common in Old Testament worship settings. The Old Testament provides the basic structure, and within this structure, certain things needed to be changed. So for the most part, it is the changes that most New Testament writing is concerned with. The New Testament builds upon the forms of Old Testament worship and lets us know of any changes or renovations that had to be done on the old structure. For example, Jesus and the apostles did away with worship centered on a priestly hierarchy, the sacrificial system, and the reliance upon buildings.[1] During His life and ministry, Jesus focused all of these things upon Himself. We no longer worship God in these old patterns, for now we worship God in Jesus Christ.

Nevertheless, not everything changed. Some of the ancient structures and patterns remained. What are these, and what are we to do with them?

OLD TESTAMENT PATTERNS THAT REMAIN

There are three main elements of Old Testament worship pat-

---

[1] See my *Close Your Church for Good* book series for detailed discussions about all of these topics, and many more besides.

terns that continued into the early church with the practice of Jesus and the apostles. The first of these elements is that everything was based on Scripture. Since God's Word is truth, it alone was the basis for what was taught and what was done. There was a reverence and respect for Scripture. It has no equal (Ps 119). When teaching occurred, it was most often by someone reading a passage of Scripture and then explaining it. What was said was always focused, grounded, and anchored in understanding and applying the Bible in sequence and in context (Neh 8:8; Isa 28:10-13; Hos 4:6; Amos 8:11). So there was a focus on learning and applying Scripture. As seen in the previous chapter, it appears that Jesus and the apostles continued this practice as they taught and trained new believers (cf. Luke 4:43-44; Acts 2:42; 6:1-7; Rom 10:8-14; 1 Cor 1:17-23; Col 1:25; 1 Tim 5:17; 2 Tim 3:15-4:4; 1 Pet 5:1-4).

Second, it was expected and assumed that biblical education began in the home with the fathers teaching their wives and children (Exod 12:26-27; Deut 4:9-10; 6:7). Father-guided biblical education constituted the essential pattern of Old Testament worship. The father was the spiritual bread-winner for the family. He did not rely on priests or schools to provide religious instruction, but did it himself. The priests and schools were supplemental. This also is what we see in the New Testament. If a man does not provide (financially, emotionally, and spiritually) for his family, he is worse than an unbeliever (1 Tim 5:8) and has no business trying to lead or teach others in the church (1 Tim 3:4-5).

Third, there was a hierarchy. This was not a hierarchy made of individuals, but a hierarchy of teams (Exod 18). We see this system set up by Moses in the wilderness when he could not handle all the problems of the Israelites. He set up groups to help deal with the various issues. A lone leader, handling all the problems, doing all the teaching, meeting with all the people, planning all the programs, will quickly burn out and will no longer be able to lead. So Moses set up teams of leaders to share the joy of leading, teaching, and helping others in the family of God (cf. Exod 19:7; Lev 4:15; Num 11:16; Deut 19:12; 21:19; 27:1; 31:28; etc.).

These are only three of the main elements to Old Testament worship. There are many other things that could be mentioned, like the pattern of music (see Psalms), tithing (this principle is changed in the New Testament), ministry training (done by the congregation) and mentor-disciple leadership selection (Moses-Joshua, Elijah-Elisha, etc.). Most of these, however, are also mentioned in the New Testament (see Eph 4; 2 Cor 8–9; Acts, 1 and 2 Timothy).

So the three Old Testament patterns mentioned above are enough to transform church as we know it today. Imagine how much healthier the worldwide church would be if we all followed some of these basic Old Testament patterns for teaching, training, and living? Imagine what the church would be like if Scripture formed the backbone to what we preach and teach, if parents taught and trained their children at home, and if teams of spiritual leaders shared the responsibilities of guiding the church into what God wants. Such a church would transform the world.

But the Old Testament is not the only, or even the primary, place which teaches about what the church is supposed to be and do. While the Old Testament must not be neglected in any study of the church, the New Testament is the primary source for the proper form and function of the church.

It is important to understand the difference between form and function. Most of the disagreements and arguments in the church are due to the fact that many Christians fail to recognize the difference between form and function. Even if they do, they fail to make a distinction between general functions of the universal church, and specific applications of these functions to their time and culture. The rest of this chapter will provide some clarity on these issues by giving the general, overarching form and function of the entire church.

THE CHURCH'S FORM

"Form" is what something is in its essence. As already discussed in this book, the church can be defined as the people of God who follow Jesus into the world. Yet although this is a good definition of the church, what does this mean in reality? What does it look like? What is its essence? How can we recognize "the church"? This sections seeks to provide some clarity to these questions by looking at two distinct characteristics of the church.

Universal and Local (Spiritual and Physical)

The first form that characterizes the church is that it is both universal and local. The New Testament speaks of the church being both universal and invisible, but also being local and made of individual bodies of believers (1 Thess 1:1; Local: Gal 1:22; Universal: Eph 1:22-23; Col 1:18). In other words, while it is true that the church is a spiritual reality that is present everywhere, it nevertheless has a very local and physical reality as well when individual believers meet to fulfill the functions of the church (discussed below).

So on the one hand, the church is universal. It consists of all

Christians worldwide and throughout time. Since the church did not exist prior to Pentecost, all believers since Pentecost are members of the church. This is because the church is a spiritual organism. A Christian can be locked away in a prison cell in China for their entire life, and never attend a church service, and still be part of the universal church. Everyone who has believed in Jesus for eternal life is part of the spiritual church, even if they never attend church.

But the church is also local and physical. The church is only functioning when local believers gather together at specific times and places to accomplish the things Jesus wants them to do. Some Christians seem to think that since the church is universal, they can "do church" on their own as they take a walk in the forest, or go for a bike-ride along a bubbling stream. Some Christians seem to think that church is happening when they pray and sing alone in their bedroom, or study their Bible by themselves on a lunch break at work. Yet while such practices are wonderful times of personal worship and devotion to God, they do not actually qualify as church, because there is no community or gathering of believers that is taking place. There is no mutual edification in such settings.

Although the church is spiritual and universal, it is also physical and local. God wants all believers of a local area to meet regularly in a physical setting. People who worship God on the bass lake are not accountable to anyone else. They are not being encouraged or taught by anyone else. They are not equipping anyone else. They are not using their spiritual gifts to serve others. They are not supporting the work of the kingdom with their time, talents, or money. People who overemphasize the universal aspects of the church must be reminded that the church is also local.

Yet we must not let the pendulum swing too far. There are those who overemphasize the local and physical aspect of church. When they think of church, they think of a building that they sit in on Sunday morning. But a building or worship service is not church either. They fail to realize that this building is just one place the church can gather during the week, and when they leave that place, the church goes with them. Rick Warren says these Christians sing "Onward Christian Soldiers" on Sunday, but then go AWOL on Monday.

We must not be "Dr. Jekyll and Mr. Hyde Christians" who regularly sit in a pew on Sunday morning to sing, bow our heads in prayer, listen to a sermon, put some money in a plate, say a few pleasantries to the pastor after the service, and then rush home for the pot roast or the football game. For the rest of the week not a thought about God or His Word enters their minds until the next Saturday night when they set their alarm clocks for Sunday morning. Such Christians think they have "gone to church," but they have done nothing of the sort. Since they view "church" as nothing more than a geographical location they visit on a certain day of the week, the compartments of "church" and "life" never mix. These people must be reminded of the universal and spiritual aspects of church.

The biblical truth is that all believers in Jesus Christ are a part of the church. Even those Christians who are no longer on this earth are part of the church. This is because scripturally, the church is universal and spiritual, physical and local. The universal, spiritual church meets regularly in local, physical locations to fulfill the functions of the church, which will be looked at below.

Before we move on, however, is should be noted that Matthew

18:20 is not the definition of what constitutes a church gathering. Many people use this verse to say that for church to exist, all you need is two or three people gathered in the name of Jesus. But this is not what Jesus is talking about in this text. The passage is about church discipline, and two or three people coming together to reconcile differences between believers. Jesus wants His followers to know that when two or three people gather in this way, to create peace and unity between Christians who are arguing and disagreeing with each other, Jesus is there with them, helping to resolve the situation.

I am all in favor of the home group churches which are sprouting up all over the world, but those who meet this way need to understand that they are not more biblical simply because they meet in a home. While many of the local New Testament believes met in homes, there were many others who met in larger, public buildings as well (cf. Acts 5:12; 13:44). Church is not about where you meet or how many meet, but simply about gathering to encourage and edify one another as we all seek to follow Jesus into the world.

This then leads to the second main form of the church, which is that we are all under the headship of Jesus Christ.

Under the Headship of Jesus Christ

To be under the headship of Jesus Christ means that He is the leader and director of the church. Just as a head tells the body what to do and where to go, Jesus tells the church what to do and where to go.

While many local churches teach that Jesus Christ is the head of the church, in actual practice, someone else often servers as the head. But we do not take our marching orders from a pastor, the

Pope, or any other person. Jesus Christ alone is the head of the church. Jesus Christ alone must be listened to and obeyed. He tells us what to do and how to do it. He gives us our instructions.

One of the biblical pictures that best represents this is the human body. The head is the control center for the body. The legs take the body where the head tells it to. The arms do the work the head wants. The eyes look at what the head wants to see. The mouth eats and feeds the body according to the head's instructions.

If a person's head is not controlling the body, the person normally ends up in an assisted living program or mental institution. When the head does not function properly, a person cannot take care of themselves. Similarly, when Jesus Christ is not allowed to be the head of the church, chaos reigns. When Christ is not allowed to rule the church, we have an arm trying to tell everybody what to do. Most of the time, the arm wants everybody to act like an arm. Or if the mouth takes control, the mouth wants everybody to look like and act like a mouth.

But when Christ is in control, He enables each member to be what it is supposed to be so that it can do what it is supposed to do. There can be peace, unity, and harmony. When the head tells the body what to do, the body must obey. The church is the universal and local body of believers under the headship of Jesus Christ. As such, He tells us how we are to function.

THE CHURCH'S FUNCTION

According to the Great Commission in Matthew 28:19-20, the overall function and purpose of the church is to make disciples. The church is an assembly plant (Heb 10:24-25) where the end product is mature disciples. According to Scripture, disciple making involves three components: The Exaltation of God, the Edification of Believers, and the Evangelism of the world. These are the three main functions of the church, but they will be applied differently in different cultures and at different times. Let's look at all three in more detail.

Exaltation of God

The exaltation of God is accomplished by bringing glory to God. Everything we do, everything we say should bring glory to God.

Johann Sebastian Bach composed music. He said, "All music should have no other end and aim than the glory of God and the soul's refreshment; where this is not remembered there is no real music but only a devilish hub-bub." He headed his compositions: "J.J." "Jesus Juva" which means "Jesus help me." He ended them "S.D.G." "Soli Dei Gratia" which means "To God alone the praise." He began and ended every composition with the glory of God.

Now when most people think of exalting God, they think of singing songs. But this is only one way to worship and exalt God. While the church service is one place we can exalt God, every second of every day should be lived to exalt God. The exaltation of God can take place all the time in a variety of ways. You can exalt God by thanking Him for your food that you eat, by working hard at your job, by loving your spouse and children, and by just enjoying His presence throughout the day. You can worship God through creative works of art, sculpting, and landscaping, or through baking and cooking. You can exalt God by how you take care of animals and plants. Though the exaltation of God is one of the main functions of the church, there are a myriad of ways to accomplish this function.

Every member of the church must do everything to the glory of God. Our constant prayer must be, "God, let what I do be used for your glory." When we live every second of every day this way, our every action is worship and the exaltation of God.

Edification of the Saints

In 1 Corinthians 14 where Paul is talking about how to use spiritual gifts, he writes over and over that all the gifts must be used for the purpose of edifying one another. Whether it is a speaking gift or serving gift, it must be used in a way that brings edification to other people.

Edification means to build up. When we edify someone, we build them up. There are numerous ways to build up and edify one another. First, we can edify by encouraging them. We praise others when progress is made in the Christian faith. We challenge one another in a positive way to press on (Heb 10:25). Will Rogers once said that we can't all be heroes because somebody has to sit on the curb and clap as they go by. Encouraging others is a wonderful way to build others up.

I once read of an elderly widow who was restricted in her activities but was eager to encourage others. After praying about this, she realized that she could bring blessing to others by playing the piano. The next day she placed this small ad in the Oakland Tribune: "Pianist will play hymns by phone daily for those who are sick and despondent—the service is free."

The notice included the number to dial. When people called, she would ask, "What hymn would you like to hear?" Within a few months her playing had brought cheer to several hundred people. Many of them freely poured out their hearts to her and she was able to help and encourage them. Encouraging others is one way to edify. And some people have the spiritual gift of encouragement which makes them wonderful at edifying others in this way.

We can also edify others by equipping them. This is different than encouraging. Encouraging is when you come alongside someone to help them press on and keep up the fight. Equipping is coming along side to give them some training or some new tools to help them be more effective in their ministry. One of the primary responsibilities of the pastor-teacher, is to equip the saints for ministry (Eph 4:11-16). This will be dealt with in much more detail in chapters 7–11.

Evangelization of the World

If exaltation is God focused and edification is church focused, evangelization is world focused. Evangelism is the ministry of all believers toward lost people. It is sharing with them through our words and actions that even though we are all sinners, God loves us and offers eternal life to anyone who simply believes in Jesus Christ for it. This is the good news that all of us are to take part in sharing.

One way to do this is by supporting mission work being done around the world. We can either go ourselves, or support those who have gone by praying and giving money to support their work. Beyond this, all of us are to be witnesses in our own communities. Each Christian should evangelize at work or in their neighborhood. Some can even evangelize at home with their spouse or parents.

For many Christians, evangelism and witnessing are the most

difficult things to do. It is scary to talk to someone. It is difficult to know what to say. But this is why evangelism is third on the list. If a Christian focuses their life on exalting God, then people will see that light naturally. God's love will be evident around unbelievers. The process of evangelizing in this way can take lots of time to produce results, often up to several years, but such relational forms of evangelism are the most effective and loving ways to introduce people to Jesus and the kingdom of God.

A young salesman was disappointed about losing a big sale, and as he talked with his sales manager he lamented, "I guess it just proves you can lead a horse to water but you can't make him drink." The manager replied, "Son, take my advice: your job is not to make him drink. Your job is to make him thirsty." So it is with evangelism. Our lives should be so filled with Jesus Christ that they create a thirst for the gospel. When a Christian exalts, they will automatically be a testimony to others. The world thirsts for what Christians have when they see us exalting God and loving one another. If a Christian struggles with evangelism, they must focus first on exaltation and edification. When they do this, evangelism will naturally result.

CONCLUSION

The entire Bible has a lot to say about the church. The Old Testament gives us a pattern. The New Testament gives us some changes and renovations. Both must be considered to get a healthy picture of the church so that we can build on the foundation laid out for us.

In this way, we see the church's form and function. It is formed by every Christian around the world and throughout time who serves under the headship of Jesus Christ. However, this universal church meets in local places to fulfill its function. The church's function is to exalt God, edify one another, and evangelize the world. These are the three main functions of the church as we follow Jesus into the world, but the specific applications of exaltation, edification, and evangelism will look different among different people at different times in different places and cultures.

So let us all stop thinking that we have "the one right way" of doing church. Instead, let us recognize that the local body of believers down the street might worship God differently than we do, but their method of exalting God is just as acceptable to Him as ours. Similarly, when we see methods of edification or evangelism on the other side of the world that cause us to raise our eyebrows a bit, it is worth remembering that they probably raise their eyebrows at how we perform these functions here. As long as we are all part of the Body of Christ, following His leadership, and focusing on encouraging one another to exalt God, edify each other, and evangelize the world, we can rejoice in our differences and praise God that He uses different people with different customs to reach different people with different customs. If this is fine with God, who are we to disagree?

DISCUSSION QUESTIONS

1. What is the best way to structure a church?

2. What is the best place to start when looking for guidance and instructions on how to structure the church?

3. What are the three main elements of Old Testament worship that continued into the early church and would make our churches so much healthier if we had them today?

4. What is the difference between the universal church and the local church?

5. Why does "going to church" mean more than entering a building a few times a week?

6. Why does being part of the universal church require more than just believing in Jesus?

7. Is it right to over-emphasize either the universal or the local aspect of the church?

8. What is Matthew 18:20 *really* talking about?

9. What picture best represents the church with Jesus as the head?

10. What are the three components of disciple making? In what order should we seek to master them?

11. Will everyone in all cultures apply these three components the same way? Why or why not? How does this help us?

PART 3: CONSTRUCTING

CHAPTER 7

THE FOREMEN

And He Himself gave some to be apostles, some prophets, some evangelists, and some pastors and teachers.
Ephesians 4:11

Once upon a time, in a local church, there were four people named Everybody, Somebody, Anybody, and Nobody. There was an important job to be done and Everybody was asked to do it. But Everybody was sure that Somebody would do it. Anybody could have done it, but Nobody did it.

Then Somebody got angry about it, because it was Everybody's job. But since Everybody thought that Anybody could do it, and Nobody realized that Everybody wouldn't do it, it ended up that Everybody blamed Somebody and Nobody did the job that Anybody could have done in the first place.

Right about this time, a fifth person visited the church. This person's name was Confused. He looked around, saw what was happening, and never came back.

All too often, this describes life in the local church. It is unclear who is supposed to do what, and this leads to confusion, frustration, and hurt feelings. But church is not supposed to be this way. God never intended for church to be so confusing. God describes in Scripture who is to oversee the building of the church and who is supposed to do the work. God very carefully delineates in Scripture who should be doing what in His church. Since God is the architect of the church, He gets to determine how the church is formed and how the church grows and functions.

One of the premier passages in Scripture which lays out God's plan for church growth is Ephesians 4:11-16. This passage lays out several essential elements to church growth. It first describes the leaders on the construction site, which we can think of as the Foremen (Eph 4:11). It then explains who performs the work, which is the Crew (Eph 4:12). Third, it reveals the construction Model that we are imitating and turning into a reality (Eph 4:13). Finally, it explains the Program goal that the church will fulfill once it is constructed (Eph 4:14-16). When all of these pieces are in place, the church will grow as God wants and desires.

This chapter considers the first element to the construction site, the Foremen. Every construction site has Foremen. On any work site, the Foremen make sure that everybody knows what they need to know, does what they are supposed to do, and does it in unison so that the task gets done right. They make sure that the foundation is laid correctly, the walls go up square, and that the wiring and plumbing are put in correctly. They also make sure that things get done in the right order—the sheet rock goes on after the plumbing and the electrical work—and that the right people do the right job—you don't want the plumber doing the roofing. Without Foremen, the construction site would be chaos.

The same is true for the church. There are four specific spiritual gifts God has given to various Overseers (see chapter 4) so that they can better shepherd the church. Ephesians 4:11 provides us with the list of four gifts.

> *And He Himself gave some to be apostles, some prophets, some evangelists, and some pastors and teachers.*

In English, it appears that there are five gifts mentioned here: apostles, prophets, evangelists, pastors, and teachers. But in Greek, many scholars agree that there are only four gifts listed. The last two, pastors and teachers, are very likely combined in the Greek to form one gift known as pastor-teacher.

In chapter 4, we learned about the qualifications for Overseers. In addition to these necessary qualifications, Ephesians 4:11 now tells us that the spiritual leaders of the church must also have at least one of these four spiritual gifts. While all of the Foremen will also have the qualifications of an Overseer, not all Overseers will be gifted as a Foreman, but will have other spiritual gifts and skill sets that can be used in other ways within the church. To properly understand the role of the Foremen, let us consider each in turn, to see how God invites them to lead His church into growth.

APOSTLES

The first of the Foremen are the apostles. We know the apostles were the twelve disciples chosen by Jesus in John 6. Judas, who betrayed Christ, was later replaced by Matthias (Acts 1:15-26).[1]

---

[1] There is some question as to whether or not this replacement was warranted. After this, the book of Acts never mentions Matthias again. Some think that maybe Paul was actually God's choice. Or possibly there was not supposed to be a replacement at all. Maybe Judas served his role as an apostle, and so there was

Yet the number of apostles in the early church was not limited to just these twelve. Paul was an apostle (Gal 1:15-17; 1 Cor 15:8) as was Barnabas (Acts 14:14). Two members of the church in Rome were also called apostles (Rom 16:7), one of whom appears to be a woman. So with these five additional apostles, there are at least seventeen apostles in the Bible. Yet when we discover what makes an apostle and what an apostle was supposed to do, we can assume that there were more than just these seventeen.

The Roman Catholic Church teaches what is known as apostolic succession. They believe that the apostles were able to pass on their position of authority and leadership to other people. This is usually done by the church after an apostle dies, as we see happen with Matthias replacing Judas in Acts 1. In accordance with this, they teach that the Pope is the successor of Peter.

The logical consequence of this is the Catholic doctrine of Papal Infallibility. Catholics teach that since apostles have the ability to speak and write the Word of God, and since the Pope is the successor of the apostle Peter, then anything the Pope says or writes is without error and is equal to the Bible. This has gotten the Catholic Church into some problems over the years, and it all stems back to the belief that there are still apostles today who speak and act with the authority of God.

Yet even many so-called "Protestant" churches and denominations have their fair share of problems even without apostolic succession. Just as apostolic succession has not kept the church free from error and problems, the absence of apostolic succession has

---

no need to replace him, in which case, the Bible does not endorse "apostolic succession."

not done any better. Some pastors and Ph.D.'s have created just as many problems for the church as have various Popes. There are even a number of "Protestant" churches that are led by self-proclaimed apostles who are thought to speak with just as much authority as the Catholic Pope.

The issue of apostolic authority can be cleared up by learning from Scripture what an apostle is and what an apostle does. When we understand the apostolic requirements and responsibilities, we are then able to see why they are important for the church and what role they serve in the church today.

What Makes an Apostle?

The term "apostle" is one of those English words that has not been properly translated from the Greek. (In fact, there are three of these words in Ephesians 4:11, "apostle," "prophet," and "evangelist." Other such words include "Christ" and "baptism"). The Greek word is *apostolos*, and rather than translate this word from Greek into English, the word has simply been transliterated, so that the Greek letters are changed into English letters, and then the word is left as it is (minus the word endings). So when we seek to understand what an apostle is and does, we must begin by understanding what the word "apostle" means.

The best translation for *apostolos* is "sent one." It refers to some sort of official or ambassador who is sent out by a group or individual to another place with a message to declare or task to perform. When translating this term, words like "messenger" or "delegate" would be good English equivalents. The apostles, therefore, were a special class of believers who were chosen by God to carry out a specific task and deliver a specific message to the world. There could, of course, be different types of apostles who were sent to perform different tasks. Jesus even referred to Himself as one sent (John 17:18; 20:21) from God, and so it could be said that He was an apostle of God.

For example, one type of apostle is the *apostle of Jesus Christ*, which is someone who was specifically called by Jesus and sent by Jesus to perform a specific task for Jesus. The New Testament records three conditions for being an *apostle of Jesus Christ*.

First of all, the Bible tells us that an apostle of Christ must have had personal contact with Jesus Christ (Acts 1:8, 21-23). This, of course, immediately eliminates everyone born after 33 A.D. Although we do not know if Paul had any physical contact with Jesus (some speculate that he was the Rich Young Ruler in Matthew 19 and Luke 18), he did have personal contact with the risen Christ on the road to Damascus (Acts 9:3-9, 15-16). This is why Paul refers to himself as one abnormally born (1 Cor 15:8).

Yet there were thousands who had personal contact with Jesus during His thirty-three years on earth, but not all of them are apostles. This is due to the second qualification. An apostle must also have personally seen the resurrected Jesus Christ (Acts 1:21-22; Luke 24:48; 1 Cor 9:1-2). This narrows the number of people down to just a couple hundred (1 Cor 15:5-8).

The final qualification for becoming an apostle of Jesus narrows it down to a select few. An apostle must be a person who received a direct appointment to the office by Jesus Christ Himself (Luke 6:13-16; 1 Cor. 15:8-9).[2] Jesus Christ handpicked His apostles (cf. John 6:70).

---

[2] Robert L. Thomas, *Understanding Spiritual Gifts* (Grand Rapids: Kregel, 1991), 175-176.

These three requirements reveal that the official office of "apostle of Jesus Christ" cannot exist today, because nobody alive today can fulfill all three requirements. This does not mean that there cannot be apostles today; there can be. But to see this, we must understand what apostles do.

What Apostles Do

Since the word "apostle" means "sent one" the church can send out people to be their messengers. God can also send out people with His message. Though such "sent ones" (apostles) might not have the official title of "Apostle of Jesus Christ," they are still "sent ones." We see various instances of these types of "sent ones" elsewhere in the New Testament. Barnabas and the two unnamed apostles in Rome are examples. So while these are "sent ones," they were sent out by the church, not specifically by Jesus Christ. Hence, they would not carry the official title of "apostle of Jesus Christ."

These "sent ones" are sent out by the church to carry the gospel to unreached people groups. Today, we would call them "missionaries." Missionaries are sent by the church to carry the gospel to new geographical areas and deliver it to new groups of people. So are there apostles today? In this missionary sense, yes. Just as there were some "apostles" in the days of Paul who were not "apostles of Jesus Christ," there can be apostles today who can be considered as "sent ones" and yet do not have the same authority as the "apostles of Jesus."

But Paul is not referring to the "missionary" type of apostle in Ephesians 4:11. Though Paul only refers to them as "apostles" here, he has in mind the authoritative and foundation-laying "apostles of Jesus Christ." In context, he refers to the "holy apostles" (Eph 3:5), as a way of speaking about the apostles who were called and sent by Jesus Christ to lay the foundation for the church by teaching and writing about Jesus Christ and the gospel (Eph 2:20). We also know that this is what Paul means because he refers to the "prophets" next in verse 11.

So these apostles in Ephesians 4:11 were the apostles of Jesus Christ. Jesus called them and chose them to carry the news about His life and ministry into the rest of the world. But something happened as they went out performing this task. After Jesus died, rose, and ascended, they travelled around, teaching others about Jesus and the Kingdom of God which He inaugurated. Yet they expected that Jesus Christ would return during their lifetime. They hoped that the second coming of Jesus Christ would occur within a few years, or a couple decades at most. But it didn't. The years went by, and Jesus did not return. As the apostles aged, they realized that the task of spreading the gospel to the entire world would require more than their lifetimes, and that it was increasingly unlikely that Jesus would return before they died.

So the apostles of Jesus Christ set out to record with pen and paper the message they had been given so that it could continue to go into all the world even after the apostles had left this world. These writings of the apostles are what we now call the New Testament. The apostles of Jesus received, declared, and recorded God's written word (John 14:26; Acts 11:28; 21:10-11; Eph 3:5).

Therefore, when Paul writes about the apostles in Ephesians 4:11, he is referring not only to the official apostles of Jesus, but also to their authoritative, apostolic writings, which have now been complied by the church into the New Testament. Further evidence that this is what Paul means is seen by the next term he uses: the prophets.

PROPHETS

The prophets are the second group of Foremen. Like "apostles," the term "prophets" is another transliteration from Greek. The Greek word is *prophetēs,* and refers to someone who declares a message from God. The word is similar to "apostle" but places more emphasis on the spoken message. Prophets were not often "sent" to another people or region (though occasionally they were, as with Jonah). Instead, they usually stayed in their home region and declared God's message to their own people.

There were two main types of messages which a prophet might declare. To put it another way, there are two facets of prophecy. To most people, a prophet is someone who predicts the future, and foretells what will happen. But this is only a relatively small part of a prophetic message. The vast majority of biblical prophecy is concerned with calling God's people back to a proper obedience to God. This is not foretelling future events, but forthtelling God's righteous requirements. While prophecy can refer to telling the future, it mostly refers to telling the truth. It is not primarily about predicting events, but rather about proclaiming God's Word.

Are there prophets today? Well, just as with the apostles, the short answer is "Yes," but not in the way that many assume. There are people today who have the spiritual gifts of apostleship or prophesy. But these gifts are used today when missionaries are sent to unreached people groups, or when certain people call the church to repent and return to a proper way of living with God. So while we do have these types of apostles and prophets (we should call them missionaries and preachers), we do not have the types of apostles and prophets that Paul refers to in Ephesians

4:11. The ones he writes about in this verse were those who wrote Scripture. The canon is closed. Scripture is written. So although there can be prophets today, this is not what Paul had in mind when he wrote about prophets here.

Just as with his term apostles, Paul has a very specific type of prophet in mind. Paul did not have in mind the various prophets who might have been alive in his day, but was instead referring to the prophets who wrote the Hebrew Scriptures, which we call the Old Testament. Jewish people typically referred to the Hebrew Bible as "the law and the prophets." Jesus Himself spoke about the Hebrew Scriptures this way (cf. Matt 5:17; 7:12; 11:13; etc.). The "law" referred to the first five books of the Bible, which is sometimes called the Torah, or the Pentateuch, and the "prophets" referred to everything else.

Modern scholars tend to divide up the "prophets" into three divisions of historical books, poetic books, and prophetic books. Jewish scholars separate the prophets into two categories, the prophets and the writings, so that the entire Hebrew Bible was called the Tanakh (TNK, shorthand for Torah, Nevi'im, and Ketuvim). But since all the historical writings were written by Jewish prophets, it was not uncommon to speak about the writings and the prophets as "the prophets." In fact, since the law itself was written by Moses, the greatest Jewish prophet (Deut 34:10; Acts 7:37), it too can be considered "prophetic," and therefore, included within the overarching term of "the prophets."

So when Paul writes here about prophets, he is thinking about the people who wrote the Hebrew Scriptures. Just as "apostles" refers to the writings of the apostles of Jesus Christ, "prophets" refers to the writings of the Hebrew prophets, which make up the

Old Testament (cf. 2 Pet 3:2). And all of this refers to the testimony about Jesus Christ (John 5:39; Rev 19:10)

Therefore, by referring to the apostles and prophets, Paul reveals his conviction about the centrality of Scripture for the church. No work that the church does can be successful in the eyes of God if not built on the foundation as laid by the apostles and prophets. And as we recall, the foundation is Jesus Christ Himself, but we read and learn about Him within Scripture. This is why the church should place a large emphasis on the Word of God. By doing so, the church is building on the foundation of Jesus Christ as we learn about Him from the pages of Scripture as recorded by the apostles and prophets. This is the good and solid foundation upon which we can build.

Many years ago, I worked at a summer Bible camp as a counselor and director. The camp is located on a lake, and about 50 years ago, when they built the kitchen and dining hall, they thought it would be nice to situate the building on the lakeshore so that people could look at God's glorious creation while cooking or eating. And it was glorious. I have many fond memories of eating my meals while listening to the waves lap at the foundation of that building.

But over the years, the shore of the lake slowly eroded away from beneath the foundation. As a result, the foundation started to crumble. But the eroding lakeshore was not all to blame. Part of this problem was due to a poor foundation. They did not dig the foundation hole deep enough, and when they poured the concrete, they failed to use any supporting rebar. As a result, very large cracks eventually developed in the foundation until eventually the building was condemned as being too unsafe to use and the camp had to tear down that beautiful dining hall on the shore.

Thankfully, the apostles and prophets laid a good foundation for the church. The prophets laid the foundation as we find it in the writings of the Old Testament. The apostles continued to lay the foundation through writing about Jesus Christ, and these writings have now been collected into the New Testament. And if the church is going to grow and thrive, we must make sure that we build upon the good and solid foundation which was laid out for us.

So we have a good foundation in the writings of the apostles and prophets. But a building is not built with just a foundation. Though a foundation is important and necessary, it is not a building. It is just a concrete slab. A building also needs walls and a roof, windows and floors. It needs plumbing and lighting. So how do all these things get added to the church? How does God's church get put together? God's church is not made of wood, concrete, glass, paint, carpet, and shingles, but of people who are called by God to follow Jesus into the world. So how is it that the church as God's people is built and formed upon the foundation of Jesus Christ as recorded in Scripture?

Well, the first thing needed is to get people into the church and show them how to live. This is done through the work and ministry of evangelists, who are the third group of God's Foremen.

EVANGELISTS

Just as with apostles and prophets, the word "evangelist" is not a translation from the Greek, but a transliteration. The Greek word is *euangelistēs,* and is closely related to the word for gospel, *euangelion.* To emphasize this close connection, I have suggested elsewhere that the term "gospelist" might be a better translation than "evangelist,"[3] but since this word is unlikely to receive wide acceptance, maybe the word could be translated as "one who teaches the gospel." However, since the gospel is about much more than just words and ideas—for also contains instructions on how to live life as a member of God's family—it might be best to include some sort of element of "proper living" in the translation of *euangelistēs,* such as "one who lives the gospel." Living the gospel would, of course, include both words and actions.

An evangelist, then, is someone who both understands the call of the gospel as found in Scripture and lives it out in their own life as a way to invite other people to believe in Jesus and live out the gospel as well. It would not be wrong to think of an evangelist as a disciplemaker. They live as a follower of Jesus themselves, and through their words and actions, invite others to also become followers of Jesus. Since the gospel is about all of life, then the evangelist who lives the gospel will be showing others how the gospel affects their entire life as well.

Notice that when we understand an evangelist in this way, the work of evangelist is not accomplished by preaching on a street corner, knocking on doors, or handing out gospel tracts. The work of an evangelist is not primarily accomplished through inviting people to believe in Jesus for eternal life. While this is cer-

---

[3] See my books *The Gospel According to Scripture* (Dallas, OR: Redeeming Press, 2020) and *The Gospel Dictionary* (Dallas, OR: Redeeming Press, 2021). There are online courses related to both books, which can be found at RedeemingGod.com/courses/

tainly *part* of the work of an evangelist, for the offer of eternal life is part of the gospel, it is not the entire work of an evangelist. Through their words and actions, an evangelist helps bring unbelievers to believe in Jesus for eternal life, and then brings believers to follow Jesus in their life.

This is what Paul writes about in 2 Timothy 4:5 when he invites Timothy to "do the work of an evangelist." Paul is instructing Timothy to do the work of living out the gospel in his life. And since Timothy is a leader in the church, this means that Timothy is providing an example to the people in his church about how to live out the gospel in their own lives as well.

So how does the work of living out the gospel fit with the foundation that has been laid by the apostles and prophets? The answer is that just as the apostles and prophets laid the foundation, the evangelists prepare to build upon that foundation by bringing people into the church and showing them how to live as members of God's family. The evangelist is the supplier. The evangelist brings the boards and siding and shingles of the spiritual church building so that they are ready and available to be put together into a structure.

And who are the evangelists? The truth is that every Christian is to be an evangelist. Since all Christians are to be living out the gospel in their life, this means that all Christians are evangelists, for "evangelism" means "living the gospel." But thankfully, as we have already seen, this does not necessarily mean that you have to pass out gospel tracts, go door-to-door, or preach on street corners. Evangelism happens when you live out the gospel in this world in front of your family, friends, neighbors, and coworkers. While words might often be used, the gospel can also be lived out in front of others by loving them and serving them in tangible ways, or simply by being a good neighbor, an honest employee, or a cheerful friend. As we live the gospel in various ways, people see our good deeds and glorify our Father who is in heaven, and are invited into the Kingdom of God along with us.

So the apostles and prophets laid the foundation of Jesus by writing Scripture. The evangelists prepare to build on this foundation by bringing the building resources to the construction site. Evangelists follow Jesus and invite others to do the same. But of course, we are still missing one element before construction can begin. The foundation has been laid, the construction materials have all been delivered. But right now, all the materials are all just lying around as piles of lumber and boxes of nails. There is no order, structure, vision, or direction for how all the pieces come together. This is why God provided the fourth foreman, the pastor-teacher.

PASTOR-TEACHERS

As was previously indicated, these two terms in Ephesians 4:11 are best understood as complimentary to one another. They are not two separate titles. Linguistically, the Greek indicates that they must at least be complimentary if not synonymous. Greek scholar and teacher Daniel Wallace, in a detailed and thorough analysis of this Greek construct, says that although the Greek does not demand these two terms be synonymous, neither does it imply their separation. Ultimately, he comes to the following conclusion:

> In light of the fact that elders and pastors had similar functions in the NT, since elders were to be teachers, the pastors were also to be

teachers. Conversely, not all teachers were said to be pastors. This evidence seems to suggest that the [pastors] were a part of the [teachers] in Eph 4:11 ... all pastors are to be teachers, though not all teachers are to be pastors."[4]

In other words, while there are various types of teachers in the church, some of them will be of a special type, which Paul calls the pastor-teacher. While not all teachers are pastors, all pastors will be teachers, and therefore, it is best to think of them as pastor-teachers.

So what do the two words mean? We know what a teacher is. A teacher is someone who imparts information to others. But what about the word "pastor"? The word "pastor" is not just a title. It comes from the world of shepherding, and is related to taking sheep to pasture. In fact, the Greek word for pastor is *poimenos*, which can also be translated "shepherd." A pastor is to the shepherd of the flock of God's people under his care. As Philip Keller so poignantly reveals in his book, one of the primary tasks of a shepherd is providing proper nourishment and protection for his sheep.

> He will go to no end of trouble and labor to supply them with the finest grazing, the richest pasturage, ample winter feed, and clean water. He will spare Himself no pains to provide shelter from storms, protection from ruthless enemies and the diseases and para-

---

[4] Daniel B. Wallace, "The Semantic Range of the Article-Noun-Kai-Noun Plural Construction in the New Testament," *Grace Theological Journal* 4:1 (Spring 1983), 83.

sites to which sheep are so susceptible.[5]

A pastor, then, shepherds the flock. When used in reference to shepherding people, a pastor leads people to green pastures where they can be fed, shows them where the calm and clean waters are from which they can drink, and protects them from dangerous predators and thieves who only want to kill, steal, and destroy. Jesus is the great Shepherd, and His under-shepherds are pastor-teachers.

The fact that Paul equates the work of the pastor with teaching indicates that teaching is a primary function of shepherding. All the functions of a spiritual shepherd can be accomplished through good teaching. Through teaching, the pastor guides his flock to green pastures where they can eat healthy spiritual food. Through teaching, the pastor takes his flock to clean and calm water from which they can safely drink. And through teaching, the pastor warns and protects his flock against false ideas, damaging and destructive philosophies, and wolves in sheep's clothing who want to kill and destroy the flock.

What is it then that the pastor should teach? Well, by inference, since the apostles and prophets laid the foundation for the church through writing Scripture, the pastor-teacher should focus on teaching Scripture. And who is it that the pastor should teach? Here again, since the evangelist gathered together the construction materials which will form the church, and these materials are the people of God, then the pastor-teacher focuses time and at-

---

[5] Philip Keller, *A Shepherd Looks at Psalm 23; The Classic Works of Philip Keller* (Grand Rapids: Family Christian, 1970), 24.

tention on teaching Scripture to God's people (cf. Acts 6:4; 1 Tim 5:17; 2 Tim 4:2). Almost every time the New Testament talks about the roles and responsibilities of the spiritual leaders of the church, teaching Scripture is at the top of the list (cf. Acts 20:28; 1 Tim 3:2; 4:6-16; 2 Tim 4:1-4; Titus 1:3; 2:1; 1 Pet 5:2). For the spiritual shepherd, this feeding and protecting is best accomplished through teaching the Word of God. It is impossible to be a good shepherd without feeding the flock of God with the Word of God.[6]

The apostles and prophets poured the foundation. Through both words and actions, the evangelist gathers together the building materials. The pastor-teacher then explains Scripture in a way to guide and instruct these building materials on how they are to be put together in a logical and useful way for God's church. He guides and protects the people so that together, they begin to form the church. We could almost say that if it is the evangelist's job to bring people into the church, it is the pastor-teacher's job to raise them up in the church. The evangelist brings a person to faith; the pastor-teacher trains a person about the faith. The evangelist increases the quantity of people in the church; the pastor-teacher increases the quality.[7]

Just as with the other three Foremen, the pastor-teacher's job is vitally important. If the pastor-teacher fails to instruct the people of God about the Word of God, those Christians will never

---

[6] Gene Getz, *Sharpening the Focus of the Church* (Wheaton: Victor, 1988), 121-150.

[7] Chester McCalley, *Commentary and Outline of Ephesians* (Kansas City: Word of Truth, no date), 43.

grow into maturity. They will forever be baby Christians. They will always remain a disorderly and confusing heap of building materials. If a pastor does not faithfully and systematically teach Scripture to Christians, they will always be bottle-fed Christians who want only milk rather than meat, and who base their decisions on feelings and emotions rather than on the truth of the Word of God. Every pastor-teacher should want the people in his church to become mature Christians, and the only way to do that is to prepare and serve all-you-can-eat-steak-and-potato meals from Scripture. But when a pastor fails to provide good meals, the people become weak and sickly. The church is weak because it has failed to understand that the primary role of a pastor is to teach, and to teach effectively.[8]

Part of the problem stems from the fact that most pastors separate the two terms Paul lists in Ephesians 4:11. Rather than see the two terms as connected (pastor-teachers), they think of two different groups, pastors and teachers. When separated in this way, some get the idea that there are some leaders in the church called "pastors" and there are others who do the teaching. In the first case, when we have pastors who are not teachers, but are just care providers, we end up with Christians who feel cared for, but who don't know much, and so cannot properly live or function as a follower of Jesus. They might be happy, but they are not very healthy. They remain immature babes for most of their life.

At the same time, the other extreme is just as dangerous. Some think that they are teachers who do not need to pastor. Then a

---

[8] Michael Fabarez, *Preaching that Changes Lives* (Nashville: Thomas Nelson, 2002), 5, 19.

pastor says "I am called to teach; not to pastor," their teaching ends up lacking love and care for their flock, which is essential for their health and well-being. Such loveless teaching often degenerates into bashing sheep over the head with the bat of legalism every week, which leads only to fear, shame, and guilt, rather than into Christlike maturity. While it is possible to have teachers who are not pastors, they should not be given roles of leadership within the church, but should instead seek positions in colleges or seminaries where they can focus on teaching.

Pastor-teachers must remember that their two roles are actually one. A true pastor-teacher is one who knows the primary way of feeding and caring for his flock is through faithful and systematic teaching of Scripture. At the same time, the teaching of Scripture is not an end in itself which is solely an academic pursuit, but is for the purpose of loving and caring for other people. Pastor-teachers will spend a lot of time with their nose in the books, but they will also spend time with the people of the community.

There is no room in God's church for the unapproachable, ivory tower personality who stands on a pedestal to deliver a message from God and then retreats back to his chambers in order to avoid mingling with the masses. While it is a wonderful idea to have times set aside for the uninterrupted study of Scripture, every pastor-teacher should also have times where people can drop in for a visit, or where the pastor goes out to visit the people where they are at.

Richard Baxter, a great preacher himself, wrote a book called *The Reformed Pastor*. In it, he says:

> That work which is our great end must be done, whatever be left

undone. It is a very desirable thing for a physician to be thoroughly studied in his art; and to be able to see the reason of his practice, and to resolve such difficult controversies as are before him. But if he had the charge of a hospital, or lived in a city where the pestilence was raging, if he would be studying fermentation, the circulation of the blood, blisters, and the like, and such like excellent points, when he should be visiting his patients, and saving men's lives; if he should even turn them away, and let them perish, and tell them that he has not time to give them advice, because he must follow his own studies, I would consider that man as a most preposterous student, who preferred the remote means before the end itself of his studies: indeed, I would think him but a civil kind of murderer.[9]

Although Baxter first published this in 1656, the truths are the same now as they were then.

George Herbert lived about the same time. When he became a pastor, he set down for himself some rules to live by. His book, called *The Country Parson*, is filled with sound, practical advice for every pastor. He says at one point that "the Country Parson upon the afternoons in the weekdays takes occasion sometimes to visit in person, now one quarter of his Parish, now another. For there he shall find his flock most naturally as they are, wallowing in the midst of their affairs ..."[10]

In a popular journal on leadership-related issues, Warren Wiersbe gave advice on how to preach practical sermons. "The experiences we preachers go through are not accidents; they are

---

[9] Richard Baxter, *The Reformed Pastor* (Carlisle, PA: Banner of Truth Trust, 1999), 312.

[10] George Herbert, *The Country Parson* (New York: Paulist, 1981), 75.

appointments. They do not interrupt our studies; they are an essential part of our studies ... It is difficult to preach to people you do not know."[11]

All of this is simply to reinforce that a pastor-teacher is primarily a teacher of Scripture, but this teaching must be warmed by personal encounters with the people under his care. Through a firm grasp of Scripture, the pastor-teacher will be able to see which building materials have been gathered together by the evangelist, and will then be able to teach, guide, and direct the people of the church to come together and build the church that God wants and desires. This will be the topic of the next chapter.

CONCLUSION

Ephesians 4:11 lists the four Foremen: apostles, prophets, evangelists, and pastor-teachers. Before any church can grow, it needs to have a firm grasp on the identity and tasks of these Foremen, and be committed to following them where they lead. The apostles and prophets wrote Scripture. The evangelist lives out the gospel in front of others as a way of gathering people together as the church. The pastor-teachers gets to know these people so that they can be taught Scripture and trained in how to function and grow as the Body of Christ in the world. With these Foremen in place, the church is ready to understand who does the actual work of the ministry. If you think we've been talking about the work of the ministry in this chapter, make sure you move on to the next chapter to see the next shocking truth from Ephesians 4:12.

[11] Warren Wiersbe, "The Patented Preacher," *Leadership* (Winter 1994), 70.

DISCUSSION QUESTIONS

1. What does a foreman do on a construction site?

2. Who are the four Foremen of the church?

3. Briefly describe the job descriptions of the four Foremen.

4. Are there official "apostles of Jesus Christ" today? What do we have instead? How do modern "sent ones" differ from the apostles that Paul is writing about?

5. Although Paul does have people in view when he refers to apostles and prophets, to what is Paul *actually* referring?

6. Can the work of an evangelist be accomplished through preaching on a corner? Why or why not?

7. Who are the evangelists?

8. What is a pastor-teacher's responsibility? Why can we not separate the pastor-teacher into two different groups, pastors and teachers?

CHAPTER 8

THE CREW

... for the equipping of the saints for the work of service, to the building up of the body of Christ.
Ephesians 4:12

John F. Kennedy once told our nation, "Ask not what your country can do for you. Ask what you can do for your country." And for a while, we followed his advice. But consumerism's viselike grip upon our lives has us once more asking, "What will the government do for me?" According to the Christian philosopher Francis Schaeffer, this me-first, entitlement mentality is the type of thinking that led to the downfall of the Roman Empire.[1] If things continue as they are, it will lead to our downfall as well.

But before that happens, this same mindset will lead to the downfall of the church. Most Christians come to church with the same consumer mentality that motivates them in the rest of life. "What does this church ... or that church have to offer me?

---

[1] Francis Schaeffer, *How Should We Then Live?* (Wheaton: Crossway, 1976), 227. He is summarizing Edward Gibbon's *Decline and Fall of the Roman Empire*. There are five stages of decline. The fifth and final is an increasing desire to live off the state. In other words, "What can the government do for me?"

Whichever one offers to meet my needs, I will go there." Even the term "Church Service" no longer means, "A place where I can serve" but rather, "A place where I am served."[2]

Pastors and churches that want to be large often cater to this mentality. They give up biblical preaching. They only speak to felt needs. They rarely talk about sin, judgment, the marriage of Christianity and politics, or anything that might make a person feel uncomfortable. Since people do not seem to come to church to get what they really need, many churches have started to offer what people think they want.

Yet nationally, church numbers are still shrinking. Why? Because God did not design His church to be a place that focuses primarily on meeting felt needs. God wants us to meet needs that most people do not even know they have. For unbelievers, their greatest spiritual need is to hear that God loves them, forgives them, and thinks nothing but good about them. They need to hear that they can have eternal life and a relationship with God simply by believing in Jesus. And one of the best ways for the church to share this message of God's love and acceptance is to show it to them. We are the hands and feet of God, and people primarily learn about God's love for them by how we love them. This is to be the primary function of the church.

But the church also has another function, and that is to teach and train those who believe in Jesus. God designed His church as a place where all believers can be taught God's Word and be given opportunities to put it into practice. The Great Commission in

---

[2] See my book, *Put Service Back into the Church Service* (Dallas, OR: Redeeming Press, 2015).

Matthew 28:19-20 commands us to make disciples—not just converts. So the primary functions of the church are to invite unbelievers to believe in Jesus for eternal life, and then to invite believers to follow Jesus in this life. This entire process is called "salvation" in the Bible, and it is not just about how to go to heaven when you die, but also how to serve God and others while you live on earth. The church must tell people how to be saved so that they can serve.

This understanding is critical for the life, health, and future of the church. If we want to get back to being a victorious, life-changing church, each and every person within the church needs to begin by asking, in the words of John F. Kennedy, not what your church can do for you, but what you can do for your church. And that is exactly what Ephesians 4:12 calls us to do.

As we look at God's Blueprints for Church Growth in Ephesians 4:11-16, we have seen that on the construction site that is Christ's Church, there are four Foremen who oversee the building site. The first two Foremen, the apostles and prophets, led the way in centuries past by writing Scripture. They laid the foundation according to Ephesians 2:20. The third Foreman is made up of all those who have the gift of evangelism. Evangelists speak the Scriptures with power to those who have not heard. As these people believe in Jesus Christ alone for eternal life, they become part of the church structure—they become what we could term the walls and the roof of God's church. And then we learned that the pastor/teachers are responsible for providing light and heat to the church. They do this by speaking the Word of God to Christians, thereby training Christians not just to know the Word of God, but to apply it to their lives.

In this chapter, by looking at Ephesians 4:12, we learn specifically what the pastor/teachers train the church members to do on the Construction site. If verse 11 listed the Foremen, verse 12 talks about the Crew. It says that God has provided the Foremen *for the equipping of the saints for the work of ministry, for the edifying of the body of Christ.*

Ephesians 4:12 shows us that the Foremen are to do one thing, and one thing only. They are to equip the saints. The rest of verse 12 indicates what the saints are supposed to do. The KJV has caused much confusion in this area because of an unfortunate comma inserted after the word "saints." It reads *For the perfecting of the saints, for the work of the ministry, for the edifying of the body of Christ.* When read this way, it appears that the Foremen are to do all three things mentioned in verse 12.

The Foremen are to:
(1) equip the saints,
(2) do the work of the ministry, and
(3) edify the body of Christ.

With this comma placement, many Christians think that everything is the responsibility of the Evangelists and Pastors/Teachers. Those who happen to not be an Evangelist or Pastor/Teacher believe they can come to church and just soak up all the teaching and worship. So they sit back, relax, and enjoy the show. They adopt a "Here I am; Serve me" mentality." They let others do the work of the ministry. After all, "the ministry" is what the pastor gets paid to do. As people adopt this mentality, the church begins to look like a football game—50,000 onlookers in the stands desperately in need of exercise, watching twenty-two people on the field who desperately need rest. All of this is the result of a misplaced comma.

But with the comma removed (punctuation is not part of the inspired text, but a simple grammatical diagram of the Greek shows that the comma should not be there) we see that the Foremen have only one task, and the Crew have two. When we remove the comma, as it should be grammatically, we get a much different picture. Visually, the verse layout now looks like this:

The Foremen are to equip the saints to:
(1) do the work of the ministry and
(2) edify the body of Christ.

This is different, isn't it? The comma determines whose job is it to do the work of the ministry. When the comma is left in, all the work of the ministry belongs to the Foremen. But when taken out, the work of the ministry belongs to all the saints, leaving the Foremen to simply equip them to do it. For the Pastor/Teacher, this is quite a relief!

THE TASK OF THE FOREMEN

Ephesians 4:12 shows that God has provided Foremen for the equipping of the saints. The word equipping means to train, to prepare, to restore, to make fully ready. Equipping is basically just providing the tools and training that the crew needs for the job. And just like on any construction site, God has given us the necessary tools for the job.

There are a wide variety of tools, but all tools can basically be boiled down into three categories: tools that cut (saws and drills), tools that connect (nail and hammer, screwdriver and screw, glue, and every man's secret weapon, duct tape) and tools that cover (caulking, mud, wood putty). For the church, these same tools are present in the preaching of the Word (cut), praying to God (connect) and fellowshipping with other believers (cover).

Cut

Cutting is done by the teaching and preaching of the Word of God. Often times in Scripture, God's Word spoken "cuts to the heart" (Acts 2:37; Heb 4:12). Sometimes the cutting is painful when things we are quite attached to must be cut off and removed. But other times, the cutting is a relief and a joy as deadweight is removed and burdens are lifted.

Connect

We connect with God through prayer. Prayer is the glue that keeps us in close contact with God. It attaches us to God as we communicate with Him. It helps us remain in constant fellowship. As we pray, God conforms our thoughts and desires to His will so that the more time we spend in prayer, the more like Christ we live. Prayer connects us with God in a way that nothing else can because spiritual intimacy is born when we pray.

Cover

Fellowship among Christians allows us to get to know one another and develop loving relationships with one another. As we do this, we learn to love another. And love covers a multitude of sins (1 Pet 4:8). As we spend time with each other, we forgive one another, and bear one another's burdens and fulfill all of the "one another's" of Scripture.

Does your church make these tools top priority? To be properly equipped, you must make sure that you have tools that cut, connect, and cover. An equipping church makes sure that they are teaching the Word of God, praying to God, and fellowshipping with one another. Incidentally, these are the three things the early church focused on (Acts 2:42)[3] and was one of the keys to their power and effectiveness. Churches can do a lot of things, but if these three are not provided then the church is just spinning its wheels and will not get anything done.

If a church is struggling, the first thing pastors and church leaders should do is determine whether they are adequately teaching the Word of God, providing times for prayer and getting the church together for fellowship. Where one or more of these are absent, you will find a church that is either struggling to survive or is built on the power and ideas of man rather than God.

Once the Foremen have adequately equipped the Crew, the church is then ready to send the Crew out to work. But what is it that the Crew does?

THE TASKS OF THE CREW

On a construction site, it is not enough to have the best-trained work crew if they don't do any work. They may have the necessary knowledge and all the best tools and resources, but if they don't do any work, there will not be any progress on the building.

When I lived in Chicago, there was a joke among some of my friends that Chicago only had two seasons—winter and construction. It seemed like the construction crews were always doing

---

[3] I take the breaking of bread from house to house to be part of the fellowship. It simply refers to going over to each's houses to eat a meal and hang out.

some project, but they never got any work done. This was especially true of the road repair crews. I remember one crew that went to work at first light every morning right outside my dormitory window for about two months. I was greeted at dawn every morning with the sound of jack hammers, concrete saws, and yelling voices for two whole months. Every morning I looked out my window to see if I could discover what they were doing. I never did figure it out. They worked for about two months on the same twenty foot stretch of pavement. When they were finally done, it looked exactly as it had before.

Many of our churches are like this. They make a lot of noise, cause a lot of commotion, but when all is said and done, not a whole lot gets accomplished. This is because, in many cases, the Crew does not know what they are supposed to be doing. Ephesians 4:12 clears this up by giving them two tasks. They are to do the work of the ministry and edify the body of Christ.

The Work of Ministry

The first task of the Crew, after they have been equipped and trained by the Foremen, is to do the work of ministry. This is backwards from how most people view the church structure today. Most of us think that the pastors are hired as "the ministers" and they are the ones who are in "full time ministry." But Paul turns all of that upside down. The ministry of the church leaders is to teach and train the Christians within the church to be the ministers. On a construction site, it is not the Foremen who do most of the work, but the Crew. This should also be the case in the church.

While God has given the Foremen three basic tools to equip the saints, He has also given a special tool set to each Christian to be used for ministry and mutual edification in the local church. These tools may be helpful in secular endeavors, but are not given primarily for this purpose. Rick Warren, in his national best-selling book, *The Purpose Driven Life*, points out that God has shaped us for service. He uses the word SHAPE as an acronym to describe the five things that make each of us unique for our God-given ministry.[4] They are your

Spiritual Gifts
Heart
Abilities
Personality
Experiences

Let us briefly consider each.

Spiritual Gifts

A gift is something specifically given to you by somebody else. Biblically, we think of these as Spiritual gifts, and they are given to Christians by God at the moment we first believe in Jesus Christ for eternal life. Some people are given only one; others are given multiple gifts. There is a debate among Christians about which gifts there are, how many there are, and which ones are still in use today. There is also a debate on how to discover your spiritual gifts. See Appendix 1 for further discussion on all of this.

---

[4] Rick Warren, *The Purpose Driven Church* (Grand Rapids: Zondervan, 2002), 236-248.

Heart

The heart is where your desires are. The heart contains your dreams and plans for your future. You discover your heart by asking the question, "If I could do anything in life, what would it be?" When you stop and think about this, you are searching for your heart. Frequently, these desires were placed there by God. The Bible says that He will give you the desires of your heart (Ps 37:4). This means both that He has placed them there, and that if you chase after them as He intends, He will bring them to fruition.

Certain forms of Christianity have told us that our desires are evil and sinful. But if we want to follow Jesus and serve God with our lives, and be used in His Kingdom, then our desires are God-given and should be sought after and worked for.[5] Certainly, there are still evil desires within us, but the solution to overcoming them is not to get rid of all desire, but rather, to discern between desires. There is the finest of lines between the greatest of sinners and the greatest of saints. We think they are on opposite ends of the spectrum, but in reality, they are both at the pinnacle of desire. One, however, reaches for the attainment of all his fleshly desires, the other reaches for the attainment of all the spiritual desires. "Desire, a burning passion for more, is at the heart of both ... the greatest enemy of holiness is not passion; it is apathy."[6] What are your desires telling you about your heart?

---

[5] Cf. John Eldredge, *The Journey of Desire* (Nashville: Thomas Nelson, 2000).

[6] Ibid, 53-54.

Abilities

Alongside Spiritual gifts and our God given desires, each of us have abilities and talents. Everybody has these, both Christians and non-Christians. Sometimes these abilities are natural—we are born with them; other times they are acquired—we learn them through education or an apprenticeship.

Often, these abilities and talents are used by business men and women to succeed in their jobs. Some who have a good head for math become excellent scientists and engineers. People with a love for music might become musicians. Those with good people skills do well in management or sales. We all have abilities that make us better at some things than others. Rick Warren says that on average, you possess from 500 to 700 different abilities![7] As we learn of these various abilities, they will help us know more about the particular features of our SHAPE.

Personality

Many of us like to classify personalities. We talk about "Type A" personalities. We take personality assessments. We talk about the four personality types. Sometimes we think that some personalities are better suited for ministry than others, or that certain personalities are ministry handicaps. But the fact is that there is no right or wrong personality for ministry. God made you who you are, and you need to understand that so that you can be who He made you to be in whatever ministry He calls you to do. There is nothing more frustrating than trying to serve God when you act like somebody else. If we try to serve God in areas that

---

[7] Warren, 242.

require gifts we do not have, the experience is quite frustrating. Be yourself because it is *you* that God wants; not you acting like someone else.

Experiences

Finally, every single person has a unique life experience. Some people have gone through unimaginable horrors. Others have lived a life of ease and luxury. There are many who wallowed in the depths of depravity, while others lived morally upright lives. Some people experience the loss of a loved one. Some experience daily pain and sickness. Nobody, however, just has an "ordinary" life. There is no such thing. We all have some things in common, but every person has a unique set of life experiences.

God can use these experiences—even the painful ones—to teach and show you the things He wants you to know. These experiences will help you relate with others who have gone through similar experiences. So do not deny them or try to hide them. When you are honest and open about the valleys, mountains and potholes of your life, others who have gone through similar experiences will see and will join you.

Putting the Five Together for Ministry

It is the first task of the saints to do the work of the ministry. But in order to know what ministry they should be doing, every saint should understand their SHAPE. The combination of these five things will help you understand what sort of ministry you would be good at. The combinations and applications are infinite. Your spiritual gifts, plus the desires of your heart, in combination with the abilities and skills you have learned, added to the personality you have developed and the experiences in life you have gone through make you absolutely unique for a certain ministry. If you don't do what God has prepared you to do, nobody else will.

Maybe you have the gifts of teaching and service, you were raised in a good family, and you have a lot of knowledge and experience in childhood development. In that case, maybe God's will for you is for you to help other young mothers within and without the church to raise their own children in a Godly fashion.

I know of a man who had the spiritual gifts of evangelism, service, and creative communication, the heart desire to travel and be on the open road, the ability and knowledge to work on motorcycles, a fun-loving and free-spirited personality, and the life experiences of riding motorcycles. He came complete with the tattoos and scraggly beard. This SHAPE made him perfect to start a ministry to Harley riders. And God is using him greatly to fulfill this ministry.

As each and every saint discovers their spiritual gifts, heart, abilities, personality and life experiences, it will become clear to them and to others what sort of ministry God has prepared for them to do (Eph 2:10). It may be unique. It may sound crazy to others. But if God has prepared good works especially for you to do, you need to do them, because nobody else will.

Pastor/Teachers sometimes find that a person knows what they need to do without knowing what their spiritual gifts, abilities or experiences even are. The way this happens is that they often come to the office after the church service, or sometime during the week, and say something like, "You know what this church really needs to do? We need to set up a skate park for all the skaters in town. I was walking downtown yesterday, and noticed signs up all over the place saying, 'No Skateboarding.' What if we built a skate park, and put up signs that said, 'Yes, Skateboarding!' Can you get started on it right away, Pastor?"

These kinds of "helpful ideas" normally destroy a pastor. He usually tries to sound positive and encouraging, but inside, he is thinking, "Oh no! Not another criticism of what the church should really be doing. I'm swamped as it is. I can't take on another project."

I used to think that way too. But no longer. I now realize that maybe this person is sensing God's leading. So I try to see how serious they are about following. First, I affirm their sensitivity to what God wants His church to be doing. I say something like, "That's a great idea! God is really showing you what He wants this church to do. And I really liked your ideas and the suggestions on how it could be done." I might even show them from the Bible that their ideas are also God's ideas.

Then I tell them that their ideas reveal the way God has wired them. I let them know that God has given them spiritual gifts, and these gifts help them see areas of need in the church, and ministries which the church is lacking. I let them know this is why they saw this need when many other people had missed it. If I am able, I tell them what their spiritual gifts might be. If a man says the church needs to reach out more to the community through acts of service, there is a good possibility that man has gifts of evangelism, service, and mercy. If a lady wants to see more emphasis on prayer, she might have the gift of intercession.

Thirdly, I lay down a challenge. I tell them that God did not give spiritual gifts just to point out weaknesses in the church. He gave the gifts to fill these weaknesses. Seeing the weakness is simply the Holy Spirit working on the individual to find a ministry in the church. When they tell me what the church should be doing, they have just told me what God wants them to do. I tell them to change "Somebody else should …" to "God wants me to …"

Frequently, some people just like to come up with ideas, but not really do anything. So I like to see how serious they are. I ask them to put together a plan, or find someone in the church who will come on board and help them put together a plan for this ministry (After all, this person might not be an organizer/administrator).

Then I leave it up to them. I have not shoved them off into a dark corner. I have not quenched their desire to serve. Instead, I have encouraged them in what may be God's guidance, and I have given them an opportunity to get their ministry started. If they want further guidance or ideas, I make myself available. I want to teach and train them to do what God has called them to do rather than simply do their ministry for them. In this way, they become the ministers. And when they minister in such a way, they accomplish the second task of the Crew—the edification of the body.

The Edifying of the Body of Christ

Each person is to minister to others for the purpose of edifying of the body of Christ. While the ultimate goal of all service is to bring glory to God, this is the method by which it is achieved. Each person needs to use their SHAPE for the mutual edification of the other members of the body of Christ.

Edification really isn't a word we use much anymore. It means strengthening, encouraging. In construction terms, it means building up. As the Bible defines it, true church growth is caused by the mutual edification of the believers. The growth of the body of Christ is caused by people using their gifts to edify, or build up, one another. If you want the church to grow, you need to be asking yourself "What has God called me to do so that I can edify others?"

Jesus Christ has specially gifted you to do exactly what He wants you to do. It is not just that He has a will for your life, it is that He has given you the set of tools you need to do what only you can do. Think of yourselves as having a monopoly on what it is Jesus wants you to do.

Imagine how impossible it would be to get your teeth cleaned if there were only one dentist in town. Not only would he always be busy, but he could also charge whatever he wanted for his services. Worse than this, imagine if this dentist refused to work on anyone's teeth! What if he got tired of people always coming to him with their toothaches, and the teeth they hadn't brushed or flossed properly? What if he got fed up with it all, and just said, "No more! I'm not going to work on anyone else's teeth!" What would happen? Two things would happen. He would eventually go bankrupt and everybody else's teeth would rot.

That's the way it is when a person either doesn't realize what their spiritual gifts are, or refuses to use them. Since we are all unique in our SHAPE, it is as if every person is the only dentist in town. Every person has a monopoly on what they offer. If people don't know what their SHAPE is, or if they refuse to use their gifts, then not only will they become spiritually bankrupt, but everybody else will rot their spiritual teeth. Each person is unique in what they can offer, and when they fail or refuse to offer it, everybody loses.

This is so important to understand. What God desires for you, and what He has gifted you to do, *no one else can do*! Yes, others may have the same gifts, but no one else has your God-given personality; no one else has your history or your experiences that can put a particular perspective on what you are doing for God. In other words, no one can do what you do better than you. In Christ, you are unique. You have a monopoly on what God has given you.

So what are you going to do with it? God will not force you to obey Him. He will not force you to do His will. But again, if you refuse, you are the one missing out—and so is everyone who needs what you have. And when too many people neglect what they are supposed to do—people and organizations start dying.

This happened to one small community church. It was the only church in town, but the people who attended never got involved, so the pastor had to do it all. One after another, pastor after pastor got burned out and left. Year after year, the church became smaller and smaller.

The church gained quite a reputation. After a while no pastor wanted to take the church. Finally, a young pastor agreed to come. On his first Sunday, he announced to the eight people who attended that on the following Sunday they were going to have a funeral service for the church. The church had died, and they were going to bury it.

He let the local newspaper know so they could run an obituary. The newspaper thought it was newsworthy enough to put it on the front page.

The following Sunday, enough interest had been sparked, that almost the whole community showed up for the funeral service. They wanted to see what a funeral service for a church looked like. As the people entered the building, there was soft funeral music playing. In the front of the sanctuary was a casket surrounded by flowers and soft lighting. The pastor sat up front dressed all in black.

When the room was packed to overflowing, he stood up to welcome the people, and then spoke a short eulogy over the casket about the dead church. He then told the audience that as it was an open-casket funeral, they would each be allowed, one by one, to come and look into the casket to pay their last respects.

So, one by one, each person came forward—out of morbid curiosity—to look into the open casket. And each one, after glancing in, turned quickly away and walked sheepishly back to their seat.

What was in the casket for the dead church? Nothing but a mirror. As each person looked into the casket, they saw their own face staring back at them. Had the church died? Yes, it had. Why? Because the people no longer did the work of the ministry that God had called them to do.

God has given you something to do which only you can do, and if you do not do it, it will not get done, and the church will be worse off as a result. Jesus Christ has a plan to build His church, and you are in it. Will you follow the directions, or will you fall through the cracks? Because you are a saint, you are a minister. You are part of the Crew. And as a minister in this Crew, you need a ministry, a place of service. Ask not what your church can do for you, but what you can do for your church.

DISCUSSION QUESTIONS

1. What is the job of the Foremen?

2. In the church, whose job is it to do the work of the ministry?

3. What three tools are needed to equip the saints to do the work of the ministry?

4. What are the five elements to your SHAPE? Briefly describe each.

5. Why is it important for each person to recognize their own unique SHAPE? What will this help them do?

6. What happens if we ignore our talents and spiritual gifts, or if we refuse to use them?

7. When you have an idea which you believe the church should implement to better love and serve others, what is God trying to tell you with this idea?

CHAPTER 9

THE MODEL

> ... *till we all come to the unity of the faith and of the knowledge of the Son of God, to a perfect man, to the measure of the stature of the fullness of Christ ...*
> *Ephesians 4:13*

In chapter 1, I mentioned that my brother had worked on an addition to the largest church in town. During that time, I remember stopping into his office when the planning process was in its final stages. He was working on putting together a miniature chipboard model of what the church building would look like with the expansion.

He was almost done with the model at the time, and I remember looking at it in awe. He had cut out all the windows. He had made topographical contour lines and inserted little trees here and there on the model grounds. When I expressed my amazement at the details, he told me that while he didn't include them on this model, he sometimes adds little cars and people.

Upon seeing the incredible detail, I asked him how much time such a model takes. He told me that while the length of time depends on the complexity of the model. This particular model took a couple hundred hours and cost several thousand dollars.

A couple hundred hours and several thousand dollars? I wanted to gag. What this mega church spent on a model could have supported my struggling little church for several months. Aside from that, it seemed like a terrible waste of the architect's time. But I had seen other construction models of this sort before, and so I asked my brother why churches and companies spent money to have these models built. The reason, he told me, was that models help generate interest in the building project. Models help with fundraising and vision-casting. People like to see what the end result will be before they get on board to donate money. Statistics show that money spent on the model generates more money for the actual project.

As I left his office that day, it occurred to me that God also provided a model for His church. God, as the Architect of the church, in His endeavors to expand the church, created a model for us. But God's model was not for the purpose of raising funds, but was provided to inspire and show us what the church will look like. God's model helps generate interest in the building project so that we serve in the church as God intends. As we continue to look at God's Blueprints for Church Growth, we see in Ephesians 4:13, the model for the church. The verse says this: *"... till we all come to the unity of the faith and of the knowledge of the Son of God, to a perfect man, to the measure of the stature of the fullness of Christ."*

Verse 13 contains three aspects, or three dimensions to the Model God seeks for His church.[1] Just as all architectural models

---

[1] In the Greek, *eis* is repeated three times, showing that there are three aspects listed here.

are made in three dimensions, width, depth and height, God's model also has three dimensions. The width of God's model is the unity among Christians. The depth of God's model is the maturity we develop. The height of the model is our growth into Christ-likeness.

WIDTH: UNITY

The first dimension, unity, is found in Ephesians 4:13. This text continues from verses 11-12, which inform us that the Foremen equip the Crew to serve in the church until we all come to the unity of the faith and of the knowledge of the Son of God. This makes sense considering the context and structure of the book of Ephesians. Ephesians 4–6 makes up the practical application section of Paul's letter based on the truths he taught in Ephesians 1–3. Paul begins chapter 4 by instructing his readers to walk in unity. This is what the first 16 verses are all about. He wrote in 4:3 that Christians should endeavor to keep the unity of the Spirit, and now, in verse 13, he writes that the first dimension of the church model is unity.[2] In other words, unity is what should characterize the church.

Yet too often, churches are more likely to be characterized by strife, division, and personal differences of opinion. Churches are divided over theology, politics, leadership, music style, finances, ministry opportunities, community involvement, what is and isn't sin, and numerous other issues. It sometimes seems there is noth-

---

[2] These two times are the only times this word for unity (*henoites*) is used in all of the New Testament.

ing the church will not argue about.

This is why unity is the first dimension of the church that God wants to build. Since division and strife is the default position of most of the world, a church that is known for its love and unity will be a light in the darkness, showing the world how to live in peace.

When unity develops in the church, it allows all people to work together for the common purpose to which we are called. But this doesn't mean we are all clones. We do not all work in the same way on the same projects. To the contrary, biblical peace enables us to live in our own unique way and with our own unique contribution, allowing others to offer their unique insights and contributions as well. Unity occurs when everybody does what he or she is best able to do in order to serve others. Unity comes when all share a common goal, a common purpose, a common vision, and a common direction, but within a framework of letting everyone be unique.

This is how it works with any building. A building consists of a wide diversity of pieces and parts, yet everything is put together with a unified purpose. Not everything is a window or door, but all the pieces—including the windows and doors, as well as the nails, wires, pipes, beams, paint—work together to make the building functional. Where there is no common purpose or unity of theme and goal, the building will not be functional or safe for those who use it.

Several years ago, I worked as a Caretaker at a summer Bible camp. One week I was told that the camp needed a storage rack for the life-jackets and canoe paddles, and I was asked to build one. The person who asked me to build a rack never bothered to ask if I knew much about construction, and I didn't bother to tell them that I was a complete novice in such matters. In hindsight, I should have asked for a quick introductory tutorial.

Prior to this, I had never really built anything, but I figured that it couldn't be too hard to build a little rack for paddles and lifejackets. So without any sort of plan or preparation except for some vague idea in my head of what I wanted to build, I started throwing 2x4s together. I didn't really do any measuring, but just took some scrap lumber lying around that looked "about the right size" and nailed them to some trees. I then decided that since the life jackets were outside, it might be nice to protect them from the rain, so maybe I should put a roof over them. Once again, I nailed a few pieces of lumber together and then fastened some plywood on top, then found some scrap metal roofing to finish things off.

As a result of my lack of planning and knowledge, the "shack" I constructed was anything but unified. It was about eight feet square and five feet high. Yet even this was overkill, since all it had to do was store about twenty lifejackets and ten paddles. It had no foundation except a tree root and two cinder blocks. Since I knew nothing about construction, I was unaware that the 2x4 framing studs for the ceiling needed to be spaced to match the 48-inch sheets of plywood. So the plywood pieces I nailed to the ceiling overhung the 2x4 frame by about 10 inches on each side. To make matters worse, I had failed to measure the metal roofing, so that when I went to screw the metal roofing pieces to the plywood, the pieces were too long. I dealt with this by getting out the tin snips to cut them down to size, leaving sharp jagged edges. Furthermore, when I screwed the metal roofing to the roof, I used the wrong size of screw, and many of the screws punched through the plywood to the underside of the roof.

The end result of my attempt at construction was a building that was not only ugly and rickety, but also quite dangerous. The edges of the jagged metal roofing were at face level so that anyone approaching the shack had to be careful they didn't cut their face. But the danger didn't end there. If they ducked their head to get a life jacket or paddle from the shack, they had to watch out for the sharp screws sticking through the roof.

But it was the first thing I had ever built, and initially, I was quite proud of that shack. Ironically, we had a master carpenter at the Bible camp who was constructing an actual building, and so I, in my ignorance, called him over to assess my work. He had spent weeks so far on his building, but I had put mine together in a few hours and wanted to show off my little pile of scrap lumber to the master carpenter.

He was very kind. He looked at my newly-built shack, and said, "Hmm ... Well ... It'll work. All we need it to do is store the life jackets and paddles." Then he went back to constructing his building.

The primary difference between our two buildings came down to one thing: Unity of purpose and planning. I did not build my shack with all the pieces and purposes in mind. I used the same studs, plywood, and sheet metal roofing that the other carpenter used, but he put his together according to a set of blueprints that showed how all the pieces fit together as a unified whole. I had no unified plan or purpose.

Later that summer, a storm blew my shack over and it got hauled away to the burn pile. Last time I was at the camp, his building was still standing, fifteen years after it was constructed. And by all appearances, it should stand for at least another fifty.

This story of two buildings, one with a unified plan and purpose and one without, represents the two ways that the church can grow and develop. Where there is no unity, the church will crumble into chaos and conflict until the first stiff breeze blows it over. But when the church is built according to the unified model that God lays out in Ephesians 4, the church will grow strong and sturdy so that it stands the test of time.

The great problem with unity however, is that few can agree with what unity looks like. Just as Christians argue and debate about everything from creeds to carpet color, so also, Christians argue and debate about how to be unified. Everybody agrees that unity is important, but few agree on how this unity is to be achieved. For example, some Christian groups seem to think that unity can only be achieved when everybody thinks like them, talks like them, dresses like them, and behaves like them. They want everyone to sign on the dotted line, color within the lines, and toe the party line.

But is this true unity? Unity is not necessarily the same thing as uniformity. We do not all have to be identical in order to live in unity. God is not interested in cloning Christians. Instead, we can learn what true unity looks like by seeing how God designed unity in creation. All of creation works and functions together toward a common divine purpose and goal, and yet it does this with incredible diversity. Each part of God's creation allows each other part to function as designed and intended. This is the only way God's creation works.

This is also the only way God's church works. True church unity is achieved when each person recognizes that all other people have different tastes, desires, interests, and abilities, and rather than see these differences in others as weaknesses to be exploited or flaws to be fixed, this diversity is celebrated and enjoyed as part of God's plan and purpose for the church. So rather than seek uniformity, true unity celebrates diversity, letting others be who God made them to be, just as we want them to let us be who God made us to be. Unity is not when we love others *in spite* of their differences, but *in light* of them.

This means that we don't all need to be in agreement on everything or act in identical ways, in order to live together in unity. The church can be as diverse as creation and yet still serve God. Nevertheless, there are a few essentials about which all should agree. Paul lists two of these in Ephesians 3:13. He says he wants us all to come to the *unity of the faith and of the knowledge of the Son of God.*

The Faith

The first item a unified church needs to be in agreement on is *the faith*. The noun *faith* is primarily used in two ways throughout the New Testament. The first way is the way we most often think of it, as a synonym for belief. Faith is typically defined as a belief, reliance upon, confidence in, or persuasion about the truth of some claim. Therefore, to talk about faith in Jesus Christ for eternal life is to say that we believe that Jesus is speaking the truth when He says that He gives eternal life to those who believe in Him for it (John 3:16; 5:24; 6:47; etc.). We can also believe, or have faith, in the truth claims that God exists, that Jesus died and rose again, and that the Bible can be trusted. This form of the word *faith* is the most prominent way the word is used in the Bible.

However, there is a second way the word is used as well. At several places in Scripture, the word "faith" is preceded by the article—the word "the"—as Paul uses it here in Ephesians 4:13.

In these cases, "*the* faith" does not refer to believing or being persuaded that something is true. Instead, "*the* faith" refers to the body of common Christian beliefs or the essentials of Christian life and practice (cf. Acts 6:7; 13:8; 14:22; 16:5; 1 Cor 16:33; 2 Cor 13:5; Gal 1:23; 6:10; Php 1:25; Col 1:23; 1 Tim 1:2; 4:1; 5:8; 6:10, 21).

We use the phrase "the faith" similarly in our own language when we refer to other religions. For example, we might talk about the Mormon faith, the Jewish faith, or the Islamic faith. We could also speak of the Christian faith. In all of these cases, we are referring to the whole system of beliefs and practices which differentiate one system from the others. The Bible uses the term similarly. When the Bible speaks of "the faith" it is speaking of the doctrines and practices which separate followers of Jesus from those who follow something or someone other than Jesus.

So while "faith" by itself refers to being convinced or persuaded that something is true, the phrase "the faith" refers to the set of beliefs and practices that are common to all Christians. This difference is seen when a person is asked about when they became a Christian, and how long they have been a Christian. In the first case, the question could be phrased, "When did you first place faith in Jesus Christ?" In the second case, the question is sometimes phrased, "How long have you been in the faith?"

Therefore, when Paul writes that God wants Christians to come to unity of *the faith*, he is giving instructions for Christians to agree on the basic non-negotiables of Christian life and practices. But of course, this is where the problems start, for what are the basics? What are the non-negotiables? I wish Paul would have laid out a few, for this statement of his has created much disunity in the church as we all try to figure out what the central beliefs actually are. If you ask one hundred pastors to name the top 10 core essential beliefs of Christianity, you will likely receive one hundred different top ten lists.

Nevertheless, if we could all sit down and talk things over, maybe we would come up with a few basic fundamentals of the faith. We would, of course, agree that there is a God. There should probably also be a statement about the authority of Scripture (even if we didn't necessarily all agree on the inspiration and inerrancy of Scripture). There would absolutely have to be a statement about the nature and character of Jesus Christ as God incarnate, since He is, after all, the foundation and center of Christianity. Finally, it would also be important to mention one of the main things that separates us from all other religions and cults, which is the foundational Christian teaching that eternal life is by grace alone, through faith alone, in Jesus Christ alone, apart from works. Without this final truth, Christianity is nothing more than just another works-based religion.

Beyond these non-negotiables, there are other things which Christians might want to include. From a historical standpoint, we could probably do no better than to simply point to the Apostle's Creed or Nicene Creed, which uphold God as the creator of the universe, the Godhead as existing eternally in three persons, the dual nature of Jesus Christ, the virgin birth, the death, burial, and resurrection of Christ, the reign and return of Christ, and the person and work of the Holy Spirit.

There may be others that we should all agree on if we are going to become unified, but those are just a few examples of the essential beliefs of the faith which Paul mentions here in verse 13.

But as was mentioned above, "the faith" includes more than just doctrine; it is more than just a set of beliefs. "The faith" also includes how Christians behave and act toward one another. If church members are going to get along, they might need to agree on a few basic ideas on how to live and act in this world and with each another.

Yet here we must be extremely careful. One generation's morality issues can lead to sin in a later generation. For example, Paul's admonition in Ephesians 6:9 for masters to treat their slaves well, was used by a later generation as permission for slave ownership.

This is why we must be careful. We must make sure we do not go as far as some churches and denominations do, in having written dress codes, along with rules about drinking, smoking, movies, music, dancing, and cards. Most of these issues are modern parallels to the issue of eating meat sacrificed to idols which Paul writes about in Romans 14 and 1 Corinthians 10. On such issues, we would be wise to remember Paul's final admonition in Romans 14:5-14 that we are not to judge each other in these matters. God has given some people freedom to do things which others do not have. The fact that each one will stand before the judgment seat of Christ to give an account of himself to God (2 Cor 5:10) should be enough of a reminder for us to abide by our own conscience and let others do the same. Operating in this way will greatly increase the unity we have with one another.

Therefore, when it comes to issues of morality, it seems that the only rule which should govern our behavior is the rule of love. Love is the guiding principle and ethic of the person who follows Jesus. As we live and exist within relationships with other people, we do so, not with a list of Dos and Don'ts, but with a desire for love. We are to love others and live in a way that invites them to love us. Issues of morality, therefore, are determined with the whole community of Christians in mind and can shift and change from one generation to another, or from one geographic location to another. There are only two ways to live: by law or by love. The Christian way is love.

So these are some of the Christian beliefs and behaviors which will help Christians grow in unity with each other. In a later letter to the young pastor, Timothy, Paul invited him to watch his life and doctrine closely (1 Tim 4:16). Paul's admonishment to Timothy very closely reflects Paul's instructions here to the Ephesians. How Christians live and what Christians believe is what makes up "the faith." The church grows in unity when it agrees on what to believe and how to live in love for one another. But unity in "the faith" is not the only aspect to growing in unity. Unity is also developed as we grow in the knowledge of Christ, which Paul mentions next.

Knowledge of Christ

The second area which allows Christians to grow in unity with one other is *the knowledge of Christ*. For growth in unity, there is nothing better than gaining a deeper knowledge of Jesus, our Lord and Savior. But we must understand that the knowledge Paul has in view here is not just a superficial knowledge of Christ. Paul is not just talking about "book knowledge." The normal word for knowledge is *gnōsis*, but Paul uses the word *epignōsis*, which is similar, but means something closer to "knowledge upon knowledge." It is used throughout Scripture as a full, complete, and detailed knowledge (Rom 3:20; 10:2; Eph 1:17; Php 1:9; Col 1:9-10; 2:2; 3:10; 1 Tim 2:4.; 2 Tim 2:25; 3:7). It is to know something exactly, completely, through and through. It is a certain and sure knowledge. It is this kind of knowledge we are to have of Jesus Christ, and which will lead us into Christian unity.

Yet is this kind of knowledge even possible? No; not in this life. Earlier, Paul wrote that he wanted the Ephesian Christians to know that which cannot be known, namely, the love of Christ (Eph 3:18-19). But how can we know that which cannot be known? How is it that we can gain a full, detailed, and complete knowledge of Jesus Christ? How can we have knowledge upon knowledge?

The answer is to recognize that since we can never fully know or comprehend Jesus Christ, we are to do two things. First, we are to add to the knowledge of Christ that we already have. Since *epignōsis* could be translated as "knowledge upon knowledge," it could be understood to mean that we are to be constantly adding knowledge to the knowledge we already have. We are to build on our knowledge of Jesus Christ. We do this, of course, through study, prayer, and following Jesus wherever He goes.

But this constant pursuit of the knowledge of Jesus Christ is dangerous if we do not also incorporate the second element of gaining this knowledge, which is humility. Since we can never fully know Jesus Christ, this means that our knowledge of Him is never full or complete. And therefore, we are ignorant of some things regarding Jesus, and flat-out wrong about others. Anybody who has been a Christian for any length of time can think back to a day when they believed something wrong about Jesus. But through study and growth as a Christian, you grew in your knowledge of Jesus Christ, and came to believe something different today. That experience should always keep you humble about what you currently believe today. For it is only a humble student who will always be a learning student, and it is only a humble and learning Christian who will recognize that they don't know it all, and therefore, they can seek out and learn from other Christians who might have different perspectives or ideas about Jesus Christ and how to follow Him in this world.

So yes, study and learn from Scripture, while putting into practice what you learn. This will slowly and resolutely conform you to the image and likeness of Jesus Christ, which will help you grow in unity with others. But as this process unfolds over time, make sure you also remain humble, allowing the convicting and illuminating work of the Holy Spirit and the sharpening influence of other Christians to teach you ever more about Jesus. This too will help you grow in unity with God, and with other members of His church.

Unity is the first dimension to the model that God has provided for His church. It is something we are to strive for and seek after, especially as we grow in unity in the faith and in knowledge of the Son of God. As we do this, we will also be begin to develop in the second dimension of the church model, which is Christian maturity.

DEPTH: MATURITY

The second dimension of the model that we are seeking to attain is Maturity. This is found in the next part of verse 13: *to a perfect man*. The Foremen of verse 11 train the Crew in verse 12. As the Crew learns to use their God-given gifts for ministry, each one grows into maturity, and the church as a whole becomes perfect.

This does not mean that any one of us will become perfect or sinless this side of heaven. The word Paul uses here for *perfect* is *teleios,* which refers to arriving at the end, or goal, for which you were created. It is not so much about arriving at the destination, but about journeying toward it. The quest for Christian maturity is an ongoing journey as we seek to become more and more like Jesus with each passing day.

So Paul's invitation for the church to become perfect is an invitation to grow into maturity. We know this is what he means because he elaborates further in verse 14 where he writes "that we should no longer be children, tossed to and fro and carried about with every wind of doctrine, by the trickery of men, in the cunning craftiness of deceitful plotting,"

An immature Christian, a baby Christian, is someone who is not biblically and doctrinally grounded. They are not yet able to tell the difference between good theology and false theology, or good teaching and bad teaching. Baby Christians think that as long as Scripture is quoted—the teaching must be okay. Baby Christians think that as long as the pastor or the teacher has some Bible school training, some letters after or before their name, or some pastoral experience, what they are saying must be okay. Baby Christians think that as long as a teacher or a pastor has a few books published or is broadcast on the radio or television they must be correct in what they say. Baby Christians are easily swayed by fine-sounding arguments. Baby Christian do not search the Scriptures to see if what they are being taught is true.

The good news is that a baby Christian can grow up. A spiritual baby can mature just like a physical baby. Human babies mature physically as they eat healthy meals, get enough rest, receive discipline, and are trained to be physically, emotionally and socially responsible. Similarly, a baby Christian can mature by eating a healthy diet of Scripture reading and listening to sound Bible teaching. They can discipline their minds to pray and their wallets to give. A maturing Christian can get involved with other believers so they can learn to serve others. In these ways, the Christian will mature, and the church as a whole will also develop toward its goal and end.

This idea of guarding and guiding Christians will be considered more in the next chapter where we look at verse 14. For now, it is important to recognize that Christian maturity is the second dimension of the model for the church. We are to strive toward our goal, or end, for which we were created, the perfect man, the mature Body of Christ, which is what Paul describes next.

HEIGHT: CHRIST-LIKENESS

The third and final dimension, found at the end of verse 13, is Christ-likeness. Paul writes that we are to grow into *the measure of the stature of the fullness of Christ*. Previously, in verse 13, he told us to gain as much knowledge about Christ as we possibly could. Now he tells us to become as much like Christ as we possibly can. One follows the other. Before you can be like Christ, you need to know what Christ is like. Many people think that Bible reading and Bible study is a waste of time, but we are only able to become more like Jesus as we learn more about Him through Scripture. "We get no deeper into Christ than we allow Him to get into us."[3] We do this according to His measure, stature and fullness. Let's look at these one at a time.

---

[3] *Springs in the Valley*, May 21, 147.

Measure

The first way to become like Christ is in His measure. The word *measure* comes from the Greek *metron*, which is where we get our word *metric*. So Paul is saying, "Go to great lengths to become like Jesus Christ in every way. From the smallest little bit to the largest part." Become like Christ in His measure.

Stature

The word *stature* frequently refers to age, or number of years. But Jesus only lived to be 33 years old, so Paul cannot be saying then that all we have to do is live to be 33. Instead, the word can also refer to the *reputation* one gains for themselves as they grow older. In Luke 2:52, when Jesus is said to be growing in wisdom and in stature, we also see that he was beginning to gain a good reputation with other people. As Jesus aged, He gained stature, or a positive reputation, among others.

This is the way it is with all great men and women in history. Nobody knows who the great men and women are when they are first born. Nobody knew George Washington or Clara Barton when they were first born. But as they grew older and matured, they served courageously and self-sacrificially, and as a result, gained a good reputation before others. This is what it means to gain stature.

Sadly, much of Christianity has bad stature. In recent decades, survey after survey and study after study has shown that the average non-Christian has a low view of the average Christian. Christians do not have a good reputation, but are instead known for being judgmental, rude, arrogant, and hypocritical. But we can work to reverse this stigma if we do the things Paul writes about in Ephesians 4:13. If we live in unity with one another and strive to become mature Christians, we will gain a good reputation among outsiders. We will, like Christ, grow in wisdom and stature and in favor with God and men.

Fullness

Finally, we are to become like Christ in His *fullness*. This means that we become like Him in every way. We cannot pick and choose which parts of Jesus Christ we want to imitate. We are to become like Him in His fullness. God wants every aspect of the church to be like every aspect of Jesus Christ. Whenever you trying to decide how to act, talk, or behave, it is wise to stop and ask yourself which words or actions look most like Jesus. When we ask ourselves this question and live as Jesus lived, we will develop into the fullness of Jesus Christ.

Christ-likeness involves becoming like Him in His measure, stature, and fullness. Although we've seen the three dimensions of the model church which God the architect is building—unity, maturity, and Christ-likeness—when we really get down to what the model looks like, it is this last statement from verse 13 that is most prominent. The church's model is Jesus Christ. If you want to know how you should live, think, and act, all you have to do is look at Jesus. If you want to know what the church should look like, what the church should be doing, and how the church should act—all you have to do is look at Jesus Christ.

Back in Ephesians 1:22-23, Paul wrote that "[God] put all things under [Christ's] feet, and gave Him to be head over all things to the church, which is His body, the fullness of Him who fills all in all." Note the word *fullness* again. The church is the fullness of Christ. The church is Christ to the world. If people in the world want to see and know Jesus Christ, they should be able to look at the church as the reflection of Jesus. Since Jesus perfectly reveals God to us, we are to reveal Jesus to others, so that by looking at us, they see Jesus, and therefore, God in us.

So Jesus Christ is our model. Everything we do, think, and say as individuals and as a church should be patterned after what Jesus did, what Jesus thought, and what Jesus said. And as we pattern ourselves after the model of Jesus Christ, we ourselves become a model of Jesus for the world to see.

CONCLUSION

When my brother built a model for the church expansion, he said that the model helped people see what the end product would look like, which in turn helped people get excited about where the church was going. God too, has laid out a model for us in Scripture. If we want to know what we're going to look like, if we want to get excited about our future, then we need to develop a complete and thorough knowledge of Jesus Christ, and then seek to live, love, and serve like Jesus.

Only when we all do this will we all come to a unity of the faith, and of the knowledge of the Son of God, to a perfect man, to the measure of the stature of the fullness of Christ. Only then will we become like our Model, Jesus. How are you and your church doing in living like this Model and revealing Him to the world?

DISCUSSION QUESTIONS

1. What is the point of a model? Why does Paul provide us with a model for the church?

2. Describe some of the things that create division in the church. How can the church come to unity instead?

3. Does unity require that we all agree on every aspect of the church and idea of theology? If not, how we can live in unity despite areas of disagreement?

4. What does the term "the faith" refer to?

5. Since it is impossible to gain a full knowledge of Jesus Christ, why does Paul include this idea in his description of the model for the church?

6. What are some of the differences between a mature and immature Christian? How can an immature Christian grow into maturity?

7. Earlier in this book, we learn that Jesus is the pattern and foundation of the church. In this chapter we learned that Jesus is also the model for the church. Why do you think Paul places so much emphasis on Jesus for all aspects of the church?

CHAPTER 10

THE PROGRAM: GUARDING CHILDREN

> *"... that we should no longer be children, tossed to and fro and carried about with every wind of doctrine, by the trickery of men, in the cunning craftiness of deceitful plotting..."*
> Ephesians 4:14

Anyone who has been around children for very long knows that they can say and believe some of the most amazing things. One little boy came home from Sunday school very excited about the lesson he had learned in Genesis 2 about how Eve was taken from Adam's side. But a few days later, he came home from school in a very distressed mood. When his mother asked what was wrong, he replied, "My side hurts. I think I'm going to have a wife."

Another little boy, after being told that God is One, asked when He would be two.

I also read about a group of children who were asked what God does all day. One responded, "He walks on water." Another said, "He lives! He lives!" A third said, "He organizes heaven, sending people down here in cloud elevators so they can help us earth people out." One of the little boys said, "He builds boats.

All kinds of boats. Nobody knows why."

When this same group of children were asked what God creates, one little boy answered, "God makes bees with little wings all day. Probably out of mud." A different child said, "He makes grass a lot of the days. That takes up a lot of hours. Did you ever see how many pieces of grass there are?"

Then they were asked if they could name any of the Ten Commandments, here is what a few of them said:

"Buckle up for safety!"

"Don't smoke in the bowling alley."

"Don't drink beer."

"Brush your teeth."

"Don't go to work on Sundays. And if your boss says she'll fire you, call in sick."

"Don't copy someone else's paper."

"I think 'Don't kill' is one. But maybe not."

"Don't eat when you have a fever and feel like throwing up."

"Say 'No' to drugs."

"Don't talk to strangers."

"Thou shalt not stab."

This is part of the wonder and joy of working with children. They are so trusting and have such vivid imaginations. But at the same time, children have some of the most amazing misconceptions and misunderstandings. Sometimes this is the result of their own immaturity and innocence, while at other times, it is due to their gullibility. Children are easily deceived. Children can be told the most outrageous lie and they will believe it because they often don't know any different.

There was an old Peanuts comic strip where Lucy told Linus that snow didn't fall from the sky the way most people thought.

Rather, it grew up from the ground in the night like a flower and then the wind blew it around. Linus, because he didn't know any different, believed her.

Children are easily tricked. Easily deceived. And most of the time, it's a cute characteristic that children have. Almost any story can captivate a child's attention. Almost any magic trick, no matter how silly, can amaze them.

But it is far from cute when adults have the same gullibility. What is adorable in a child is not at all adorable in an adult. Children are not supposed to stay children forever. Children are to grow up and mature so that they become productive members of society. Sadly, many adults, though they may have matured physically, are still mentally, emotionally, and psychologically immature. It is a sad state of affairs when this happens.

The same thing can happen when it comes to spiritual maturity. When people first believe in Jesus, they are born again into the family of God, and are spiritual babes in Jesus Christ. No matter how old they might be physically, they are spiritual children. And just as humans are supposed to mature as they get older, the same thing is supposed to happen with people the longer they are "in Christ." But just as physical maturity can sometimes be stunted, so also, some Christians never mature into spiritual maturity.

In fact, it is a sad reality in the church that many modern Christian adults are childish in their thinking. While immature spirituality should be expected from a new believer, many Christians remain childish for far long. While every Christian starts off as a baby Christian, some Christians remain that way for most of their Christian lives.

God wants baby Christians to become mature Christians. He wants Christians to move on from "milk doctrines" that make us feel warm and fuzzy, and start ingesting the meat truths of the Word that we mull over and think about (cf. Heb 5:11–6:3). It is only when Christian do this that they lose their gullibility, and become able to discern good from evil, truth from falsehood, correct doctrine from heresy.

As we think about growing the church God's way, we have learned that God's church grows as the people of the church develop into Christlike maturity. And believe it or not, this maturing process is the main activity which God desires for the church. Though people often say that evangelism and world missions are the primary activities of the church, effective evangelism and world missions only take place as Christian mature in the faith and develop Christlikeness in their beliefs and behaviors. All of the activities of the church in this world depend upon Christians growing into spiritual maturity. The task of helping baby Christians grow into mature Christians is to be the primary program of the church.

One of the important parts of planning and constructing a building is the "Architectural Programming" phase. This phase of the design process usually begins before the blueprints are drawn up or the ground is broken. This phase of the construction process helps determine what *kind* of building will be planned and built. Architectural Programming determines how large the building will be, what materials will be used, how many people the building can hold, the number of rooms it will have, and a whole range of similar details. Therefore, it is appropriate to think of the programming of the church. And as we have just seen, "The Program" of the church is to turn baby Christians into mature followers of Jesus Christ.

God's Program for His church is not primarily about a music

program, an educational program, or a youth program. God's Program for the church He is building centers around helping people mature in the faith. While music, education, and youth events might help people mature, they are not the only ways that people do mature. God does not care so much about the number of meetings at the church, or the frequency and variety of church events. He doesn't even care about the number of people. The primary thing God cares about in the church is whether or not the people within it are developing into spiritual maturity.

So when a local gathering of believers is trying to decide whether or not they are accomplishing God's will for the church in their community, they must not look at the numbers of bodies who sit a pew, the amount of money collected in the offering, or the square feet of the building in which these things take place.[1] The only Program God wants to know about is whether or not the people who make the church look, act, and love more like Jesus this year than they did last year.

This is exactly what Paul writes about in Ephesians 4:14-16. Back in verse 13, Paul wrote about the model for the church, which is the measure, stature, and fullness of Jesus Christ. He now turns to describing the two steps for accomplishing this Program in the church. The church must first seek to guard and protect new believers (Eph 4:14), and then it must seek to help guide and grow mature believers into greater depth and Christlikeness (Eph 4:15-16).

These two aspects of the church Program will be considered in

---

[1] See my book, *Church is More than Bodies, Bucks, & Bricks* (Dallas, OR: Redeeming Press, 2015) for more on this subject.

two different chapters. This chapter looks at the topic of guarding the spiritual children in the church (Eph 4:14), and the next chapter will consider verses 15 and 16 about guiding and growing spiritually mature Christians into greater depth and Christlikeness.

NO LONGER BE CHILDREN

When Paul wrote about children in Ephesians 4:14, he was not thinking about those members of the church under the physical age of ten. He had spiritual children in mind, regardless of whatever physical age they might be. A new believer is a child in the faith, whether they are five years old or ninety-five. When we first believe in Jesus, we are born again into the family of God, and start our live as a spiritual babe in Jesus Christ. But we are not to remain in such a state.

The sad fact, however, is that many Christians remain in the infant stage for far too long. While many Christians sit in pews and sing worship songs on Sunday morning for decades on end, some of them remain immature the entire time. So Paul calls the church to help these Christians grow up so that they will no longer be children.

But how can you tell who is a spiritual child and who is not? Christian maturity comes down to two things: beliefs and behaviors. Christian maturity is not measured by how much time a person spends sitting in a pew or reading their Bible. It is measured by how well a person understands the life of God and how well their own life imitates His. Let us briefly consider both aspects, beginning with beliefs.

Beliefs are critically important for growth into maturity. We are what we know. Furthermore, sociologists and psychologists have discovered that a person's view of God largely determines how that person lives. People who believe that God is vengeful and angry will often be violent and unforgiving. People who believe that God is gracious and loving will more readily love and serve others. So the beliefs of a person help guide that person's behavior.

Yet how can we know which beliefs indicate maturity? Scripture helps us in this regard. For example, Hebrews 6:1-3 contains a list of six key doctrines which are foundational for every new Christian to understand. The author of Hebrews states that people must understand these six truths in order to move on to the true "meat" of Scripture. These foundational teachings are (1) repentance from dead works, (2) faith toward God, (3) the doctrine of baptisms, (4) the laying on of hands, (5) the resurrection of the dead, and (6) eternal judgment. Do you understand and comprehend what the Bible teaches about these six areas? If not, then according to the author of Hebrews, you are still a Kindergarten Christian. This is not wrong; it just means you have some learning to do.[2]

Sadly, by using this one instrument to measure the maturity of modern, western Christianity, it appears that the majority of Christians might very well be classified as immature. Earl Radmacher was exactly right when he once said that American

---

[2] I have written a book on all six doctrines, but it is not yet published. Join my discipleship group at RedeemingGod.com/join/ to get notified when this book is available.

Christianity is a mile wide but an inch deep. Similarly, A. W. Tozer said that much of the failures of our Christian experience can be traced back to our habit of skipping through the corridors of the kingdom like children through a marketplace, chattering about everything, but pausing to learn the value of nothing. The church has great power and influence in society, and our presence is evident by the vast number of church buildings and Christian slogans that dot our cultural landscape, but few Christians have progressed much past a milk diet of basic Christian truths. These basic truths are a great first step, but they are only the first step. We must move on to maturity. We must grow up.

But it is not just theology that indicates maturity. It is not just about what we believe. It is also about what we do. Proper Christian behavior is also required for growth into Christian maturity. Earlier in Ephesians 4, Paul revealed that spiritual maturity can be measured by involvement in ministry. Each member of the church is part of the work Crew on God's construction site, and each person only grows into Christlikeness as they discover the ministry to which God has called them and start practicing it in their life.

Church ministry is not fulfilled by sitting in a pew on Sunday morning while trying to stay awake during the sermon. Christian behavior does not consist in smiling happily while chatting with friends in the foyer for twenty minutes on Sunday. True Christian ministry and behavior consists of how we live our day-to-day lives with our friends, family, and coworkers. It is measured by how we interact with our neighbor, the server at the restaurant, and the check-out lady in the store. Ultimately, the true test of Christian maturity is love.

In fact, love brings us full circle, back to our beliefs. Christianity is known for its large diversity of beliefs. This is one of the reasons there are so many denominations. How can we know which beliefs are right and which are wrong? The answer is love. Love is the litmus test for good theology. More specifically, love that *looks like Jesus Christ* is the litmus test for good theology. If our beliefs do not lead to loving behavior toward others, then we can be sure that our beliefs are wrong. Since God is love, and everything God does is focused on revealing His love, this means that when God's life is working through us, we too will live with love for others.

But sadly, once again, much of Christianity is not known for its love. Though we Christians often describe *ourselves* as loving, the average non-Christian rarely describes us in similar terms. Instead, words like "hypocritical, judgmental, and mean" are more often used.[3] Therefore, on this basis, much of modern Christianity can be described as immature. Christians who do not have a ministry and who are not lovingly serving others through the daily and weekly use of their spiritual gifts are not living the way a mature Christian would. Many Christians are immature Christians because they are not doing what God intended the members of His church to do.

Many people seem to think that the longer they are Christians, the more mature they become as a Christian. But this is just not true. Maturity in Christianity is not measured by the length of time one has been a Christians. While it is true that a new

---

[3] See Dan Kimball, *They Like Jesus But Not the Church* (Grand Rapids: Zondervan: 207) and David Kinnaman, *UnChristian* (Grand Rapids: Baker, 2012).

Christian cannot be a mature Christian (1 Tim 3:6), a long-time Christian may not be a mature Christian either. A man who has been a Christian for forty years is not necessarily more mature than one who has been a Christian for two. Maturing in the faith takes discipline, correction, training, teaching, instruction, and lots of practice (2 Tim 3:16–4:4).

It is like anything else in life that takes time and practice. For example, I play bass guitar. I've been a bass player for thirty years. When I first started playing bass guitar, I remember talking to every bass guitarist I could about how to play the bass. I wanted tips and suggestions on how to improve my ability no the bass. One question I always asked was how long they had played bass. Most of the answers I got were in the eight to ten-year range. So as I set out to learn bass, I couldn't wait to be able to say that I had played bass for ten years, because by then, I would certainly be good.

But I never took a single lesson. I never bought an instructional book. I never took a class. In fact, after the first year of playing, I put the bass aside, and have only played about a dozen times since then. Yet I still own the bass, and I pick it up every couple years to play for twenty minutes or so. Yet I can truthfully say that I have been playing bass for almost thirty years. However, I am worse today at bass guitar then I was at the end of that first year. I have not improved because I have not practiced. So also, just as length of time does not guarantee mastery of a musical instrument, length of time as a Christian does not guarantee maturity in the Christian life.

But everybody must start somewhere. And everybody, when they first believe in Jesus for eternal life, starts out as a newborn Christian. They are an infant. A spiritual babe. As new Christians, the first thing they must do is focus on growing up. They must learn what to believe and learn how to behave.

However, just like regular children, new Christians don't really know what they need to grow up. They don't know how to talk, eat, get clean, or move around. All they really know is that sometimes they are hungry and sometimes they are tired. Sometimes they cry a lot. If given a choice, many of them would pick candy as the main element of their diet, and television as the main activity. But this is because children simply do not know what is good for them. They must be taught and trained by loving, protective adults. The children in the church must be protected and provided for. Those who are spiritually mature must guard the children and give to them what they need. This is what Paul goes describes in the rest of Ephesians 4:14.

GUARDING CHILDREN

In Ephesians 4:14, Paul mainly emphasizes the guarding of spiritual children. He writes that there are false teachers prowling about, looking for immature Christians who can be led astray. Therefore it is the responsibility of the spiritually mature Christians to make sure that this does not happen to the immature Christians. It is the responsibility of the spiritual adults to guard the spiritual children from false teachers and false doctrine.

God wants the people in His church to have correct doctrine. And although God makes all believers into new creations when we first believe, this does not mean that all of our incorrect ways of living and wrong ways of thinking are instantaneously and completely corrected. Though we pass from death to life when we believe in Jesus, this transformation does not immediately affect all our beliefs and behaviors. We still retain many bad habits and ideas. It is the responsibility of the church, and specifically the pastor-teachers, to teach and train new Christians about what they are supposed to believe and how they are supposed to behave.

God gave the ability to some Christians to use the Word of God to teach and train other Christians, so that these new Christians can start doing the work of ministry. When new and immature Christians are taught what to believe and how to behave, they grow up in the faith and start loving and serving others, so that the entire church is strengthened. But until new Christians have matured a bit, they often fall prey the false teachings that abound in our fallen world. This is why it is important for church leaders to guard immature believers from false teaching and false teachers. Let us consider both dangers more closely.

From False Teaching

Ephesians 4:14 reveals that when new Christians are not adequately guarded by mature Christians, several bad things happen. First, the immature Christians are *tossed to and fro.* Like a child in a professional wrestling match, immature Christians get tossed around in the ring when they try to stand against sin and Satan. They are easily defeated and easily deceived. This is because they have not yet been trained to correctly discern truth from error. They fall prey to false doctrine and those who teach strange ideas.

This has been true of new Christians since the very beginning of the church. The early church fought against numerous heresies. One of the earliest was the heresy of the Gnostics. In the Greek language, *gnosis* means knowledge, so the Gnostics taught that in order to receive all that God wanted for you, you had to be given a special and deeper knowledge of God. This heresy led a lot of Christians astray, and the book of 1 John was written to combat an early form of this heresy. Sadly, various forms of Gnosticism are still rampant in the church today, especially among those that place a heavy emphasis on gaining special knowledge, blessings, or experiences in the Christians life. Gnostic ideas are also found in the dualistic tendencies of some churches to emphasize the spiritual realm over the physical. Any group of believers that focus more on the Holy Spirit than on Jesus has likely succumbed in various ways to this ancient heresy. After all, the Holy Spirit does not like to take center stage, but always points people to Jesus. So mature Christians today can help immature believers avoid these ancient false teachings.

Then there was the heresy of Arianism. This teaching has nothing to do with Hitler's sadistic dream of an Arian race. Instead, this false teaching claims that Jesus Christ was not fully God, but was just a human like the rest of us. Many Christians fell into this trap in the early days of the church, and there are some even today who argue that Jesus was not God, but was just an enlightened human who shows us the way that we too can become enlightened.

Later in church history, the church struggled against the heresy of Pelagianism. Pelagius taught that humans were born sinless and that, through sinless living, could attain heaven by good works and human effort. Many followed his path, and indeed, many still do. Any time you encounter someone who teaches that good works are necessary to make it into heaven, you are encountering remnants of the Pelagian heresy. Oddly, many of those who most loudly decry the Pelagian heresy turn around and teach the necessity of good works in order to attain heaven. They say things like "Salvation is by faith alone, but not by a faith that is alone" or "Faith without works is not really faith at all." Such statements show that good works are required to attain heaven.[4] The anti-Pelagians have become Pelagian.

We could go through the centuries of church history and list one heresy after another, one false teaching after another. The truth is that the church is always being attacked by falsehood. But as every new wind of false doctrine rises, the church also rises against it, to teach the truth and call people to hold fast to what we have received. Nevertheless, there have always been those within the church who were immature, who were children, and who fall prey to these false teachings. They are the ones that Paul refers to in verse 14 who are tossed to and fro by every wind of doctrine.

The picture Paul describes is of a small boat on a stormy sea getting tossed to and fro by the waves. Those who have been on a stormy sea, or even on a stormy lake in a small boat, know that it is a very frightening experience. Every swell threatens to capsize or crush the vessel. And there seems to be no end to the threatening waves. They just keep coming, one after another, pounding, crashing, and breaking. You expend all of your energy trying to get to the safety of the shoreline without seeming to make any progress. This is how it feels to be caught in the torrential waves of false doctrine. It is frightening and exhausting.

A new Christian reads some book or hears some teacher who says one thing, and the statements seem to be logical and biblical,

---

[4] See J. D. Myers, *The Gospel According to Scripture* (Dallas, OR: Redeeming Press, 2020) for a longer explanation of why such statements are wrong.

so the new Christian thinks that what they heard was correct. They often begin to excitedly tell their friends and family about what they have learned. But it is not long before one of these friends questions or challenges some of these ideas, and suggests that the new Christian read a different book or hear a second speaker who teaches the opposite. When the new Christian follows this suggestion, these new ideas also sound logical and biblical. So the new Christian becomes confused, and a little bit scared. They want to believe what is right, but have trouble determining which teaching is right and which is wrong. After a few of these issues pile up in their minds, they begin to feel battered, beaten, and tossed about by the winds of doctrine.

But note that the waves which might toss a small boat back and forth will barely touch an ocean liner. The church is a like the giant ocean liner. Church history, tradition, and teachings provide stability in the storm and firm decks on which to stand, so that there is no fear for those on board. But those who stray from the teachings of the church will get tossed to and fro by the waves, and will face the fear and uncertainty that comes with them. It is the church's responsibility to call all new Christians to board the ocean liner, where they can gain their sea legs in a manageable and safe environment.

Paul continues this line of thinking by the next phrase in verse 14, where he describes these children as being *carried about with every wind of doctrine*. Again, picking up the imagery of a boat at sea, this would be like a boat which has no sail and no oars. A boat of that kind is at the mercy of the wind. If the wind blows east, the boat goes east. If the wind changes direction and blows west, the boat goes west. A boat without any way to maneuver is a boat that is carried about with every wind. And that is exactly what happens to children who have not been grounded in the Word of God. When people fail to become founded upon the Word, they get carried about by every wind of doctrine (cf. Jude 12; Heb 13:9).

But it is not just the winds of doctrine that blow immature Christians around, it is also the false teachers who teach these doctrines. The false teachers are the true danger that Paul focuses on in the rest of verse 14, for without false teachers, there would be no false teaching.

From False Teachers

Paul continues in verse 14 to write about *the trickery of men, in the cunning craftiness of deceitful plotting.* False teachers are tricky, cunning, and crafty. They are deceitful. They plot schemes and carry them out. Part of this is because they themselves are deceived. Many false teachers, I believe, don't set out to become a false teachers, and often do not realize they *are* false teachers.

Most people who teach false doctrine are fully convinced of the truth of it themselves. False teachers truly believe that they are right. This is what makes them so persuasive. They honestly believe that they have discovered a set of truths which everyone needs to believe. But the real truth is that they too have been deceived and tricked into teaching what they teach.

There are, of course, some who purposefully set out to deceive. The old Steve Martin movie, "Leap of Faith," though intended to be a satire of modern-day healing ministries, also revealed how some false teachers are simply in the ministry for the money and the fame. Some don't believe a word of what they are teaching, but they teach it anyway because it bring in lots of money.

Nevertheless, for the most part, false teachers do not know they are false teachers, and therefore, false teachers are hard to recognize. False teachers do not wear signs proclaiming who they are. They are, as Jesus said, wolves in sheep's clothing (Matt 7:15). Sometimes, the most vociferous and argumentative defenders of the truth, who go about accusing everyone else of being a false teacher, are false teachers themselves.

Furthermore, just as no false teacher believes they are a false teacher, nobody sitting under a false teacher believes that they are receiving false teaching. After all, if a person knew that they were learning from a false teacher, they would stop listening to them. Nobody intentionally listens to and obeys a teacher they know to be false and deceptive.

So how do false teachers become false? It happens in a variety of ways. Sometimes a teacher gets tired of not getting the attention they think they deserve. So in order to get attention, they invent or develop a brand new idea or an exciting way of teaching, and oftentimes this teaching turns out to be false. Through sly words, fine-sounding arguments, and phrases that tickle the ears, they gain support and popularity. Though they do not intend to teach falsely, they do not teach with the right motives. Rather than teach to spread the truth, they teach to gain popularity or a following for themselves. They want to be known and recognized. They want to be the largest church in town or the most popular podcast online. Often, money is a factor as well, so that rather than teaching to grow spiritual children into adults, they teach to grow their own wallet and bank account. This means that two reliable signs of a false teacher is when they only seem to care about growing the *numbers* of followers they have, or they often talk about *giving money* to support them and their ministry.

Any time a teacher starts talking a lot about numbers, red flags should go up in the minds of the mature Christian. The sad reality is that these false teachers are not just led astray themselves by the lure of power and riches; they also lead astray spiritual children who have not been grounded in good doctrine.

And lest we get too puffed up with pride about our own ability to spot false teachers and sniff out bad doctrine, we must recognize that all Christians (including you and me) have occasionally fallen prey to false teaching. In fact, we can also say with a high degree of certainty that all Christians (including you and me) currently believe some false theology. There is not a single person on the face of the earth who is 100% correct in everything they believe. This is why we must continually be learning, studying, refining, and correcting ourselves under the authority of Scripture.

If you have been caught up in error in the past, or if you are afraid of being caught up in error in the future, you can mature and protect yourself from false teachers by taking time and making effort to study good biblical teaching and listen to good biblical teachers. Ask God to reveal to you where you are wrong in your thinking and theology, and then ask Him to direct you to good resources and teachers who can help guide you into the truth. Most importantly, never be afraid to question or challenge anything you believe. You can only discover false ideas if you question those ideas.

To truly see where you are lacking in your theology, seek to put into practice what you have learned. Only by ministering and serving others will you be able to see if what you are learning is truly leading you into love. After all, love is the litmus test for good theology. When you learn and live this way, you will no longer be spiritual children (cf. 1 Cor 13:11), tossed to and fro and carried about by every wind of doctrine, but instead, you will become a mature and Christlike spiritual adult.

This is the first aspect of God's Program. It is what keeps us from false teaching and false teachers. Although Ephesians 4:14 mainly talks about the importance of guarding the spiritual children in church, the other aspect of proper parenting is giving to the children, or providing for them. Paul doesn't mention this, but it is appropriate to include it because there is so much confusion today about what exactly a new Christian needs.

GIVING TO CHILDREN

Children are not born into this world knowing what is good for them. They need to be trained to eat their vegetables rather than fill up on licorice and Twinkies. They need to be told to not sit too close to the TV, to go to bed at a decent hour, and to treat other children with respect. If parents allowed children to make all their own decisions, few children would live past the age of ten.

It is the same with spiritual children. When we first become Christians, we do not know what is good for us. We want cotton candy sermons that are light, airy, and sweet on the tongue. We want high-energy music that gives us goosebumps. We don't want to hear about getting rid of sin or practicing spiritual disciplines. We prefer to be carried everywhere, and don't want to learn how to walk in the Spirit. And oftentimes, when we don't get our way, we throw temper tantrums and get angry at the leadership of the church for not giving us what we want.

Sadly, most churches today seem to operate under the conviction that new Christians (and even non-Christians) know best what they need. They run surveys to discover what the "felt needs" are of new and non-believers, and then organize the church around these needs. When the church operates under this mentality, it functions like a family that assumes children know what they need. The end result of focusing solely on these "felt needs" is that the young Christians remain weak and sickly children who never grow up or mature.

I agree that it is critically important to meet the physical, emotional, relational, and psychological needs of new and non-Christians. After all, if we only seek to meet the spiritual needs of people, we have fallen into the ancient trap of dualism, thinking that it is only the spiritual aspects of life that matter. The church is to minister to the whole person. Nevertheless, the church must not primarily take its cues from new believers or unbelievers about what the church should be doing and offering. Why not? Because new Christians and non-Christians don't really know what they need. They know what they want, but this is quite different from what they need.

If parents met only the "felt needs" of their children (as far too many are now doing!), we would be near the end of civilization as we know it. When my daughters were young, they thought they needed a dog, a pony, a kitten, a fish, a horse, a lion, a bird, and just about every other animal they saw. When it came to food, they thought they needed jelly beans, licorice, chocolate ice cream, juice, chips, and green olives. (Yes, my oldest daughter *loved* green olives when she was two.)

But as parents in the family, my wife and I (actually, my wife *more* than I) knew what our daughters needed better than they did. Did they need food? Yes, but not junk food. They needed healthy food, and we added in sweets and candy as a treat after the healthy food was eaten. Did they need companionship and something to take care of? Yes. It is good to develop the caretaking abilities of children. But they didn't need to be Noah, gathering two of every animal they saw. Did they need time to relax and be entertained? Sure. But this doesn't mean they get to watch television all day long.

The same is true for the church. Those who are more mature in the faith and who know sound doctrine, should be the ones who decide what to teach. And those who, through constant practice, are able to discern good from evil (Heb 5:15), should be the primary decision-makers about what to give to the new and immature believers in the church.

New Christians do not know what they need. Most think they need big churches with numerous options and lots of activities to divert their energy and attention from the troubles of life. They want a large children's program and youth group, forty-five minutes of quality, heart-pounding music, and a dynamic speaker who takes them on an emotional roller-coaster complete with side-splitting jokes and tear-jerking stories. When they leave church, they want to feel all warm and fuzzy inside and as if God Himself has sung them to sleep.

None of these are bad things. Youth groups and children's programs are good. Quality music is a must. It is a sin to bore people with the sermon (the ideas in Scripture are the most exciting ideas that exist). And people should absolutely feel closer to God when they hang out with other believers. But these are not the *only* things that new Christians need.

New Christians, like new babies, need milk—and lots of it. Milk helps newborns grow, and it helps protect them from sickness and disease. There is also a bond that forms between the mother and the infant as the baby feeds. Spiritually, the mother of the new Christian is the church. So with all of these benefits, it is the responsibility of the spiritually mature adults in the church, and especially of the pastor-teacher, to make sure that milk is what new Christians get. Whether it is provided through a special service or in a small-group study, new Christians need spiritual milk.

What is spiritual milk? It is nothing but the pure and simple teaching of the Word of God, and the activity of showing them how to practice these truths in their lives. Peter writes in 1 Peter 2:2 that Christians, as newborn babes, should desire the pure milk of the Word, so that they may grow (cf. also Heb 5:11–6:3). If a church is not giving to its people the clear and systematic teaching of Scripture, complete with explanation and application, and finished off with actual practice in the community, then they are not giving to the people what they need. Such church leaders are starving their children and should not wonder why the Christians in their church never seem to mature.

And note that as a child grows and develops, they eventually should become self-feeders. That is, while it is important for parents to feed their children when they are young, people should not continue to be fed by their parents for their entire life. Part of the maturing process is that children learn to prepare their own meals and feed themselves. So while it is a valid criticism for new Christians to say that they "are not being fed" by the church, it is not valid for those Christians who think they are mature to make the same complaint. By the time a baby Christian becomes a mature Christian, they should be able to plan, prepare, and eat their own spiritual meals.

If parents continue to feed their children for 48 years after they are born (barring any special mental or psychological factors, of course), that parent is a failure. At some point or another, those parents must show their children the door, saying, "It is time to be an adult on your own." Yet ironically in the church, it is usually those Christians who consider themselves to be "mature" who complain that they are "not getting fed" by the pastor's sermons. It is important to be fed spiritually … when you are spiritual baby. But as you mature as a follower of Jesus Christ, you should learn to feed yourself.[5]

And so it is a pastor-teacher's responsibility along with the other overseers of the church, to protect the church from false teaching and false teachers. The best way to do this is to provide good teaching from good teachers, and then lead by example on how to live out these teachings in our daily lives. It is not enough to tell a child they can't have Twinkies and soda pop every day. The spiritual leaders of the church must also provide good, healthy meals to the children so that they can grow and mature. These children will ultimately be able to study Scripture for themselves and teach it to others also.

As great as children are, the main goal of child-rearing is to help them grow up to become productive members of society. This involves guarding them from harm and giving them what they need. The same is true for the church. As great as new believers are, the goal of the church is to help new Christians mature into productive members of God's kingdom. For this to

---

[5] For a longer explanation of this point, see the article here, which is mostly written by Vince Antonucci: "Waa! I'm Not Getting Fed!" https://redeeminggod.com/waaaaa-im-not-getting-fed/

happen, they need to be protected from what will harm them and they need to be guided into sound doctrine. This is what Paul goes on to explain in Ephesians 4:15-16.

DISCUSSION QUESTIONS

1. Why do we not let children run the world?

2. What is the primary goal of raising a child? When it comes to those who are spiritual children, what is the primary goal of raising a spiritual child?

3. Who are the spiritual children?

4. Does "length of time" as a Christian have anything to do with spiritual maturity? Why or why not?

5. What does determine spiritual maturity?

6. What are the six key "elementary" doctrines mentioned in Hebrews 6:1-3, and how confident are you in your knowledge of all six?

7. From what two things are spiritual adults supposed to guard spiritual children?

8. Why do spiritual children need guarding from these two things and how is the church supposed to protect children from these things?

9. Have you ever discovered that you believed some false theology? If so, what was the false teaching, how did you come to originally learn it, and how did you discover that it was false?

10. What are some of the reasons that false teachers teach their false ideas?

11. What are some of the keys to identifying a false teacher?

12. How can the church develop its programs and activities to bring spiritual babes into Christlike maturity?

CHAPTER 11

THE PROGRAM: GROWING ADULTS

> *"... but, speaking the truth in love, may grow up in all things into Him who is the head—Christ—from whom the whole body, joined and knit together by what every joint supplies, according to the effective working by which every part does its share, causes growth of the body for the edifying of itself in love."*
> Ephesians 4:15-16

When the majority of people in the United States think of "church growth" they think of a church that has more people attending the Sunday morning service this year than last year. Such numerical growth in the pews leads to a larger budget and maybe a larger building.

So it is not surprising that one popular book on church growth begins with the following statement:

> Since 1966, [our church] has grown from 125 to over 13,500 in worship. We have gone through five building programs and two complete relocation projects, the last of which cost over ninety million dollars (including land, construction costs, and architects' fees).

We have gone from an annual budget of eighteen thousand dollars to an annual budget of eighteen million dollars.[1]

This is the popular definition of church growth. According to most, church growth is measured with bodies, bucks, and bricks, with more people, more money, and bigger buildings.[2]

Since growth is one of the top priorities of every local church, those who measure church growth with bodies, bucks, and bricks will often use whatever means necessary to get such things. I have a comic strip in my office showing a pastor asking his elders for ideas on how to grow the church. He says, "Besides calling every Sunday 'Easter,' does anyone else have ideas for improving church attendance?"

I also have an article from TIME magazine about a church whose "Ultimate Goal" was to get 40% of the people in its area back to church within one year. The article reported that in order to accomplish this, the pastor sang and danced the Lord's praises in an "electric whirlwind" which he termed, "Aerobics of the Lord." He executes choreographed jumps, leaps, and twists that the faithful try to copy. And when the Spirit really moves, he

---

[1] Bob Russell, *When God Builds a Church*, (West Monroe, LA: Howard, 2000), 3. On page 8, he does qualify this statement by saying that "Although we rejoice over our numerical growth, we know that God doesn't measure success in terms of attendance, offerings, or size of buildings. He measures effectiveness in terms of faithfulness to His Word, conformity to Jesus Christ, and ministry to those in need." The rest of the book is excellent in laying out 10 principles to grow your church, but still, it seems that the basic message of the book is "Do these 10 things, and you too can have a church that grows numerically." Cf. p. 10-11.

[2] See my book, *Church is More than Bodies, Bucks, & Bricks* (Dallas, OR: Redeeming Press, 2015).

pours buckets of holy water on his ecstatic audience.[3]

Yet this is fairly mild compared to what some churches do. One pastor in California collected a file of news clippings about how churches were employing innovations to keep their worship services from becoming dull. In only five years' time, "some of America's largest evangelical churches have employed worldly gimmicks like slapstick [comedy] ... wrestling exhibitions, and even a mock striptease to spice up their Sunday meetings."[4] If churches want more bodies, bucks, and bricks, these are some of the things that churches can do to accomplish this kind of growth.

However, just because we *can* do something, doesn't mean we *should*. But maybe the real problem isn't so much in *what* these churches are doing, but *why*. Maybe the problem is that they are chasing after the wrong type of church growth. What if numeral growth is not biblical church growth? What if God's idea of church growth is not measured with bodies, bucks, and bricks, but with some other measurement entirely?

If this is the case, then most of what we do in church could possibly be wrong! After all, if our definition of church growth is wrong, then the methods we use to achieve this growth will also be wrong.

Thankfully, the solution is relatively simple. If a poor definition of church growth leads to flawed methods to achieve this growth, then the simple fix is to get a right definition of church

---

[3] Sol Biderman and Sao Paolo, "Padre Marcelo Rossi" TIME Magazine (Feb 28, 2000).

[4] John MacArthur, *Ashamed of the Gospel* (Wheaton: Crossway, 1993), xvii.

growth. Once we properly define church growth, then our methods will fall into place as well.

WHAT CHURCH GROWTH IS

The definition of church growth proposed in chapter 1 of this book was that *church growth occurs when we teach and train the people who are the church to become what God wants them to be so they can do what God wants them to do.* This definition of church growth is drawn primarily from Ephesians 4:15-16. These verses show what church growth is and how church growth is accomplished.

The definition of church growth was foreshadowed in Ephesians 4:13, where Paul described the model that church growth is patterned after. A completed building should end up looking like the model. The model in verse 13 was Christlikeness. This is what Paul states in Ephesians 4:15 as well. While the first part of the Church program requires us to protect the spiritual children, this is primarily so that the second part of the church program can be accomplished, which is to grow the children into adults. Paul wants his readers *to grow up in all things into Him who is the head—Christ.* In other words, a church is growing when the people in the church are becoming more and more like Jesus Christ.

Remember, the word "church" is not defined by *how many* people meet, or even *when* or *where* they meet. The church consists of the people of God who follow Jesus into the world. Church growth happens when spiritually immature Christians (the spiritual children of verse 14), are corrected, trained, taught, encouraged, and equipped (2 Tim 3:16–4:4) in such a way so that they become spiritually mature Christians.

Church growth happens when the individual Christians who make up the church grow into spiritual maturity as exemplified in their Christlike behavior toward other people. They grow by learning the Bible and learning to obey the Bible. They grow by learning what their spiritual gifts are and finding ways to put them into practice so that they become who God made them to be. Church growth, therefore, is about building up one another to Christlike maturity and service.[5] Ultimately, they do this by learning to live and love like Jesus. That is biblical church growth.

Logically, this means that it is possible to grow a church and actually shrink in size. If a church of 100 loses 50 members, but these 50 become more like Jesus Christ, then that church is growing. Alternately, if a church of 500 doubles in size, but few mature into Christlikeness, then that church is not growing, even though they have gone from 500 to 1000 in attendance. With this understanding, it is entirely possible that a church is still growing even if they lose most of their people, hardly have any budget, and have to sell their building. A local church with few bodies, bucks, and bricks can still be a vibrant and growing church. A church in which the people are maturing is a growing church, regardless of how many people there are, where they meet, or how much money is in their ministry budget.

It is helpful to think about church growth the way we think

---

[5] This is seen partly by the noun "growth" in verse 16: *auxesis* is only used of spiritual growth (cf. Col 2:19). The verb in verse 15, *auxano*, is sometimes used of physical growth, but always has in mind factors outside oneself, or an element of life placed within a person by God, which brings about the growth. This kind of growth is never a self-achievement.

about family growth. Nobody believes that only large families are successful. While I myself come from a family with ten children, and while I believe my parents were *very* successful in raising all ten of us, my family was not "successful" *because* there were ten children. Similarly, we don't think a family is a failure because they don't "grow" from two kids to four, or from four kids to eight. A family with only one child, or even no children, can be successful if the members of that family grow together in unity, love, and faithfulness to each other and to people in the world. This is true of a husband and wife with no children just as it is true for a family with ten or more children.

Furthermore, we don't think that a family is a failure because the parents don't get raises at their job every year or buy bigger houses. Some of the richest families in the world are also the greatest failures at being a family. Family "growth" and success is not accomplished by increasing the size or wealth of the family, but by growing in maturity and love with each passing year.

Just as with a family, so also with the church. True church growth occurs when Christians grow up into Christlike maturity, so that they love God, love each other, and love the world more with each passing year. The goal of the church, according to Ephesians 4:15, is for Christians to grow up into maturity, becoming more and more like Jesus Christ. When this happens, church growth happens as well, for the people are growing into Christlike maturity.

HOW CHURCH GROWTH IS ACCOMPLISHED

The entire paragraph of Ephesians 4:11-16 has been building up to this single point. Once the spiritual children in the church have been protected from false teachers and false teachings, it is time for them to mature and become spiritual adults. How does this happen? Paul writes that growth into maturity comes through *speaking the truth in love*. The primary method to accomplish church growth is by speaking the truth, and speaking it in love.

Speaking the Truth

The phrase *speaking the truth* is one word in Greek. This word is used only one other time in Scripture (Gal 4:16), where it refers primarily to teaching the Word of God or preaching the gospel (cf. Gal 4:13). If the phrase means the same thing here, then Paul is writing that the primary way church growth is accomplished is through speaking the truth of Scripture with an emphasis on gospel-related truths.[6] This means that teaching and learning about Scripture is one of the primary keys to church growth. One reason God provided Scripture is so that His people could learn it and grow into maturity as a result.

Yet the preaching, teaching, and learning of Scripture is often the one thing that many Christians do not want or desire. Many local gatherings of believers tend to focus on everything *but* the teaching and learning of Scripture. Yet this is simply a sign of spiritual immaturity. While new Christians desire only sweet milk, mature Christians crave the meat of the Word of God. It is

---

[6] The gospel, of course, is not simply the message about how people can go to heaven when they die. The gospel is every truth from Scripture related to the person and work of Jesus Christ. In other words, all biblical truth is gospel truth. See J. D. Myers, *The Gospel According to Scripture* (Dallas, OR: Redeeming Press, 2020).

the teaching and learning of the truths of Scripture that turns baby believers into mature adults, and helps guide adults into the proper way of life.

Yet although the church has the largest and most fascinating collection of infallible truth that exists in the world, we tend to keep the light of God's truth locked up in the closet so we can focus on the latest fads of entertainment and newest insights from popular psychology. Walter Kaiser writes this:

> In the midst of all the feverish activity to restore the church once again to her former position of influence and respect, all sorts of programs and slogans have appeared. But regardless of what new directives and emphases are periodically offered, that which is needed above everything else to make the Church more viable, authentic, and effective, is a new declaration of the Scriptures with a new purpose, passion, and power. This we believe is most important if the work of God is to be accomplished in the program of the church.[7]

If the church is going to protect children and grow adults into spiritual maturity, we must focus on the truth of Scripture. Though the church doesn't have a monopoly on truth, and while many in the world are not ready to hear the truth, it does seem strange that the church is often cautious about boldly proclaiming the truth of Scripture to the Christians in the church. Rather than offer the one unique and shining jewel that we do have, we try to keep people's attention with poor copies of worldly music, entertainment, and social clubs ... and we will always fail.

---

[7] Walter C. Kaiser Jr., *Toward an Exegetical Theology* (Grand Rapids: Baker, 1981), 242. Italics mine.

The one thing the church can offer, and the one thing the church is instructed by God to offer, is also the one thing we fail to offer. What is that one thing? It is truth. The truth of God is the one thing that sets the people of God apart from all other people on earth. We have something they need, and something they crave in their inner-most being. We should, therefore, be focusing on the truth, and specifically, the infallible truth of Scripture. When people start to hear the truth, and when their lives begin to get transformed by the truth, they cannot get enough of the truth. They soak it up like rain in a dry and thirsty desert.

Only truth transforms lives. Only the truth of God helps people grow spiritually. And when lives are transformed and people begin to mature, then the church begins to grow. But speaking the truth by itself is not enough. Paul goes on to clarify that when we speak the truth, it must be presented *in love*.

Speaking in Love

Some Christians seem to focus primarily on speaking the truth, yet with a lack of love. If they see someone who is in sin or who has a false belief, these Christians feel it is their responsibility to point it out. We all know Christians who always seem to be critical and judgmental of others. They are on the lookout for those who say or do something wrong, and when they find some real or imagined fault in others, they feel it is their responsibility to point it out. Such Christians believe that truth is the highest ideal and that they are God's appointed defenders of truth in this world.

This tendency is sometimes found in those who claim to have "discernment ministries." Such ministries seem to do little more than point out the errors of other ministries. A while back, in the span of a few weeks, I watched one of these ministries attack James Dobson and his "Focus on the Family" ministry, Mel Gibson's movie, "The Passion of the Christ," Rick Warren's book, *The Purpose Driven Life*, the theology of several well-known pastors, and the phenomenon of contemporary Christian music. Such ministries see themselves as defenders of the truth who help keep Christians on the "straight and narrow" road to heaven. Yet they do little more than divide the church.

Of course, there are some who err on the other side. The opposite extreme is found in those ministries and Christians who just want everybody to get along, to love one another, and be in agreement on all things. They only want positive words to come from their pulpits and out of their printers. They never want to rock the boat or stand up for the truth. Their greatest fear is that someone might get offended by something they say.

Jay Adams has noticed this modern tendency and writes:

> In some circles, the fear of controversy is so great that preachers, and congregations following them, will settle for peace at any cost—even at the cost of the truth, God's truth. The idea is that peace is all important. Peace is a biblical idea (Rom 12:18 makes that clear: "If possible, so far as it depends on you, be at peace with everybody"), but so is purity. The peace of the Church may never be bought at the cost of the purity of the Church. That price is too dear.

But why do we think that we can get along in the world or for that matter, even in the Church, without conflict and controversy? Jesus didn't. Paul didn't. None of the preachers of the apostolic age who faithfully served their Lord were spared controversy. Who are we to escape controversy when they did not? The story of the advance of the Church across the Mediterranean world from Jerusalem to Rome is a story of controversy. When the gospel is preached boldly, there will be controversy.[8]

These two approaches reveal two extremes. Some teach the truth without love, and others teach love without truth. But in Ephesians 4:15, Paul calls for both. He calls for a balance between truth and love. To err on one side or the other causes great problems. Truth without love is harsh judgmentalism and dogmatism. Love without truth is blind sentimentality. But truth in love is compassionate concern.

Truth without love makes Cactus Christians: they're full of good points, but prickly, and painfully difficult to be around. Love without truth makes Cotton Candy Christians: they're sweet and look good, but there's nothing of substance to anything they say or do. They're just a lot of fluff. But truth in love makes Christlike Christians. They are not afraid to speak the truth, but know that such truth must be spoken in love, and that sometimes, love requires a person to not speak at all, but live the truth instead. A Christlike Christian seeks to balance truth and love. Truth, as important as it is, must always be taught in a loving manner.

The difficulty, of course, is that every "truth-telling" Christian thinks they are speaking the truth in love. I have heard Christians say the most hateful things, and when challenged about it, have defended their words by saying, "The loving thing is to tell them

---

[8] Jay Adams, *Preaching to the Heart* (Phillipsburg, NJ: P&R Press, 1984), 17.

the truth, no matter how painful it might be."

But when it comes to speaking the truth in love, the question is not whether you think you are loving, but whether the *other* person thinks you are loving. If you speak something you believe to be true, and the other person believes your words or actions were hateful and harmful, there is a good chance you were not speaking truth.

When we properly understand God, Scripture, and correct theology, it will *always* lead us to love. This is why love is the litmus test for correct beliefs. If our beliefs, doctrine, and theology are leading us to be judgmental, mean, and rude toward other people, then the truth is not in us. Where there is no love, there also is no truth. If someone truly knows the truth, they will be the most loving person you know.

This is exactly what Paul writes in 1 Corinthians 13. He says that even if you have all knowledge, but have not love, then you have nothing. This means that even if you can win at Bible trivia, can recite hundreds of Bible verses, and can argue theology with the best theologians in the world, but have not love, then you have nothing. Without love, there is no truth. Without love, knowledge counts as nothing. If you know the truth, it will lead you to love, and love provides evidence that you know the truth.

Furthermore, I would argue that *love is the main truth* which Christians should be preaching, teaching, and revealing through our lives and actions. Since God is love (1 John 4:8), all truth about God will be wrapped in love, focused on love, revealing love, and leading people to love. If the church could focus on only one truth to teach and practice, it should be the truth of love. The main truth presented by the church should be that God loves us, accepts us, forgives us, and desires nothing more than to be in fellowship with us.

As always, Jesus is the perfect example of how this is carried out. During His life and ministry, He never avoided the truth, but spoke it plainly in the most loving words possible. Though Jesus often had disagreements with the religious leaders of His day, and though He spoke many hard words to them, I doubt that a single one of them ever thought that His words were hateful, mean, or cruel. Though the words of Jesus are often read in harsh, accusatory ways today, it is possible to read the "hard" words of Jesus with a loving, pleading, and beseeching tone. When you do this, the words of Jesus take on a completely different meaning, which better matches the overall tenor of His life and ministry. The tone and demeanor of Jesus were always full of love, even when He had hard truths to speak.

God behaves similarly, which is not surprising, for Jesus perfectly reveals God to us. What is surprising about God's revelation of truth to us, is that He rarely speaks truth to us until we are ready and willing to hear it. God does not sit us down on the first day of our Christian life and beat us over the head with every wrong thing we do and incorrect belief we hold. Instead, God reveals His truth to us slowly, over time, as we mature and become ready to hear it and respond to it. This means that it is *loving* for God to withhold the full truth from us. It is *loving* of God to slowly reveal truth to us over time.

Sometimes, God will not point out our faults to us unless we honestly ask that He do so. We all sin in various ways all the time, and often, we are unaware of the myriad ways we disobey God. But in His patience and loving kindness, He waits to reveal our faults to us until we ask for Him to search our hearts and see if there is any wicked way in us. Even then, He gently whispers to us by the Holy Spirit about the skeletons in our closet, or He kindly takes us to Scripture to reveal our faults to us. But God never beats us over the head with some harsh judgmental attitude or hurtful words. Softly and gently, tenderly and kindly, He washes our feet with the water of the Word and cleanses us from all sin.

When we seek to speak the truth in love, we must seek to follow the example of God. Just because we see faults in someone else, this does not mean we are obligated to point it out. And even when we are invited, within the boundaries of a close friendship, to lovingly correct someone else, we must never do so in harsh, judgmental, or accusatory words.

It is also critically important that we seek to be part of the solution. When we correct someone, we must also be willing to take the time and effort to help that person through their faults and mistakes. We must never "hit and run." When Jesus set out to wash the filthy feet of His disciples, He didn't simply point out the dirty condition of their feet, but actually got a basin and a towel and knelt at their feet to wash them Himself. Jesus took the role of a servant and came alongside them to wash their feet for them. When we see somebody with "dirty feet," we must be willing to help them wash their feet. If we are not willing to help, then we should keep our mouths shut.

Another example is found in Acts 9:10-13. God tells Ananias to go see Saul who has been blinded. Saul's reputation of persecuting Christians has preceded him, and so understandably, Ananias is a little scared. He says, "God, I don't think that's the best idea. If Paul doesn't kill me, he'll imprison me for sure!" Ananias clearly and blatantly rejects God's command.

Now if we were God, most of us would do one of two things

in the face of such disrespect. We would either flat-out rebuke the man, saying something like, "You sinner! Away from me you evil doer!" This response would be truthful, but not very loving. This kind of response would be truth without love. The other way to handle such disobedience would be to ignore it in the name of love. In this case, God could have said, "Ananias, I understand your fear. I would be scared too. So it's okay if you don't want to obey me right now. Maybe someone else will come along." This seems to be loving, but there's not much truth. In fact, in the name of love, such a statement actually contains a lie. It is *not okay* to disobey. Very often, when love is the goal at the expense of truth, lies creep in (which is not very loving).

These are two of the possible responses to Ananias' disobedience. The first is to be so focused on the truth, that we beat people over the head with it saying "Obey or else!" The other is to be afraid of offending people, and say, "Okay, I understand that you're scared. If you don't want to obey right now, that's fine." These are the two extremes. One reveals truth without love, and the other reveals love without truth.

But God speaks the truth in love to Ananias. In Acts 9:15, God said, "Go, for he is a chosen vessel of Mine to bear My name before Gentiles, kings, and the children of Israel. For I will show him how many things he must suffer for My name's sake." God says, "Go. And let me give you some reasons why you should. I am not rebuking your lack of wisdom for resisting My viewpoint. I am also not denying your feelings of fear. Instead, I am telling you why you should obey, and also telling you that everything will be okay." This response is both truthful and loving. So in Acts 9:17, Ananias went.

This is how God deals with us as well. He never gives us truth without love, and never hides the truth in the name of love. Instead, He always speaks the truth in love. Scripture repeatedly tells us that God is gracious and compassionate, slow to anger and wrath (Exod 34:6; Neh 9:17; Ps 86:15; Joel 2:13; Jonah 4:2). When we resist and rebel, He gives us reasons to obey. If we continue to resist and rebel, His reasons slowly but surely become much stronger, until, after a while, He begins to discipline us. Truth balanced with love is how God deals with us and how we are to deal with one another.

Here are eight tips on how to achieve this balance between truth and love. If you sense the desire to correct someone who is sinning, there are several things you need to think through before you talk to that person.[9]

> First, remember what the ultimate source of truth is. If you feel someone is in sin, you had better have a strong biblical case. You cannot base truth on what your opinion is, or on what your traditions are, or on what some pastor, teacher or author said. God's word is truth. Jesus prays in John 17:17, "Sanctify them by Your truth. Your Word is truth." Before you confront someone with the truth, make sure you have a biblical case.[10] This helps too, because then it is not you saying "I think you are wrong" but it is God's Word saying "Here is what you are doing wrong."
>
> Second, make sure God is actually calling you to address the prob-

---

[9] Modified from Cathy Miller, "Ten Questions to Ask Before you Complain to Church Leaders" (Moody Magazine, Issue 96, 1996), 80. See also, Ken Sande, *The Peacemaker* (Grand Rapids: Baker, 1997).

[10] Cf. Bob Russell, *When God Builds a Church,* (West Monroe, LA: Howard, 2000), 153.

lem. Maybe He just wants you to pray about it. In fact, it might be a good idea to do nothing but pray about it for a whole month before you say anything—just to see God work. Also, it is often true that when God points sin out to us, it is actually *our own* sin He is pointing out, but we often project this conviction of sin onto others. Recognize that when you become aware of sin in others, it might actually be your own sin that God wants you to see.

Third, ask yourself what you might have contributed to the problem. Often, the problem you see in others is a problem that you yourself contributed to (Paul wrote about this earlier in Eph 4:1-6).

Fourth, try to discover what your motive is in pointing out the error. Maybe you simply want to get noticed, or maybe you want to get back at someone, or maybe you have had a bad day and feel like lashing out at someone. If you are unsure of your motives, spend a lot of time in prayer before going to the person.

Fifth, if you confront, are you doing it in a biblical way? Have you gossiped about this to anyone or, according to Matthew 18, are you following the steps for church discipline? Always try to keep the circle small.[11]

Sixth, you might want to ask yourself if you are demanding perfection. Nobody is perfect except Christ - not even you. And remember that with the same measure you use, it will be measured out to you at the judgement day. Are you overcritical and judgmental, or are you gracious and understanding about other people's failures because you know you have your own struggles?

---

[11] This does not hold true for predatory sins that harm others, such as rape, murder, abuse, or threats of physical violence. In such cases, it is your responsibility to go straight to the police or authorities.

Seventh, if you do confront the person, can you give input in the form of constructive suggestions rather than outright criticism and complaint? Rather than just point out sin, provide some steps to correct it, or explain how you yourself struggled with this problem in the past, yet was able to experience victory over it.

Finally, are you willing to be part of the solution? God may be showing you this error because He wants you to help out, not to criticize. This final point is critically important. Since we are all part of the church body, we are all supposed to help and love each other into wholeness. If we are not willing or able to love and serve others in their areas of sin and weakness, then we probably have no business pointing out their sin to them. It is not loving to point out someone's sin if we are not also willing to help love and help them through it.

These eight ideas will help you balance truth and love, which leads to personal growth.

Since God wants His church to grow, and since the church consists of the people of God, this means that the first stage of church growth involves the personal growth of individual Christians. And people grow mentally, emotionally, psychologically, and spiritually when they encounter the truth of God spoken in love. In other words, speaking the truth in love leads to the personal growth of those who hear it

PERSONAL GROWTH

In the last half of Ephesians 4:16, Paul writes that we will *grow up in all things into Him who is the head—Christ.* This statement reveals two truths about personal growth. First, it reveals that when we grow, we *grow up in all things*. This is growth into complete maturity. When we grow in this way, everything about us changes. God wants us to grow and change from spiritual children into spiritual adults. But this requires going through spiritual adolescence.

The teenage years are a rough time for most people because it is a time in which they transition from children into adults. It is during these years that people change mentally, emotionally, and physically. Many teenagers think they have all the answers, even when they don't. Also, hormones begins to rage, which causes numerous changes. Male voices start to deepen. Hair grows in strange places. There are physical changes as well. Legs and arms get longer. Muscles begin to grow, and female bodies start to develop curves. Some kids become quite awkward as they learn to deal with all these changes.

Something similar happens as Christians mature. Our tastes and desires start to change. We develop different interests than those we once had. Like teenagers, we sometimes become "know-it-alls," condemning and criticizing everyone who believes or behaves differently than we do. We might bounce around from group to group, theology to theology, trying to find "the one." We might also enter into a stage of spiritual awkwardness. But God wants us to grow up into all things, and although He gives us everything we need for life and godliness, we need to grow into these areas so that we can become mature adults.

The second truth about growth from verse 16 concerns the goal. The goal is to become like the Head of the church, Jesus Christ. This is quite humbling, of course, since no person will ever fully be conformed to the character of Jesus while in this life. This means that we will never fully mature. Any Christian who thinks they have "arrived" in their spiritual maturity is deluding themselves. As long as we compare ourselves to Jesus Christ, we will always fall short.

Teenagers provide another good example. Teenagers often have heroes, whether they are musicians, sports stars, or movie actors and actresses. It is not uncommon to see Junior High girls trying to look and act like some famous female musician or movie star, while Junior High boys attempt to emulate NFL quarterbacks or rock stars. As a result, teenagers often copy the behavior and antics of these "heroes," whether good or bad. However, regardless of how well a fourteen-year old boy throws the football, he will fall short of throwing like Tom Brady. There is always room to grow.

It is the same for us as Christians. Our hero should be Jesus Christ, and we should want to talk like Him, be like Him, and live like Him. But we should also realize that there will always be room for growth and development. We can never stop striving after the goal of maturity in Jesus Christ. We should make decisions and choices in our lives with this goal in mind. When people look at us, they should be reminded of Jesus Christ. With Jesus Christ as our head, we will experience personal growth into all things.

This finally leads us to church growth. When individual Christians grow into Christlike maturity as described above, the church grows as well.

CHURCH GROWTH

Paul concludes this revolutionary passage on church growth by summarizing and reminding his readers that all growth is accomplished only when every part does its share. Just as a body will never mature if the arms refuse to work, so also a church will never grow if certain members refuse to take part in God's work. Paul writes that:

> ... the whole body, joined and knit together by what every joint supplies, according to the effective working by which every part does its share, causes growth of the body for the edifying of itself in love.

Verse 16 is a summary of everything Paul has taught up to this point. He previously mentioned the spiritual gifts God provided to help church leaders train the rest of the church body to carry out church ministry. Here, Paul basically says the same thing, and points out that when each member does its share, church growth will occur.

Church growth is not primarily when more and more people are added to the church, but when each individual person in the church grows into Christlike maturity and starts using their spiritual gifts to love and serve other people within the church. When every part does its share, the church grows into health and love. This causes the growth of the body, which is true church growth.

A healthy and mature body knows what each part does best and how to use those parts correctly. An eye does the seeing, the ear the hearing, the mouth the talking, the feet the walking, and the hands the working. And according to verse 16, every part, even down to the joints, needs to do its share if the body is going to grow into health and effectiveness.

God is the one who created the church, just as He created our physical bodies. And He put the church together the same way

He put our bodies together. Each part of our body is like each person in the church. Each part serves a purpose and has a function, and each part is connected to every other part so that the whole body works together as a whole to accomplish what God wants and desires. When every part does what it is supposed to do, then the body grows into a healthy, mature, and complete person, glorifying God and serving the world. It works exactly the same way for the church body.

Furthermore, when it comes to the health and growth of the church, it is best to follow the Golden Rule: Do unto others as you would have them do unto you. If you feel like you are not being helped, loved, served, or fed in the church, rather than complain about it, make sure you are doing what you can to help, love, serve, or feed others. It may be that you are not being edified in the church because the person who should be edifying you, is not being edified by you.

In this way, church relationships are symbiotic. Other parts of the body of Christ may be weak and sickly because you are not doing what you are supposed to be doing to help them. And since they are weak and sick, they cannot do what they are supposed to do to help you. Since someone needs to step up and serve, it might as well be you. The best way to have your own needs met is to start meeting the needs of other people. When you help, love, and serve others, this allows them to grow in health and maturity, which allows them to start helping, loving, and serving you.

When each part does its share, then each part is cared for by all the others and so the body remains healthy. The mouth could not eat if the hands did not bring food to the mouth. But if the mouth refused to eat, the hands would not have enough energy to bring food to the mouth. When every part does its share, the entire body is strengthened, so that every part can function for the benefit of every other part. When every part serves, the whole body grows.

This is when church growth occurs. Whether we're talking about two people, two-hundred, or two-million, when those people love and serve each other, it causes the church to grow. This type of church growth does not require gimmicks, ingenuity, creativity, cleverness, or fancy marketing schemes. Every part of the body has a task, and if every part does its task, the church grows. It is so simple—only God could have designed it. These are His blueprints for church growth.

THE END IS LOVE

Paul's instructions on church grown ends with love. As Paul laid the groundwork for what he would write about church growth, he frequently mentioned the importance place of love in the life and health of the church. We are to be rooted and grounded love (Eph 3:17), to know the love of Christ which passes knowledge (Eph 3:19), and bear with one another in love (Eph 4:2).

As Paul concludes the section of his letter about church growth, he returns to the centrality of love. We are to speak the truth in love so that we may all work for the edification of the body in love. Church growth only happens within the context of love. Love is the beginning, middle, and end of church growth. Love causes Christian maturity, and Christian maturity results in love.

If you want your church to grow, don't focus on programs, budgets, or attendance numbers. Instead, just focus on love. As we love and are loved, we will all grow into the love of Christ, and each person will become mature spiritual adults, who are able to love God, love each other, and love the world just like Jesus Christ. This is true church growth.

DISCUSSION QUESTIONS

1. What have we learned so far in this book about how church growth occurs?

2. Can church growth occur even if there are fewer people attending this year than last year? Why or why not?

3. Describe how you would decide whether or not a family is growing and functioning properly? Can the same principles be applied to the church? Why or why not?

4. Is it possible to speak the truth without being loving? Why or why not?

5. Is it possible to speak loving words while not being truthful? Why or why not?

6. Describe how to find the right balance between truth and love.

7. Of the eight tips provided to help you speak the truth in love, which one was most helpful to you? Why?

8. How does speaking the truth in love lead to church growth?

9. What is the beginning and ending goal for church growth? Why is this so important?

PART 4: FRANCHISING

CHAPTER 12

GRAND OPENING

Normally by this point in a book on church growth, you would have read how the author started his church with three people meeting in an alley behind the supermarket, but followed ten simple steps and grew the church to over 24,000 members in only two years. Then you would be encouraged to follow these same ten steps to see similar results in your community.

This book contains nothing of the sort. You have not learned how to increase Sunday morning church attendance, the amount of money that gets deposited into the offering plate, or the square footage of your church building. You have, however, learned several principles for true church growth. You have learned that true church growth occurs when the people who make up the church grow spiritually into Christlike maturity through loving service toward others. When you think about church growth in this way, you too can experience true church growth, whether your local church community has 10 or 10,000 people, and regardless of whether these attendance numbers are increasing or decreasing from last year.

And just like many other church-growth experts, I too have an example of a church that experienced true church growth. But it is not an example from my own ministry (though many such examples could be provided), but is instead an example from Scripture. The principles of church growth as taught in this book were first seen in the practices of the early church. The church growth principles taught in this book are biblical principles as first seen in the New Testament church.

THE GROWTH OF THE EARLY CHURCH

Acts 2 records the Grand Opening of the church. Acts 2 reveals the birth of the church when the Holy Spirit came upon the disciples in the upper room. Immediately following the birth of the church, Luke records what sorts of practices the early church engaged in. He writes in Acts 2:42 that the church focused on four things. They "continued steadfastly in the apostle's doctrine and fellowship, in the breaking of bread, and prayers." Let us briefly consider all four activities.

1. The Apostle's Doctrine

The first thing that the early church focused upon was the apostle's doctrine. This means they spent lots of time listening to the teachings of the apostles. In chapter 7 of this book, we discovered that the church is built upon the teachings of the apostles, prophets, evangelists, and pastor-teachers. Here in Acts 2 we see the very same thing.

Since the New Testament did not yet exist, the apostles would have spent time preaching and teaching from the Hebrew Scriptures, which consists of the writings of Hebrew prophets. And since many of the apostles were also evangelists and pastor-teachers, this means that all four roles of the Foremen are present within the description of Acts 2:42.

The stance of the early church on the truth of God, as recorded in the Hebrew Scriptures and explained by Jesus, was a clear factor in the success and spiritual growth of the early church. They focused on listening to the teachings of the apostles, and such teachings transformed their theology and thinking, which in turn transformed their lives and actions.

The same thing is true today. The truth of God has not changed and will not change. Scripture is the lighthouse that guides us through the storms of life. It is the North Star that can always be trusted to point the way we should go. It is a lamp unto our feet and a light unto our path. Scripture is living and active and sharper than a double-edged sword, helping us discern truth from error. When the church focuses on teaching and living out the Scriptures, the members of the church will experience great spiritual growth.

2. Fellowship

But teaching is not the only important activity for church growth. Acts 2:42 says that the early church also devoted themselves to fellowship. But what is fellowship? Does it mean that they spent a minute or two shaking hands and welcoming each other before the Sunday morning church service? No. That is not true fellowship.

The Greek word used in Acts 2:42 (*koinōnia*) refers to a deep and abiding friendship. It has in mind the relationships between people who love to spend lots of time together. It refers to those who live life together. When two or more people live in fellowship with each other, they hang out with each other, eat together, and engage in various activities together. They do this multiple times a week, if not every day. People who are in fellowship with each other are good friends.

Many Christians struggle with this today, because some Christians seem to think that whenever Christians gather together, there needs to be prayer and Bible study. But it is impossible to develop a true and abiding friendship with others if you always do the same thing every time you meet. Good friends live life together, regardless of what activities or events they might be doing. Such variety creates excitement for the friendship, and also provides memories and experiences that allow the friendships to grow even further. Fellowship does not require Bible study and prayer. We can fellowship with others by sharing a meal, going to a movie, playing sports, and simply sharing all aspects of life with one another.

This is what the members of the early church did. They didn't just gather when an apostle was teaching, but at numerous other times as well. We know from Acts 2:46 that they met daily in the temple and that they went around from house to house to share meals with each other. It is also likely that they met each other at their places of work, as well as for holidays, celebrations, and major life events (such as weddings and births). They connected in as many ways and times as possible, as good friends tend to do.

It is only within such friendships that people can find the love and care they long for and so desperately need. When we live within loving friendships with others, it is then that true personal and spiritual growth occurs. Humans were made for relationships, and it is within the safe boundaries of a loving friendship that sin can be corrected, that proper behavior can be encouraged, and that each person can develop and practice their gifts and talents to their full potential. So it is here, in loving friendships, that true church growth takes place.

Furthermore, it is through such loving friendships that we will be recognized as disciples of Jesus. Jesus said that all people would know we are His disciples if we love one another (John 13:34-35). So loving friendships are the clear mark of being a disciple of Jesus. Loving friendship are also what draws people into the church. Since the entire world is longing for loving and trusting relationships, when we develop these friendships amongst ourselves, it is then that the world wants to join us and participate in the church. It is friendships based on the deep and unconditional love of God for each other that the world finds most inviting.

3. The Breaking of Bread

The third activity the early church focused upon was the breaking of bread. Some Christians equate this with "the Lord's Supper" or "taking communion." But as Acts 2:46 makes clear, the breaking of bread does not refer to getting a little sip of grape juice or wine and a tiny morsel of tasteless bread. It instead refers to eating an entire meal, usually in someone's home.

The reason that the early church engaged in this practice is because they loved spending time together. Since the early church consisted of friends who lived in fellowship with each other, eating meals together was an easy and natural way of expressing that friendship.

But more than that, the early church likely discovered (or simply knew from experience) that friendships often develop when there is food involved. Food is one of the best catalysts for building friendships. There is something magical that happens to human relationships when they share a meal together. The act of eating food with others loosens the lips so that people can talk and laugh. Even the presence of the food itself provides a conversation topic during the early stages of friendship, for all people can easily talk about food.

Furthermore, it is in the preparing, serving, sharing, eating, and cleaning up after a meal that many of the spiritual gifts can be exercised and used. Gifts such as hospitality, service, helps, and wisdom can all be put into practice while people eat and talk during the meal. Great personal, relationship, and spiritual growth can occur when people regularly gather together to share a meal. If one is not careful, great physical growth can occur this way too, but that is another matter.

4. Prayer

The final element that the early church focused upon was prayer. They understood that communication with God was essential for the health and growth of the church. They prayed for God's protection and guidance, as well as for boldness and power to preach, love, and serve others (cf. Acts 4:24-31). Just as Jesus sought the will of God so that He only did what He saw His Father doing (John 5:19), so also, the early church maintained constant communication with God so that they too could see what God was doing and align themselves with His actions in the world.

If Christians today want to grow in strength and wisdom, conviction and power, boldness and clarity, then they must maintain constant communication with God. Prayer should not be a strange practice in which we speak to God at set times with religious terminology, but should be an ongoing conversation with God in which we present our requests and needs to Him, and also seek guidance from Him about what He wants us to do in the world. Prayer is nothing more than talking to God as we would talk to a friend.[1] When we communicate with God in this way, we come to understand His heart and will for our lives. We also begin to see His hand at work as never before. Inviting God to get involved in our lives through prayer and asking how we can get involved with what He is doing is key to seeing the church grow in the world.

Result

As a result of these four activities, the early church experienced exponential numerical expansion. From a small band of 120 people praying in the upper room of a house in Jerusalem, the church quickly expanded to thousands of people (Acts 2:41, 47; 4:4; 5:14; 6:1). Acts 2:47 says that "the Lord added to the church daily those who were being saved."

Note that this numerical increase was not the goal or purpose of the early church. The new believers simply wanted to tell others what God had done for the world in Jesus Christ, and sought to live out the reality of this revelation through their own personal lives and in their relationships with others. Their goal was to love and serve others as they had been loved and served by God. Toward this end, they devoted themselves to the teaching of the apostles, fellowship with one another, sharing meals in each other's homes, and communicating with God through prayer. And as a result, God added people to the church.

When numerical growth of the church is the goal, the church does not grow. But when the people of God seek to grow, mature, and develop in their spiritual lives, then the church grows,

---

[1] See J. D. Myers, *What is Prayer?* (Dallas, OR: Redeeming Press, 2017).

and people are also added to the church. Numerical growth cannot be a goal of the church, but numerical growth can occur (but it doesn't always occur) when the members of the church mature and grow spiritually.

When the church focuses on growing into healthy spirituality and Christlike maturity, it is then that God will work to add more people to the church as He sees fit. This will likely happen at a greater rate among unreached people groups or in geographical areas where the gospel is being preached for the first time, but ultimately, such numerical growth is not up to the church at all, but is entirely up to God.

GOD GIVES THE INCREASE

I admit that it is nice to see more people showing up this year than last year. This is not only true for pastors and teachers, but also for bloggers, authors, and podcasters. I engage in all of these activities, and I am always thrilled to see more people buying and reading my books, downloading and listening to my podcasts, or visiting and joining my online discipleship group. I believe my teachings will help people find freedom in their lives, and so I am glad when more people are reading or listening to what I teach.

But in the decades I have been engaged in these activities, I have learned that all I can do is study hard and publish my content to the best of my ability. The only thing I have any control over is whether or not I am growing spiritually. As I learn from Scripture, I grow and mature, and seek to help others do the same. But I cannot control the numbers of readers, listeners, or subscribers. I try to leave all of that up to God, because only God can provide the increase.

Jesus taught something similar in Mark 4:26-29 with the parable of the growing seed. In this story, Jesus compared the kingdom of God to a man who scatters seed on the ground. Then the man goes to bed and sleeps. The next morning, he gets up and goes about his day. But whether he is awake or asleep, the seeds begin to grow and sprout. They come up out of the soil and become a plant. And then as soon as the grain is ripe, the man harvests it. The point of the story is that there is really nothing we can do to force the seed to grow or become a bountiful harvest. All of that is up to God. The *one* thing we can do is the *only* thing we should do, which is to scatter the seed. Yes, the farmer can also water the field and remove the weeds, but when all is said and done, it is not the man who does the growing, but God.

Paul offers a similar picture in 1 Corinthians 3:5-9 when he writes that while he planted the seed and Apollos watered, it was God who made it grow. The reason God brings the growth, Paul says, is because the church is God's field. One person plants the seed, another waters the seed, but it is God who adds people to the church and helps the church spread into the world (cf. Col 2:19).

When we focus on growing the church God's way, we must realize that while we do have a part in church growth, it is only God who brings the people and causes the church to expand over the face of the earth. Our part is simply to focus on our own spiritual growth, development, and maturity into Christlikeness. As we do this, we will be spreading seeds of the gospel to those around us through our words and our works. Then Jesus will take that seed, and make it sprout. Jesus will build His church (Matt 16:18). And Jesus will causes to spread and expand throughout the world.

DISCUSSION QUESTIONS

1. According to Acts 2, what four activities did the early church focus upon?

2. What is the Apostle's doctrine? Where do we find this today? How can the church today also focus upon the Apostle's doctrine?

3. What is fellowship? How is it different than the "fellowship" that is often talked about at a typical modern church gathering? How can Christians fellowship today?

4. What is the breaking of bread? How is this different than communion or "the Lord's Supper"? How can Christians participate in the breaking of bread today?

5. What is prayer? What do you think of the suggestion that prayer is nothing more than talking to God as you would talk to a friend? Why did the early church engage in prayer?

6. If we focus on these four activities, are we guaranteed to see numeral growth in the church? What are we guaranteed to experience? Will this be true church growth?

CHAPTER 13

THE EXPANSION OF THE CHURCH

As people begin to grow and mature spiritually, and as God starts to bring more and more people into the church, it is inevitable that the church will begin to spread and expand over the face of the earth. It will begin to make headway into new geographical areas and among new groups of people. In business terms, this sort of expansion is known as "Franchising." For example, the first McDonald's opened in Monrovia, CA in 1937. But through franchising, McDonald's has now spread to nearly every corner of the globe.

The church spreads in a similar way, but with a few differences. Just as a local business seeks to expand its reach and influence through franchising, local churches can expand the reach and influence of the universal church through church planting. But church planting does not occur the way many assume.

CHURCH PLANTING

In recent years, various church planting organizations have sought to recruit, teach, and train entrepreneurial Christian leaders to go out and plant more churches in various communities around the world. This process generally works as follows: The church planters find a community in which they want to live and minister, and then follow a series of guidelines and principles to launch a new local church in that community. Although most of these new church plants fail within 3-5 years, some of them become quite large. The pastors of these "successful" churches become famous and are invited to speak at church planting conferences and write church planting books.

Several years ago, I decided to become one of these church planters. I read all the books and attended all the conferences. I became friends with some of the best "church planters" in the country. I picked a location of the country in which I wanted to plant a church. I even started raising funds to support my church planting efforts.

Then I took a "church planter's assessment." This assessment was a personality test published by a large church planting organization. It was designed to help people discover whether or not they were likely to be successful in church planting. I failed the assessment. Miserably. The test told me that I was definitely *not* cut out to be a church planter.

But I disagreed with the results of the test. I decided the problem was not with me, but with the test. I didn't liked how some of the ways the questions were phrased, and figured that I had misunderstood the questions and answered them poorly. So I took a different assessment from a different church planting organization. I failed that one too. But again, my complaint was that the questions seemed to be weighted in a particular direction.

So I did some research and discovered that the church planter assessment test had been developed by interviewing and performing personality inventories on the pastors of some of the fastest-growing megachurches in the country. The church planting organizations then created the church planter assessment tests to find other people who had similar traits and characteristics as these megachurch pastors. In other words, the creators of the test were only looking for one type of church leader who could lead one type of church. They were looking for church leaders who would do well in a rapidly-growing megachurch setting, usually found in rapidly-growing suburban and metropolis areas.

Since this is what the church planting organization were looking for, then it made perfect sense why I failed both tests. The tests were designed to find Type-A personalities, who wanted to live in high-density areas, could lead lots of people, raise large sums of money, and gain lots of media attention. I was (and still am) unable to do any of these things. I am *not* Type-A. I go insane living in cities or suburban areas. I don't thrive in crowds of people, nor do I speak loudly and passionately enough to get people to follow me. I absolutely stink at fundraising, and I don't think I've ever been in the news. So I failed all the tests.

However, it turns out that the tests were indeed flawed. For while it is true that megachurches get lots of media attention and money, it is also true that the vast majority of Christianity does not find true spiritual fulfilment or meaningful connections with God in a megachurch experience. After all, while megachurches are able to gather lots of people together for spectacular and entertaining events, most megachurches do a poor job of actually *being* the church in their community. While they often attempt to serve their community, the lack of relationship building in the church means that these service projects are often little more than membership drives to get more people to attend the church.

Related to this, most megachurches are not actually helping the expansion of the church around the world. The numerical growth that many megachurches experience tends to come through transfer growth instead of conversion growth. Rather than bringing people into the family of God by helping them believe in Jesus for eternal life, much of the numerical growth in a megachurch occurs through Christians leaving their smaller, less exciting Sunday morning event so they can start attending the large, more thrilling event down the street at the megachurch.

Furthermore, the megachurch usually does a poor job of helping its members develop close, interpersonal relationships. It is easy for a person to attend a megachurch for years on end without ever developing a close friendship with anyone. Yet this is nearly impossible in a small church. Small local churches thrive and survive on the bonds of close relationships.

It is also extremely difficult for megachurches to lead the masses of people who attend into any sort of meaningful process of discipleship. A twenty-minute Sunday sermon which is mostly filled with colorful anecdotes and humorous stories is not enough for proper discipleship. Though smaller churches often struggle to make disciples as well, they do a bit better job of it *per capita* than do the megachurches because there is more accountability.

There are also numerous weakness in the leaders of megachurches. While it is true that they have a skillset which allows them to gather large crowds, gain lots of media attention, and raise large sums of money, such leaders are often quite poor at caring for people. Pastors with Type-A personalities are generally not adept at many of the "shepherding" aspects of pastoral ministry such as interpersonal relationships, tenderness, compassion, humility, and patience.

None of this is intended to bash megachurches or their pastors. Both have accomplished many good things for the kingdom of God. But we must recognize that the megachurch model is not the only church model, and therefore, the megachurch pastor is not the only type of person who can plant a church, or even pastor the church. Just as it takes all kinds of churches to reach all kinds of people, it also takes all types of pastors to lead and minister in all types of local churches. Megachurch pastors are not to be the model for all other types of pastors.

Once I realized all of this, I also realized that it was okay for me to fail those church planter assessment tests. All they really told me is what I already knew: that I didn't want to pastor a megachurch. As long as I served as a pastor the way Jesus called me to, I would be faithfully serving Him and the people He placed within my care, regardless of how many people there were. About this time I learned this, I encountered another pastor in town who was a church planter. As I got to know him and looked at his life, I discovered that he too would have failed all of these "church planter assessment" tests. And when I heard how his church was doing, I realized he was probably the best church planter the world has ever known.

THE BEST CHURCH PLANTER

I had always known this pastor was in town, but I recently heard some rumors about what he was doing, so I met with him to ask about his church. What he said blew me away. He began by saying that he only has a dozen people in his "core group." This isn't that impressive until you hear who they are. One is a member of the Black Panthers. Another belongs to the Klu Klux Klan. Somehow, they both worship together.

But this is only the beginning. One guy in the church is a

mega-wealthy Democratic Wall Street banker, and another is an unemployed construction laborer who has a concealed-carry gun permit and "TRUMP" bumper stickers all over his pickup. Furthermore, an illegal immigrant worships next to a Federal ICE agent. In a recent service, a cocaine-using prostitute gave her Bible to the visiting police officer. Somehow, all of these people are part of this church and they all worship God together.

When I expressed shock at how this sort of unity and love occurs in his church, the man told me that there are three secret keys to church planting. These keys are the ground rules he laid out for his church plant from day one. Here are the three keys:

1. All are welcome.

The first ground rule for this man's church plant was that all are welcome. And he really meant this. Though many churches say "Come as you are," what they often really mean is "Come as you are ... as long as you look like us, talk like us, and act like us." But this pastor's church really allows all people to participate, regardless of how they look, acts, or talk.

What is more, there is never any pressure to change. There is never any hidden agenda to take people from where they are at and turn them into something more socially acceptable. Each person is welcome just as they are, and they are *always* welcome just as they are. Yes, some people do change over time, but the pastor of this church points out that change is the Holy Spirit's job; not the church's job. So he teaches and models the first conviction that all are welcome in the church.

2. The only rule is to love one another.

The second key is related to the first. The only rule in this church is that they love one another. There are no standards of conduct. There is no dress code. There are no forbidden topics, questions, or issues. The church does not even have a doctrinal statement. The only rule is that they live by love. Everything must be done in love and for love.

Of course, living according to love is easier said than done, and so the pastor goes to great length to teach by word and example to show what this love looks like and how it is lived out in daily living. While mistakes are often made by the people in the church, his love for them shows them how to live in loving ways toward each other and toward the community.

Speaking of which, they not only agree to love one another, but also find ways to love the community in tangible ways on a regular basis. To me, this seemed to be the glue that bound such diverse people together. People will often put aside the greatest differences if they have a common mission and purpose. As these people lovingly work together to love the community, the vast differences between them all disappear.

3. The Bible will be the primary source for inspiration and discussion.

Finally, the church has agreed to spend time focusing on Scripture. But this doesn't mean they listen to lots of sermons and attend numerous Bible studies each week. Very rarely do they sit in rows, sing songs, share prayer requests, and listen to a message delivered by the pastor. Instead, the church functions more like a group of friends hanging out on weekends and in the evenings.

When they gather as friends, they talk about current events in the news, on their minds, or taking place in their lives. As they talk, they often try to include God in the conversation by discussing biblical principles that speak to the issue at hand. They know that Scripture is the best written revelation of God that exists, and so they agree to discuss Scripture as a way to understand God and each other.

They don't all agree on what Scripture teaches, but they do all agree to read and interpret it together. The key, they have found, is not to agree on everything they discuss, but stay together even when they disagree.

Who is this Pastor?

When the pastor explained these three keys to his church, I pointed out that it sounded very similar to what the early church was doing in Acts 2. The pastor gently smiled and said, "Of course! Where do you think I got the ideas?"

As we talked, I asked the pastor what the biggest challenge was for the church. He said that the biggest challenge was dealing with all the criticism he received from other churches in town. Though this was not too surprising from the fundamentalist and evangelical churches, he even received criticism from the mainline liberal churches. All of them agree that his church was doing everything wrong. Some critics say this new church has gathered the wrong people and needs to focus on getting some trained leaders who are spiritually mature into the church so they can disciple the church members on how to behave. Other critics say that the new church needs to get a building and a website so more people will come to the church. There are some who say the church needs a doctrinal statement. Some of the leaders say that while they appreciate the pastor's effort to welcome absolutely anyone into the church, he needs to be realistic and recognize that some people are beyond redemption. Of course, the various leaders who voice this criticism do not agree on who those hopeless people are.

The pastor and I discussed his church for a bit longer, and then went our separate ways with plans to meet again another time. I heard later that he had been arrested and imprisoned and was facing a death sentence. But I am pretty sure he is innocent and was framed by some of the church leaders in town. Are you curious to know more about this church? Do you want to know who this church planter is? You have probably heard of him.

The church planter is Jesus. And of course, the church He planted is the only church there is … the universal church which began in Acts 2. And since Jesus planted the only church there is, this makes Jesus the only real church planter in history.

THE ONLY CHURCH PLANTER

Along with being the best church planter the world has ever seen, Jesus is also the only church planter the world will ever need. Though it is quite popular to talk about church planting, the reality is that the church has already been planted and it was planted by Jesus. There is only one church, and it is the universal church that was started and founded by Jesus Christ. In Matthew 16:18, Jesus said, "I will build My church," and this is exactly what He started doing in the early chapters of Acts. In Acts 2, Jesus planted the church, and He has been building it ever since.

So we don't need more church plants or church planters. We also cannot truly speak about church multiplication, for there is only one church and it does not multiply; it expands. Since the church is a universal and spiritual gathering of all believers which transcends time and space, local gatherings are just small parts of the body meeting in a particular place and time. Though the number of local gatherings may increase, all such gatherings are still part of the one, universal Body of Christ in this world.

Therefore, we no longer have to spend time or money focusing on church planting. Instead, we can grow the church by focusing on our own spiritual growth and maturity. We can expand the church by simply being the church in our community.

EXPAND THE CHURCH BY BEING THE CHURCH

Along with church planting, there has been a lot of talk over the past several years about the importance of "being" the church. It is common to hear people say, "Don't go to church … *be* the church." While I agree with this slogan, the reality is that most Christians don't actually know *how* to be the church. But it really is not that difficult. To be the church, all you really need to do is be yourself.

Since the church is the people of God who follow Jesus into the world, this means you are acting as the church whenever you are acting as a person. Sometimes you might be a good representative of the church, while other times you might be a poor representative. But in either case, you live and act as the church wherever you go and whatever you do. Since the church goes with you wherever you go, you are the church wherever you go. It really is that simple.

So the issue is not how to be the church, but how to be the *best* representative of the church as you go about your day. The answer is that you can best represent the church when you remember that as a member of the church, you are to simply love others like Jesus. The *way* you do this might look different from day to day, and will definitely look different from the way other Christians love others like Jesus, but it doesn't need to be anything big or grand. You simply need to look for opportunities throughout your day to love and serve others with your gifts, talents, abilities, and desires. When you do this, you will be the church.

A friend of mine described his experience of being the church this way:

> After my wife came home from work we walked through our neighborhood before leaving for our evening class. We greeted several neighbors, then drove to class. After class, we discovered a backpack in the parking lot next to our car. We opened it (No, it didn't explode) and found a driver's license, credit card, and other personal items for a person vacationing from out of the area. With the help of a friend who has a smart phone app that found a phone number for the address on the driver's license, we reached the owner of the backpack and arranged for her to pick up her backpack.[1]

Do you see? There is nothing special to being the church. All you have to do is be yourself while focusing on loving others like Jesus. To be the church, all you have to do is keep your eyes and ears open to the people around you, and try to show them love in whatever ways you can. When you live as the church in this way, you will be spreading seeds of the gospel, and will be growing in spiritual maturity and Christlikeness. Those who see your good deeds will glorify God (Matt 5:16). Then maybe they too will

---

[1] See the "How to Be the Church in Your Community" series of posts by Sam Riviera. https://redeeminggod.com/be-the-church-community/

start to live in a way that reflects the love of God for others, so that the influence of the church spreads and expands to the very ends of the earth (Acts 1:8).

CONCLUSION

Church growth is no longer a mystery to be solved, or a lottery to be won. It is not that some lucky pastors experience massive church growth while others experience none. All Christians in all parts of the world in every local gathering can (and should) experience great strides in seeing the church grow.

How?

By not focusing on numbers at all, but instead by focusing on what God is doing in our lives and in our midst. You don't need to plant a church or grow the church. All you need to do is be the best representative of Jesus that you can be in this world. As you focus on learning from Scripture, building loving relationships with other people, and regularly communicating with God, you will grow in spiritual strength and maturity, which is true church growth.

When the church is a living witness of God's love to a lost and dying world, the church is everything that God wants it to be. So whether you gather with 3, 300, or 30,000 Christians, know that you can grow the church by focusing on growing yourself and loving others. This is true church growth.

So get out there and start loving others, so that the church can start growing and expanding upon the earth. Jesus said, "I will build my church," so let us focus on building ourselves into the image and likeness of Jesus Christ, so that He can work with us to build His church as He promised.

DISCUSSION QUESTIONS

1. Though this book has discussed that church growth does not mean numerical growth, it is nevertheless true that the church should expand upon the face of the earth, reaching new people and spreading to new areas. This is often done with church planting. Describe how church planting often occurs.

2. What sorts of traits do church planting organizations look for in church planters? How did they decide that these were the preferred character traits?

3. Is a pastor only a successful pastor if he or she pastors a megachurch? Why or why not?

4. What are some of the strengths and weakness of megachurches?

5. What are some of the strengths and weakness of small churches?

6. What three things did the church planting "pastor" in my town focus on in his church? Describe each.

7. If the only church in existence is the universal church which Jesus planted in Acts 2 and which He has been building ever since, do we need "church planters" today? Why or why not?

8. Since the church is already planted, how can the church expand on the face of the earth, reaching new people and new geographical areas?

9. What is your role in helping the church grow? How does the church grow through you?

APPENDIX

SPIRITUAL GIFTS

The following appendix is a summary of my book,
What are the Spiritual Gifts?
The book provides an expanded explanation of the gifts as well as an entire chapter on the gift of tongues. Get it on Amazon or wherever books are sold.

As discussed in chapter 8, God gave spiritual gifts to the church so that we could properly function. Just as the various parts of our physical body allow us to live, exist, and function within this world, so also, spiritual gifts allow the church to live, move, and have being within this world. But in order for this to happen, we must first know what the gifts are, and how to discover which gifts God has given to each of us. Let us begin with a brief explanation of the various spiritual gifts.

WHAT ARE THE SPIRITUAL GIFTS?

There is some debate among Christians about how many spiritual gifts there are. Some people think that the Bible includes an exhaustive list of spiritual gifts, while others think that the gift lists are only a small sample of a much larger number of gifts, most of which are not mentioned in the Bible. Along with this, some people divide the gifts up into various categories, such as the two categories of ministry gifts and miraculous gifts, or into the three categories of teaching, service, and sign gifts. Furthermore, some argue that certain spiritual gifts are no longer in use.

My belief is that the Bible lists all the spiritual gifts. There are twenty-six of them. When people feel they might have a spiritual gift that is not listed in Scripture, what they actually have is a skill, hobby, talent, or ability which they are especially good at doing. They can use the spiritual gifts in coordination with their skills and abilities to do unique and amazing work in this world.

For example, some people excel at math. But "math" is not listed in Scripture as a spiritual gift. So a person who loves and enjoys math should also seek to discover their spiritual gifts so that they can partner their love of math with their spiritual gift as a way to discover the perfect ministry God has for them. In this way, while math is not a spiritual gift, it is part of their overall "SHAPE," as discussed in chapter 8 of this book. Other talents and abilities are important considerations for the type of ministry you will perform, but these talents, interests, skills, and abilities are not spiritual gifts themselves, but work together *with* the spiritual gifts as listed in Scripture.

Below is the list of spiritual gifts mentioned in Scripture. The brief list is then followed by an alphabetically arranged list, which includes an explanation of each gift.

Romans 12	1 Corinthians 12
Exhortation	Administration
Giving	Apostleship

Leadership Mercy Prophecy Service Teaching	Discernment Faith Healing Helping Knowledge Miracles Prophecy Teaching Tongues Interpretation Wisdom

Ephesians 4	Misc. Passages

Apostleship
Evangelism
Pastor-Teacher
Prophecy
	Celibacy (1 Cor 7:7-8)
	Hospitality (1 Pet 4:9-10)
	Martyrdom (1 Cor 13:1-3)
	Voluntary poverty
	  (1 Cor 13:1-3)
	Craftsmanship (Exod 31:3-5)
	Creative communication
	  (Acts 16:25; 1 Cor
	  14:26; Eph 5:19)

Administration: To steer a group toward the accomplishment of God-given goals and directives by planning, organizing and supervising others (1 Cor 12:28; cf. Acts 15:12-21). It is based on the Greek word, *kubernēsis*, which means "to steer, guide" and can be used in reference to the helmsman of a ship. Those with this gift understand the goals of the group, and the steps needed to achieve those goals. The group could consist of anything from a country or multi-national business to a local outreach ministry or a family. Politicians, CEOs, and mothers often have the gift of administration.

Apostleship (Missionary): To be sent forth to new frontiers with the gospel, providing leadership over church bodies and maintaining authority over spiritual matters pertaining to the church (Eph 4:11; 1 Cor 12:28; cf. 1 Cor 9:19-23; cf. Acts 12:1-5; 14:21-23). The word is based on the Greek word *apostolos,* which means "one sent forth." While the office of "Apostle" is no longer in use today, the gift of apostleship is still given by God in the form of missionaries who take the gospel to unreached people groups (See Chapter 7 in my book, *God's Blueprints for Church Growth*).

Craftsmanship: To make, construct, or build things (Exod 28:3-4; 31:3-5). Those with the gift of craftsmanship will often be skilled at using tools to help and inspire others through artistic, creative means. Those with this gift will also be good at making or fixing things, and will often find themselves drawn toward jobs such as architecture, engineering, construction, creative design, and culinary arts.

Creative Communication: To teach and share biblical and spiritual truths in creative ways that rely less on words and books and more on art, music, poetry, plays, photography, dance, and other similar outlets (Mark 14:26; Acts 16:25; 1 Cor 14:26; Eph 5:19). Nearly all artists, designers, actors, and musicians have the gift of creative communication. As people who capture God's creative beauty and wonder through the experience of the five senses, they use their gift to create beauty and inspire change in others.

Celibacy: To voluntarily remain single without regret and with the ability to maintain controlled sexual impulses so as to serve the Lord without distraction (1 Cor 7:7-8). Those with the gift of celibacy often devote their lives to a single cause, task, or mission, so that all of their time and energy can be devoted to this purpose, without the risk of neglecting a spouse and children. Just because someone is unmarried this does not mean they have the gift of celibacy. Those who desire to get married can and should do so. However, while looking and praying for the spouse that God has for them, they can use their time of singleness to focus on serving God and others.

Discernment: To clearly distinguish truth from error by judging whether a certain behavior or teaching has a divine, satanic, or human origin (1 Cor 12:10; cf. Acts 5:3-6; 16:16-18). Those with the gift of discernment also tend to be helpful in helping others know and understand their own spiritual giftedness. People with the gift of discernment often work as life coaches, counselors, and mentors.

Evangelism: To be a messenger of the good news of the gospel with their words, lives, and actions (Eph 4:11; cf. Acts 8:26-40). The Greek word, *euangelistēs*, means "preacher of the gospel" but since the gospel includes instructions for all of life and theology, the evangelist will not only preach the gospel, but will live out the truths of the gospel in a way that inspires others to do the same (See Chapter 7 in my book, *God's Blueprints for Church Growth*). Their life serves as a guiding light to others in this dark world. The evangelist is also proficient at discipleship, as they walk alongside others to help them practice the gospel in their lives. They will often live a transparent life, showing their failures and weaknesses to others, so that others can learn about God's grace, love, and forgiveness through them.

Exhortation (Encouragement): To come along side of someone with words of encouragement, comfort, consolation, and counsel to help them be all God wants them to be (Rom 12:8; cf. Acts 11:23-24; 14:21-22). The Greek word, *paraklēsis*, means "calling to one's side," and is related to the work of the Holy Spirit as our Paraclete, our Comforter or Encourager (John 14:16, 26). Just as there are people who serve with their hands, these people serve and encourage with their words. Those with the gift of encouragement include coaches and teachers who see the potential in others, and cheer them on to rise to this potential.

Faith: To be firmly persuaded of God's power and promises to accomplish His will and purpose and to display such a confidence in Him and His Word which cannot be shaken by circumstances or obstacles (1 Cor 12:8-10; cf. Heb 11). Those with the gift of faith know what they believe and why they believe it, and are able to inspire action in others based on their beliefs. They are often called upon to encourage others to step out in faith and follow God to accomplish seemingly impossible tasks. Other people are drawn to those with the gift of faith because they find hope and strength in their presence. Those with the gift of faith often find themselves in positions of visionary leadership.

Giving: To share what material resources you have with liberality and cheerfulness without thought of return (Rom 12:8; cf. Acts

4:36-37; 2 Cor 8:1-5). They give without ulterior motive or conditions attached to how the money should be spent. Some believe that when God gives the gift of giving, He also gives the gift of making lots of money so that the giver can financially support multiple ministries and missionaries around the world. Givers often give away the vast majority of their substantial income, sometimes up to 90% or more. In ancient Roman society, those with the gift of giving would be called Patrons.

Healing: To be used as a means through which God makes people whole and restores health to the sick, whether they are physically, emotionally, mentally, or spiritually ill (1 Cor 12:9, 28, 30; cf. Luke 9:1-2; Jas 5:13-16). Note that healing is not just miraculous healing, but the ability to use modern medicine and science to bring about healing in someone's mind or body. As a result, those with the gift of healing often find themselves in the fields of medicine and psychology.

Helping: To render support or assistance to others so as to free them for other work (1 Cor 12:28; cf. Acts 6:2-4). They bear the burdens of others to help them accomplish their work more effectively. Those with the gift of helping find great satisfaction in doing menial jobs behind the scenes so that others can be freed up to do other tasks. While those with the gift of helping rarely receive much recognition or praise, the truth is that without their gifts, the people who often receive recognition and praise would not have the time or energy to do what they do. Therefore, the gift of helping actually allows the other more "flashy" gifts to function. People such as janitors, custodians, nurses, parents, classroom aids, assistant coaches, secretaries, and all other "behind the scenes" staff likely have the gift of helping.

Hospitality: To warmly welcome people, even strangers, into one's home as a means of serving people who need food or lodging (1 Pet 4:9-10; cf. Gen 18:1-15). They cheerfully open their homes to care for other people. True hospitality is not standing behind a counter at the "Hospitality Center" that exists in some church buildings, but requires you to open your own home to other people so they can share your food and enjoy a roof over their heads. The Greek word, *philoxenos*, means "love of strangers." Note that in biblical times, these "strangers" were usually Christians who were traveling from town to town and came with letters of introduction, but it does not have to limited to only Christians. Non-Christians can (and should) be welcomed into your home as well. However, wisdom dictates that you should know something about the people you invite into your home, for it is always unwise to welcome *complete* strangers into one's home.

Interpretation of Tongues: To translate the message of someone who has spoken in another language for those who do not understand what was said (1 Cor 12:10; 14:27-28). As will be discussed briefly below, the gift of tongues is speaking in an actual foreign language. Therefore, in order for what is said to make sense to other people, it must be interpreted. Those with the gift of interpretation are sometimes able to understand what foreigners are saying, even if they have never learned the other language. Some who have the gift of interpreting tongues also find that they can quickly and easily learn foreign languages.

Knowledge: To seek to learn as much about a particular subject as possible through the gathering of information and the analysis of that data (1 Cor 12:8; cf. Eph 3:14-19). Those with the gift of knowledge enjoy reading and studying, and find that they are able to easily learn, retain, and recall facts. Those with the gift of knowledge are also able to synthesize various streams of learning to develop new ideas and insightful ways of looking at difficult topics. People with the gift of knowledge find themselves in the fields of science, mathematics, literature, history, and theology.

Leadership: To live in front of people in such a way as to motivate others to change their lives, follow directions, influence decisions, and get involved in their community and the world so that all harmoniously work together to accomplish common goals (Rom 12:8; cf. Exod 18:13-16; Judg 3:10; Heb 13:7). Those with the gift of leadership inspire others to follow without feeling the need to command, threaten, or cajole. Those with the gift of leadership often become actual leaders in their communities, businesses, or countries.

Martyrdom: To give over one's life to death for the cause of Christ (1 Cor 13:3). Those who give their life in this way are called "martyrs," from the Greek word, *marturos,* meaning "witness." Giving one's life for Jesus is a great way to be a witness for Him. Nevertheless, while one can feel that they would be willing to die for Jesus Christ, it is not something which you can plan, prepare, or practice. Therefore, a person cannot know if they have the gift of martyrdom until they actually become a martyr. As a result, the Spiritual Gift inventory test at the end of this book does not contain any questions about martyrdom.

Mercy: To be sensitive toward those who are suffering, whether physically, mentally, or emotionally, so that you feel genuine empathy and compassion for others in their misery (Rom 12:8; cf. Luke 10:30-37). Those with the gift of mercy are able to empathize with those in pain, so that they speak words of compassion and offer acts of love to help alleviate others in their distress. Those with the gift of mercy often devote large amounts of time to help others in need, and can typically be found in the positions as counselors, mentors, and service positions where they work with the sick, elderly, mentally ill, and handicapped.

Miracles: To be enabled by God to perform mighty deeds which witnesses acknowledge to be of supernatural origin and means (1 Cor 12:10, 28). Those with the gift of miracles cannot promise that God will work miracles in their life, or the life of someone else, but often see God work the impossible in response to their prayers and acts of faith. This gift often works in coordination with the gifts of faith and healing.

Pastor-Teacher: To be responsible for the spiritual care, protection, guidance, and provision of a group of believers entrusted to one's care (Eph 4:11; cf. 1 Pet 5:1-11). Since the word *pastor* is related to the word for *shepherd,* the pastor-teacher often uses preaching and teaching as a way to lead, guide, and protect others (See Chapter 7 in my book, *God's Blueprints for Church Growth*). Those with the gift of pastor-teacher tend to be more relational than the teacher, and are therefore better at providing overall care for the spiritual well-being of the church.

Prophecy: To speak forth the message of God to His people (Rom 12:6; 1 Cor 12:10; Eph 4:11; cf. Isaiah–Malachi; 1 Cor 14:1-5, 30-40). The Greek word, *prophētēs,* refers to the forth-telling of the will and word of God. It does not primarily refer to foretelling the future, but to forth-telling God's will (See Chapter 7 in my book, *God's Blueprints for Church Growth*). One with the gift of prophecy will speak God's Word with boldness and clarity to call God's people to repent from sin and return to God's ways.

Service: To identify undone tasks in God's work, however menial, and use available resources to get the job done (Rom 12:7; cf. Gal 6:1-2). The Greek word, *diakonia,* means "servant, attendant," and refers to someone who runs errands for others. They take care of the day-to-day physical details for leaders and spiritual directors to free them up to take care of spiritual matters. Though this spiritual gift sounds lowly, it is one of the backbone gifts of any community or group. Without people to take care of these routine tasks, no business or organization would be able to properly function.

Teaching: To instruct others in a passionate, logical, succinct, and systematic way so as to communicate pertinent information for true understanding and personal growth in others (Rom 12:7; 1 Cor 12:28; cf. Heb 5:12-14). The gift of teaching differs from that of pastor-teacher in one main way: the pastor-teacher usually teaches with "pastoral" concerns in mind. The preaching and teaching of the pastor-teacher tends to be more practical, attempting to address the needs and concerns of the average Christian. The teacher, however, might be more academic and will often lack the interpersonal skills necessary to serve as a pastor-teacher.

Most skilled teachers and professors have the gift of teaching.

Tongues: To speak in a language not previously learned so unbelievers can hear God's message in their own language (Acts 2:4; 1 Cor 12:10; 14:27-28). If those who are present do not understand what is said, tongues must always be interpreted. If there is no interpreter, the speaker must remain silent. There is no evidence anywhere in Scripture that the gift of tongues causes a person to speak in a secret prayer language. Speaking in tongues always involves speaking in another "tongue," or language. As such, it might be more precise to speak of people having the gift of *languages*, which helps them quickly learn foreign languages. (See the chapter on tongues later in this book.)

Voluntary Poverty: To purposely live in an impoverished lifestyle to serve and aid others with your material resources (1 Cor 13:3). Those with the gift of poverty love to give away their money and possessions so that they might live simply, generously, and sacrificially. They often view possessions and money as a hindrance to ministry, and use their money to meet the needs of those poorer than themselves. Voluntary poverty differs from the gift of giving in that those with the gift of giving might be rich, whereas those with the gift of voluntary poverty tend to live among the poor so that they might love, serve, and identify with them.

Wisdom: To apply knowledge to life in such a way as to make spiritual truths quite relevant and practical in proper decision-making and daily life situations (1 Cor 12:8; cf. Jas 3:13-17). Those with the gift of wisdom are often very good in counseling situations, and find that people often come to them for advice. They are very good at understanding God's will in various situations, and helping people understand the right decisions to make in life.

As you read through the descriptions of the spiritual gifts, you might have recognized one or two as describing your interests, skills, and strengths. This might be a good indication of what gifts you have. But how can you know for sure? How can you know your spiritual gifts?

HOW CAN I KNOW MY SPIRITUAL GIFTS?

There are many ways to discover your spiritual gifts. I encourage you to use all of them as a way to identify and confirm your spiritual gifts. If you use just one method, there is a chance of improperly identifying your spiritual gifts, thereby leading to frustration in life and ministry. But if you start with one method of identification, and then use the other methods to confirm or change the results of the first method, you will often end up properly identifying your spiritual gifts.

Self-Analysis

The first (and preferred) method for identifying your spiritual gift is to look into your own heart and mind and consider which spiritual gifts you would like to have. Of course, when you do this, you are not just trusting your own heart and mind to "figure it out," but are actually looking for the still small voice of the Holy Spirit to point out to you which gifts you have been given. As these gifts are *spiritual* gifts, we must first look to the Holy Spirit for leading in this matter.

Even if you are uncomfortable or unaware of how to listen to the voice and leading of the Spirit, it is still important to try. The Spirit is always whispering to you, and you will only learn to sense His leading and direction as you attempt to listen to what He is saying. Furthermore, once you discover your spiritual gift, it will be important to continue to rely on the leading of the Holy Spirit for how He wants you to use your spiritual gift. So you might as well begin by seeking His input on the identification of your gifts.

To do this, just return to the previous chapter where the spiritual gifts are listed and read through them slowly, trying to discern which ones might be true of you. As you read the descriptions, look for ones that might be interesting or that sound intriguing. Look for gifts that pull on you heart or that seem to describe your interests and desires. The gifts that you feel drawn to are possibly the gifts that God has given to you.

Remember, of course, that there is a difference between the gifts you *want* and the gifts you *have*. You can be wrong in your feelings and desires. So as you read through the spiritual gifts, not only think about the gifts you would like to have, but also the sorts of things you have actually done in life which have given you joy and satisfaction. For example, almost everybody wants the gift of giving since it is often accompanied by wealth. But if you have never been rich, and do not see that you are likely to become rich, and do not have a history of giving away large sums of money, then these are good indications that even though you desire the gift of giving, you likely do not have it. Pairing the gifts you desire with the sorts of activities and actions you have actually done provides the best self-analysis of the spiritual gifts you might have.

Once you have done this self-analysis, you can move on to the next four ways of identifying your spiritual gifts, as they help confirm which spiritual gifts you might have.

Seek the Input of Others

Since the gifts are given for the edification of others, one way you can gain insight into which gifts you might have is by seeking the input of others. This is especially effective when you seek the input of people who know you well, and who have seen you serve and interact with other people.

This method of discovering your spiritual gifts is especially effective if you can ask someone who has the spiritual gift of discernment. God has specifically enabled those with the gift of discernment to see, understand, and recognize the various spiritual gifts in other people. Of course, they don't do this through some sort of magical "fortune-telling" experience where their eyes roll back in their head and they read tea leaves in a cup. No, they discern these things by getting to know you and observing your life. So even here, if you are going to ask for the input of others, you must not ask strangers.

This shows why it is important to be involved in the lives of other people. It is only with other people that you can practice your spiritual gifts, and it is only with other people that you can ask for their input about your gifts. If you are not part of a gathering of believers, it may be difficult for you to discover your spiritual gifts, or for others to provide input on what your gifts might be.

Remember, of course, that the smallest, most basic gathering of believers is your immediate family. So as you seek the input of others about your spiritual gifts, start with your parents, children, spouse, and siblings. They know you best, and will be able to provide some of the most helpful input and advice about your spiritual gifts. Other than family, you can also ask your close friends and coworkers. It will not be of any benefit to ask people who rarely see you or interact with you on a daily or weekly basis.

Spiritual Void Analysis

One of the very best ways to discover your spiritual gifts is to take note of your criticisms and complaints about church. When you look at the local church body you are part of (or the worldwide church as a whole), and see areas of weakness, fault, or neglect, you have just discovered what God wants you to be doing in the church. In other words, if there is something you think that everybody in the church should be doing (but aren't), then you have just discovered what it is *you* should be doing.

For example, if you think the church is doing a poor job of teaching Scripture to others, then this likely means that you have the spiritual gift of teaching, and you are supposed to start using it. If you think the church should be serving the poor in your community, this probably means you have the gifts of service, mercy, or hospitality. If you complain that the church is not creative and artistic enough in its music, programs, or decorations, this likely means that you have the gift of creative communication.

As you can see, this method of discovering your spiritual gifts is extremely helpful, for it not only allows you to accurately identify your spiritual gifts, but it also spurs you on to actually use your gifts to meet the need that you see, rather than just sit on the sideline (or in the pew) complaining about all the things the church should do differently. If you see a void in the church, it is likely because God wants you to fill it and has specially gifted you to do so.

Spiritual Gift Analysis

You can, of course, always take a spiritual gift inventory test as a way of discovering your spiritual gifts. There is one such test at the end of this book (see Appendix 1). Many of these tests are somewhat like personality tests, where the person answers a series of questions and then scores the test based on their answers. The scores provide insight into which spiritual gifts the person might have.

However, it is necessary to state a warning about these sorts of tests. Of the five available ways for discovering your spiritual gifts, this method is the least reliable. This is simply due to the fact that test results are easily undermined by various outside factors. Not only is it possible for the questions to be misunderstood, but when a person takes the test, a whole host of outside factors can drastically alter the outcome of these sorts of tests, such as where they took it, how they are feeling at the time they took it, and what they just heard or read before they took it.

I once ran a little experiment where I decided to test a group of men by giving them the same exact test two weeks apart. During the first week, I taught a 30-minute lesson about the miracles of Jesus and the importance of faith for seeing miracles today. Then I gave the men the test, and had them turn it in to me for scoring. The next week, I told the men that I had somehow misplaced the tests, and I apologetically asked them to take it again. But this time, I preceded the test with a 30-minute lesson on the importance of Scripture memorization, Bible study, and reading good books about theology. Then they took the test a second time.

The (unsurprising) results of these two tests were that even though the same men took it only two weeks apart, the results from the first week showed that the majority of the men had spiritual gifts of miracles and faith, while the results from the second week showed that the majority of them had spiritual gifts of teaching and knowledge. The clear influencing factor which explains the difference was the lesson they had just heard me teach.

So it is fine to take spiritual gift inventories like the one at the end of this book, but you must recognize that these tests are easily skewed by how you are feeling, what you have been reading or hearing, and a wide variety of other factors. If you take a spiritual gift inventory test, it is best to take it multiple times over the span of a several months or years, and to use it in coordination with the other four ways of discovering your spiritual gifts. It is especially important to use the fifth and final way, discussed below.

Serve and Experiment

The last and most important way of discovering your spiritual gifts is simply to use the spiritual gifts you think you have. There is no better way to discover and strengthen your spiritual gifts than by serving and experimenting with them in the context of a local body of believers. Regardless of what other method you might use for discovering your spiritual gifts, this is the one method you must not neglect.

The reason this method is so critical is because it will either confirm or contradict the initial identification of your spiritual gifts. When you find your spiritual gift and start putting it into practice, you will experience greater excitement and energy in the ways you interact with others, and find that they grow closer to Jesus as a result of your work with them. Furthermore, as you practice your gifts, you will get better and better at using them, and will begin to influence and edify more and more people.

The exact opposite happens, however, when you try to use gifts that you think you might have, but in fact do not. For example, if you think you have the spiritual gift of teaching, but people fall asleep when you teach, and few return to hear you teach, then this might be a good sign that teaching is not your gift. If you think you have the gift of mercy, but you get upset and angry at people who don't seem to take your advice and don't change fast enough to suit your expectations, then this might be a good sign that you don't have the gift of mercy.

So if you think you have certain spiritual gifts, but when you attempt to put them into practice, you get frustrated and angry while other people are not encouraged or edified, then this is a good sign that the spiritual gift you are trying to practice is not actually your spiritual gift. If you initially misdiagnose your spiritual gift, do not be discouraged, but simply go back and try to discover your spiritual gift again. It usually will not take more than two or three attempts before you find the spiritual gift God has given to you, and you begin to see Him work through your life to touch the lives of others.

Now that you have learned what the spiritual gifts are and how you can discover and use your spiritual gifts, let me provide you with a Spiritual Gift Inventory which you can take if you feel so inclined. Remember, a test like this is probably the least accurate way of determining your spiritual gifts, but when used in coordination with the other methods, a gift inventory can provide some guidance as you seek to discover and practice your spiritual gifts.

Enjoy!

SPIRITUAL GIFTS INVENTORY

Instructions for Use:

1. There are a total of 125 statements below. For each statement, circle whether you *Strongly Agree, Somewhat Agree,* are *Undecided, Somewhat Disagree,* or *Completely Disagree.* Try to use *Undecided* no more than five times.

2. When you have completed all 125 statements, transfer your answers to the profile sheet at the end of this document.

3. Total your scores for each of the gifts. Each gift will have a score between ZERO and TWENTY.

4. Order the gifts in descending order of score. Higher scores indicate your more dominant gifts.

5. For more information on your gift and how to use it, look at the chapter titled "What Are the Spiritual Gifts?"

1) *I enjoy the responsibility of making important decisions that affect others.*

      4-Strongly Agree
      3-Somewhat Agree
      2-Undecided

1-Somewhat Disagree
0-Completely Disagree

2) *I often think God is calling me to take the gospel to people who haven't heard about Jesus.*

4-Strongly Agree
3-Somewhat Agree
2-Undecided
1-Somewhat Disagree
0-Completely Disagree

3) *I enjoy working creatively with wood, cloth, paints, metal, glass, or other materials.*

4-Strongly Agree
3-Somewhat Agree
2-Undecided
1-Somewhat Disagree
0-Completely Disagree

4) *I enjoy developing and using my artistic skills (art, drama, music, photography, etc.).*

4-Strongly Agree
3-Somewhat Agree
2-Undecided
1-Somewhat Disagree
0-Completely Disagree

5) *It is easy for me to recognize talents and gifts in other people.*

> 4-Strongly Agree
> 3-Somewhat Agree
> 2-Undecided
> 1-Somewhat Disagree
> 0-Completely Disagree

6) *I live out the truths of gospel with words and actions so that others see and understand God's love and grace in their lives.*

> 4-Strongly Agree
> 3-Somewhat Agree
> 2-Undecided
> 1-Somewhat Disagree
> 0-Completely Disagree

7) *It is enjoyable to motivate people to help them take the next step in following Jesus.*

> 4-Strongly Agree
> 3-Somewhat Agree
> 2-Undecided
> 1-Somewhat Disagree
> 0-Completely Disagree

8) *I often step out to attempt the impossible.*

> 4-Strongly Agree
> 3-Somewhat Agree

2-Undecided
1-Somewhat Disagree
0-Completely Disagree

9) *I give liberally and joyfully to people in financial need or to projects requiring support.*

4-Strongly Agree
3-Somewhat Agree
2-Undecided
1-Somewhat Disagree
0-Completely Disagree

10) *I often know what is wrong with people physically, and know what steps are needed to help them recover to full health.*

4-Strongly Agree
3-Somewhat Agree
2-Undecided
1-Somewhat Disagree
0-Completely Disagree

11) *I enjoy working behind the scenes in order to support the work of others.*

4-Strongly Agree
3-Somewhat Agree
2-Undecided
1-Somewhat Disagree
0-Completely Disagree

12) *I view my home as a place to love and serve other people.*

    4-Strongly Agree
    3-Somewhat Agree
    2-Undecided
    1-Somewhat Disagree
    0-Completely Disagree

13) *I often wonder why people struggle with sexual urges, since these are not a temptation for me.*

    4-Strongly Agree
    3-Somewhat Agree
    2-Undecided
    1-Somewhat Disagree
    0-Completely Disagree

14) *It is easy for me to learn foreign languages.*

    4-Strongly Agree
    3-Somewhat Agree
    2-Undecided
    1-Somewhat Disagree
    0-Completely Disagree

15) *I am often approached by people who want to know my perspective on a certain Bible passage or theological concept.*

    4-Strongly Agree

3-Somewhat Agree
2-Undecided
1-Somewhat Disagree
0-Completely Disagree

16) *I am able to motivate others to accomplish a goal.*

4-Strongly Agree
3-Somewhat Agree
2-Undecided
1-Somewhat Disagree
0-Completely Disagree

17) *I empathize with hurting people and desire to help in their healing process.*

4-Strongly Agree
3-Somewhat Agree
2-Undecided
1-Somewhat Disagree
0-Completely Disagree

18) *I very frequently see God miraculously alter circumstances when I pray.*

4-Strongly Agree
3-Somewhat Agree
2-Undecided
1-Somewhat Disagree
0-Completely Disagree

19) *My wallet and bank account are nearly always empty because I give so much money away.*

    4-Strongly Agree
    3-Somewhat Agree
    2-Undecided
    1-Somewhat Disagree
    0-Completely Disagree

20) *It is enjoyable to have the responsibility of leading other people in their spiritual life.*

    4-Strongly Agree
    3-Somewhat Agree
    2-Undecided
    1-Somewhat Disagree
    0-Completely Disagree

21) *I often speak in a way that results in conviction and a change of life in others.*

    4-Strongly Agree
    3-Somewhat Agree
    2-Undecided
    1-Somewhat Disagree
    0-Completely Disagree

22) *There is great joy in doing little jobs for other people and helping with day-to-day tasks.*

4-Strongly Agree
3-Somewhat Agree
2-Undecided
1-Somewhat Disagree
0-Completely Disagree

23) *I love to read and study God's Word and then share with others what I have learned.*

4-Strongly Agree
3-Somewhat Agree
2-Undecided
1-Somewhat Disagree
0-Completely Disagree

24) *Sometimes I am able to speak to a person in their own language even though I have never studied it.*

4-Strongly Agree
3-Somewhat Agree
2-Undecided
1-Somewhat Disagree
0-Completely Disagree

25) *I am often sought out for advice on personal or spiritual matters.*

4-Strongly Agree
3-Somewhat Agree
2-Undecided

1-Somewhat Disagree
0-Completely Disagree

26) *I enjoy organizing people and harnessing their gifts and talents to solve a particular problem.*

4-Strongly Agree
3-Somewhat Agree
2-Undecided
1-Somewhat Disagree
0-Completely Disagree

27) *I have a strong burden to share the gospel with the unreached people groups of the world.*

4-Strongly Agree
3-Somewhat Agree
2-Undecided
1-Somewhat Disagree
0-Completely Disagree

28) *I am skilled in working with different kinds of tools.*

4-Strongly Agree
3-Somewhat Agree
2-Undecided
1-Somewhat Disagree
0-Completely Disagree

29) *I use art, plays, pictures, or music to help people understand*

God, themselves, this world, and their relationships.

> 4-Strongly Agree
> 3-Somewhat Agree
> 2-Undecided
> 1-Somewhat Disagree
> 0-Completely Disagree

30) *I usually detect spiritual truth from spiritual error before fellow believers.*

> 4-Strongly Agree
> 3-Somewhat Agree
> 2-Undecided
> 1-Somewhat Disagree
> 0-Completely Disagree

31) *I find it easier to build relationships with non-believers than with believers.*

> 4-Strongly Agree
> 3-Somewhat Agree
> 2-Undecided
> 1-Somewhat Disagree
> 0-Completely Disagree

32) *I like to encourage people to revitalize their spiritual life through Bible study, prayer, or getting involved in community service.*

> 4-Strongly Agree

3-Somewhat Agree
2-Undecided
1-Somewhat Disagree
0-Completely Disagree

33) *I find it natural and easy to know that God is hearing and answering my prayers.*

4-Strongly Agree
3-Somewhat Agree
2-Undecided
1-Somewhat Disagree
0-Completely Disagree

34) *I manage my money well in order to free more of it for giving.*

4-Strongly Agree
3-Somewhat Agree
2-Undecided
1-Somewhat Disagree
0-Completely Disagree

35) *When someone is sick or injured, I pray for them and check up on them until they recover.*

4-Strongly Agree
3-Somewhat Agree
2-Undecided
1-Somewhat Disagree
0-Completely Disagree

36) *In life, I gravitate toward undone work, even if unpopular.*

>   4-Strongly Agree
>   3-Somewhat Agree
>   2-Undecided
>   1-Somewhat Disagree
>   0-Completely Disagree

37) *I enjoy meeting new people and helping them feel welcomed.*

>   4-Strongly Agree
>   3-Somewhat Agree
>   2-Undecided
>   1-Somewhat Disagree
>   0-Completely Disagree

38) *I want to serve God with all my time and energy, and am sometimes afraid that marriage or children might get in the way.*

>   4-Strongly Agree
>   3-Somewhat Agree
>   2-Undecided
>   1-Somewhat Disagree
>   0-Completely Disagree

39) *I often feel like I can understand what a person from another country is saying even though I have never studied their language.*

>   4-Strongly Agree

3-Somewhat Agree

2-Undecided

1-Somewhat Disagree

0-Completely Disagree

40) *I am committed to spending large blocks of time on reading and studying Scripture so that I might know biblical truth more fully and accurately.*

4-Strongly Agree

3-Somewhat Agree

2-Undecided

1-Somewhat Disagree

0-Completely Disagree

41) *I know where groups of people should be headed and the steps they need to take to accomplish the goals of the group.*

4-Strongly Agree

3-Somewhat Agree

2-Undecided

1-Somewhat Disagree

0-Completely Disagree

42) *I can patiently support those going through painful experiences as they try to stabilize their lives.*

4-Strongly Agree

3-Somewhat Agree

2-Undecided

1-Somewhat Disagree
0-Completely Disagree

43) *I have often seen God work in desperate life situations by miraculous intervention when I pray.*

4-Strongly Agree
3-Somewhat Agree
2-Undecided
1-Somewhat Disagree
0-Completely Disagree

44) *I have no desire to own a car, wear nice clothes, buy a house, or go on vacations.*

4-Strongly Agree
3-Somewhat Agree
2-Undecided
1-Somewhat Disagree
0-Completely Disagree

45) *I have a strong desire to seek out wayward believers and restore them to fellowship with Jesus and the church.*

4-Strongly Agree
3-Somewhat Agree
2-Undecided
1-Somewhat Disagree
0-Completely Disagree

46) *I often am able to predict the consequences of a particular sinful behavior if a person continues engaging in it.*

>   4-Strongly Agree
>   3-Somewhat Agree
>   2-Undecided
>   1-Somewhat Disagree
>   0-Completely Disagree

47) *I enjoy doing routine tasks to help others.*

>   4-Strongly Agree
>   3-Somewhat Agree
>   2-Undecided
>   1-Somewhat Disagree
>   0-Completely Disagree

48) *People often tell me I am able to share difficult truths in ways that are easy to understand.*

>   4-Strongly Agree
>   3-Somewhat Agree
>   2-Undecided
>   1-Somewhat Disagree
>   0-Completely Disagree

49) *Sometimes when I do not know what to pray, words come out of my mouth which I do not understand.*

>   4-Strongly Agree

3-Somewhat Agree
2-Undecided
1-Somewhat Disagree
0-Completely Disagree

50) *I often find simple, practical solutions in the midst of conflict or confusion.*

4-Strongly Agree
3-Somewhat Agree
2-Undecided
1-Somewhat Disagree
0-Completely Disagree

51) *People often look to me for guidance in coordination, organization, and ministry opportunities.*

4-Strongly Agree
3-Somewhat Agree
2-Undecided
1-Somewhat Disagree
0-Completely Disagree

52) *I desire to learn another language, culture, or religion so that I can better connect the truths of the gospel with the people in that culture.*

4-Strongly Agree
3-Somewhat Agree
2-Undecided

1-Somewhat Disagree
0-Completely Disagree

53) *I enjoy making things with my hands.*

4-Strongly Agree
3-Somewhat Agree
2-Undecided
1-Somewhat Disagree
0-Completely Disagree

54) *I have enjoyed being involved in local musical productions or plays.*

4-Strongly Agree
3-Somewhat Agree
2-Undecided
1-Somewhat Disagree
0-Completely Disagree

55) *It is easy for me to tell if a person is honest or dishonest.*

4-Strongly Agree
3-Somewhat Agree
2-Undecided
1-Somewhat Disagree
0-Completely Disagree

56) *I am effective at adapting the gospel message to fit a person's needs or current situation.*

4-Strongly Agree
3-Somewhat Agree
2-Undecided
1-Somewhat Disagree
0-Completely Disagree

57) *I can challenge others without making them feel condemned.*

4-Strongly Agree
3-Somewhat Agree
2-Undecided
1-Somewhat Disagree
0-Completely Disagree

58) *I have unwavering confidence in God's continuing provision to help, even in difficult times.*

4-Strongly Agree
3-Somewhat Agree
2-Undecided
1-Somewhat Disagree
0-Completely Disagree

59) *I like knowing my financial support is making a real difference in the lives of others.*

4-Strongly Agree
3-Somewhat Agree
2-Undecided

1-Somewhat Disagree
0-Completely Disagree

60) *I have prayed for an emotionally ill person and seen the person get better.*

4-Strongly Agree
3-Somewhat Agree
2-Undecided
1-Somewhat Disagree
0-Completely Disagree

61) *I cannot stand idly by while things go undone.*

4-Strongly Agree
3-Somewhat Agree
2-Undecided
1-Somewhat Disagree
0-Completely Disagree

62) *I like to create a place where people do not feel they are alone.*

4-Strongly Agree
3-Somewhat Agree
2-Undecided
1-Somewhat Disagree
0-Completely Disagree

63) *I have never had problems with lust or strong sexual desires.*

4-Strongly Agree
3-Somewhat Agree
2-Undecided
1-Somewhat Disagree
0-Completely Disagree

64) *It is a strong desire of mine to have all Christians of all languages communicate together.*

4-Strongly Agree
3-Somewhat Agree
2-Undecided
1-Somewhat Disagree
0-Completely Disagree

65) *I am able to grasp and understand passages in Scripture which others find difficult.*

4-Strongly Agree
3-Somewhat Agree
2-Undecided
1-Somewhat Disagree
0-Completely Disagree

66) *I am able to influence others to achieve a goal.*

4-Strongly Agree
3-Somewhat Agree
2-Undecided
1-Somewhat Disagree

0-Completely Disagree

67) *I enjoy helping people sometimes regarded as undeserving or beyond help.*

    4-Strongly Agree
    3-Somewhat Agree
    2-Undecided
    1-Somewhat Disagree
    0-Completely Disagree

68) *I believe that if we trusted God more, we would see dramatic, public miracles like in the New Testament.*

    4-Strongly Agree
    3-Somewhat Agree
    2-Undecided
    1-Somewhat Disagree
    0-Completely Disagree

69) *I live in communal housing and get my clothes from thrift shops so that I can give more of my income away.*

    4-Strongly Agree
    3-Somewhat Agree
    2-Undecided
    1-Somewhat Disagree
    0-Completely Disagree

70) *In the past, when helping someone, I try to provide direction for*

the whole person—relationally, emotionally, spiritually, etc.

> 4-Strongly Agree
> 3-Somewhat Agree
> 2-Undecided
> 1-Somewhat Disagree
> 0-Completely Disagree

71) *I frequently, boldly, and verbally expose cultural trends, teachings, or events to other Christians which contradict biblical principles.*

> 4-Strongly Agree
> 3-Somewhat Agree
> 2-Undecided
> 1-Somewhat Disagree
> 0-Completely Disagree

72) *I receive great satisfaction in doing small or trivial tasks for others that need to be done.*

> 4-Strongly Agree
> 3-Somewhat Agree
> 2-Undecided
> 1-Somewhat Disagree
> 0-Completely Disagree

73) *I pay close attention to the words, phrases and meanings of those who teach God's Word.*

4-Strongly Agree
3-Somewhat Agree
2-Undecided
1-Somewhat Disagree
0-Completely Disagree

74) *I frequently speak or pray in a language that I have not learned.*

4-Strongly Agree
3-Somewhat Agree
2-Undecided
1-Somewhat Disagree
0-Completely Disagree

75) *I can anticipate the likely consequence of an individual's or group's action.*

4-Strongly Agree
3-Somewhat Agree
2-Undecided
1-Somewhat Disagree
0-Completely Disagree

76) *The development of effective plans for church ministry or community service gives me great satisfaction.*

4-Strongly Agree
3-Somewhat Agree
2-Undecided
1-Somewhat Disagree

0-Completely Disagree

77) *It is easy for me to move into a new community and make friends.*

    4-Strongly Agree
    3-Somewhat Agree
    2-Undecided
    1-Somewhat Disagree
    0-Completely Disagree

78) *I am good at and enjoy working with my hands.*

    4-Strongly Agree
    3-Somewhat Agree
    2-Undecided
    1-Somewhat Disagree
    0-Completely Disagree

79) *If a truth cannot be presented creatively, it would be better to not present it at all.*

    4-Strongly Agree
    3-Somewhat Agree
    2-Undecided
    1-Somewhat Disagree
    0-Completely Disagree

80) *God has used me to warn others of the danger of a certain teaching.*

4-Strongly Agree
3-Somewhat Agree
2-Undecided
1-Somewhat Disagree
0-Completely Disagree

81) *I openly and confidently tell others what Jesus has done for me, and want others to ask me about my faith.*

4-Strongly Agree
3-Somewhat Agree
2-Undecided
1-Somewhat Disagree
0-Completely Disagree

82) *People express to me how much I've helped or encouraged them in a time of need.*

4-Strongly Agree
3-Somewhat Agree
2-Undecided
1-Somewhat Disagree
0-Completely Disagree

83) *I believe God will help me accomplish great things.*

4-Strongly Agree
3-Somewhat Agree
2-Undecided

1-Somewhat Disagree
0-Completely Disagree

84) *I believe I have been given an abundance of resources so that I may give more to help with the financial needs of others.*

4-Strongly Agree
3-Somewhat Agree
2-Undecided
1-Somewhat Disagree
0-Completely Disagree

85) *When I visit and help those who are sick and pray that God would make them physically whole, they nearly always recover.*

4-Strongly Agree
3-Somewhat Agree
2-Undecided
1-Somewhat Disagree
0-Completely Disagree

86) *The church needs to stop talking so much and start helping people in practical ways.*

4-Strongly Agree
3-Somewhat Agree
2-Undecided
1-Somewhat Disagree
0-Completely Disagree

87) *I make people feel at ease even in unfamiliar surroundings.*

    4-Strongly Agree
    3-Somewhat Agree
    2-Undecided
    1-Somewhat Disagree
    0-Completely Disagree

88) *When I imagine my future, I rarely envision a spouse or family,*

    4-Strongly Agree
    3-Somewhat Agree
    2-Undecided
    1-Somewhat Disagree
    0-Completely Disagree

89) *If I hear a Christian speaking in a different language, I find I can understand what they are saying.*

    4-Strongly Agree
    3-Somewhat Agree
    2-Undecided
    1-Somewhat Disagree
    0-Completely Disagree

90) *I discover important biblical truths when reading or studying Scripture which benefit others in the church.*

    4-Strongly Agree
    3-Somewhat Agree

2-Undecided
1-Somewhat Disagree
0-Completely Disagree

91) *I can manage people and resources effectively to accomplish set goals.*

4-Strongly Agree
3-Somewhat Agree
2-Undecided
1-Somewhat Disagree
0-Completely Disagree

92) *I enjoy doing practical things for people who are in need.*

4-Strongly Agree
3-Somewhat Agree
2-Undecided
1-Somewhat Disagree
0-Completely Disagree

93) *I often pray for impossible things which actually come true.*

4-Strongly Agree
3-Somewhat Agree
2-Undecided
1-Somewhat Disagree
0-Completely Disagree

94) *I think that materialism, consumerism, capitalism, and greed*

are some of the greatest problems in the world today.

> 4-Strongly Agree
> 3-Somewhat Agree
> 2-Undecided
> 1-Somewhat Disagree
> 0-Completely Disagree

95) *I often see other believers respond spiritually to my direction and leadership.*

> 4-Strongly Agree
> 3-Somewhat Agree
> 2-Undecided
> 1-Somewhat Disagree
> 0-Completely Disagree

96) *I am able to understand how key current events around the world tie into Bible prophecy and how these events will affect the future.*

> 4-Strongly Agree
> 3-Somewhat Agree
> 2-Undecided
> 1-Somewhat Disagree
> 0-Completely Disagree

97) *I often recognize ways that I can care for others indirectly without speaking or teaching.*

4-Strongly Agree
3-Somewhat Agree
2-Undecided
1-Somewhat Disagree
0-Completely Disagree

98) *I take a systematic approach to my daily study of the Bible.*

4-Strongly Agree
3-Somewhat Agree
2-Undecided
1-Somewhat Disagree
0-Completely Disagree

99) *God has used me to witness to other people whose language I did not know.*

4-Strongly Agree
3-Somewhat Agree
2-Undecided
1-Somewhat Disagree
0-Completely Disagree

100) *I have a strong sense of confidence in my solution to problems.*

4-Strongly Agree
3-Somewhat Agree
2-Undecided
1-Somewhat Disagree
0-Completely Disagree

101) *I would rather make a decision for a group than persuade them to reach the same decision.*

> 4-Strongly Agree
> 3-Somewhat Agree
> 2-Undecided
> 1-Somewhat Disagree
> 0-Completely Disagree

102) *The thought of moving to a new community and making new friends is exciting to me.*

> 4-Strongly Agree
> 3-Somewhat Agree
> 2-Undecided
> 1-Somewhat Disagree
> 0-Completely Disagree

103) *I am able to design and construct things that help others.*

> 4-Strongly Agree
> 3-Somewhat Agree
> 2-Undecided
> 1-Somewhat Disagree
> 0-Completely Disagree

104) *I regularly need to get away from people so that I can reflect and develop my imagination.*

4-Strongly Agree
3-Somewhat Agree
2-Undecided
1-Somewhat Disagree
0-Completely Disagree

105) *I often have insights into a person's character or motives, and receive confirmation of my perceptions at a later date.*

4-Strongly Agree
3-Somewhat Agree
2-Undecided
1-Somewhat Disagree
0-Completely Disagree

106) *I seem to be able to determine when a person is prepared to receive Jesus Christ.*

4-Strongly Agree
3-Somewhat Agree
2-Undecided
1-Somewhat Disagree
0-Completely Disagree

107) *I would rather develop a friendship with a Christian person than a non-Christian.*

4-Strongly Agree
3-Somewhat Agree
2-Undecided

1-Somewhat Disagree
0-Completely Disagree

108) *I am regularly challenging others to trust God and step out in faith to do difficult things.*

4-Strongly Agree
3-Somewhat Agree
2-Undecided
1-Somewhat Disagree
0-Completely Disagree

109) *I have great satisfaction in giving large amounts of money to others in need.*

4-Strongly Agree
3-Somewhat Agree
2-Undecided
1-Somewhat Disagree
0-Completely Disagree

110) *I feel strongly that my prayers for a sick person bring wholeness to that person.*

4-Strongly Agree
3-Somewhat Agree
2-Undecided
1-Somewhat Disagree
0-Completely Disagree

111) *I would rather support someone in their ministry than lead a ministry of my own.*

> 4-Strongly Agree
> 3-Somewhat Agree
> 2-Undecided
> 1-Somewhat Disagree
> 0-Completely Disagree

112) *I enjoy cooking meals and preparing my house so that I can share my house with other people.*

> 4-Strongly Agree
> 3-Somewhat Agree
> 2-Undecided
> 1-Somewhat Disagree
> 0-Completely Disagree

113) *I am currently single, and am fine with never being married or having children.*

> 4-Strongly Agree
> 3-Somewhat Agree
> 2-Undecided
> 1-Somewhat Disagree
> 0-Completely Disagree

114) *When visiting other countries, I find it easy to communicate even though I don't know the language.*

4-Strongly Agree
3-Somewhat Agree
2-Undecided
1-Somewhat Disagree
0-Completely Disagree

115) *It is easy for me to learn difficult truths.*

4-Strongly Agree
3-Somewhat Agree
2-Undecided
1-Somewhat Disagree
0-Completely Disagree

116) *People seem to enjoy following me to do an important task.*

4-Strongly Agree
3-Somewhat Agree
2-Undecided
1-Somewhat Disagree
0-Completely Disagree

117) *I enjoy ministering to a person who is sick in the hospital.*

4-Strongly Agree
3-Somewhat Agree
2-Undecided
1-Somewhat Disagree
0-Completely Disagree

118) *God often provides answers to my prayers with unordinary means.*

    4-Strongly Agree
    3-Somewhat Agree
    2-Undecided
    1-Somewhat Disagree
    0-Completely Disagree

119) *If I die with more than $1000 to my name, I will consider my ministry a failure.*

    4-Strongly Agree
    3-Somewhat Agree
    2-Undecided
    1-Somewhat Disagree
    0-Completely Disagree

120) *Other Christians frequently come to me with their cares and spiritual worries.*

    4-Strongly Agree
    3-Somewhat Agree
    2-Undecided
    1-Somewhat Disagree
    0-Completely Disagree

121) *I often speak the truth, even in places where it is unpopular or difficult for people to accept.*

4-Strongly Agree
3-Somewhat Agree
2-Undecided
1-Somewhat Disagree
0-Completely Disagree

122) *I don't mind helping others even if they are undeserving or take advantage of me.*

4-Strongly Agree
3-Somewhat Agree
2-Undecided
1-Somewhat Disagree
0-Completely Disagree

123) *I am always looking for better ways to explain things to people so they can grow spiritually and personally.*

4-Strongly Agree
3-Somewhat Agree
2-Undecided
1-Somewhat Disagree
0-Completely Disagree

124) *I find it easy to quickly learn foreign languages.*

4-Strongly Agree
3-Somewhat Agree
2-Undecided
1-Somewhat Disagree

0-Completely Disagree

125) *When people follow my advice in difficult situations, things often turn out well.*

    4-Strongly Agree
    3-Somewhat Agree
    2-Undecided
    1-Somewhat Disagree
    0-Completely Disagree

GIFT PROFILE ANSWER SHEET

1	Administration	1	26	51	76	101	=
2	Apostleship (Missionary)	2	27	52	77	102	=
3	Craftsmanship	3	28	53	78	103	=
4	Creative Communication	4	29	54	79	104	=
5	Discernment	5	30	55	80	105	=
6	Evangelism	6	31	56	81	106	=
7	Exhortation or Encouragement	7	32	57	82	107	=
8	Faith	8	33	58	83	108	=

9	Giving	9	34	59	84	109	=
10	Healing	10	35	60	85	110	=
11	Helping	11	36	61	86	111	=
12	Hospitality	12	37	62	87	112	=
13	Celibacy	13	38	63	88	113	=
14	Interpretation	14	39	64	89	114	=
15	Knowledge	15	40	65	90	115	=
16	Leadership	16	41	66	91	116	=
17	Mercy or Compassion	17	42	67	92	117	=
18	Miracles	18	43	68	93	118	=
19	Voluntary Poverty	19	44	69	94	119	=
20	Pastor-Teacher	20	45	70	95	120	=
21	Prophecy	21	46	71	96	121	=
22	Service	22	47	72	97	122	=
23	Teaching	23	48	73	98	123	=
24	Tongues	24	49	74	99	124	=

| 25 | Wisdom | 25 | 50 | 75 | 100 | 125 | = |

PLEASE NOTE:

This test is not infallible.

Confirmation comes only through repeated cycles of practice and reassessment.

DOMINANT GIFTS

_____

_____

_____

_____

_____

ABOUT THE AUTHOR

Jeremy Myers is a popular author, blogger, podcaster, and Bible teacher who lives in Oregon with his wife and three daughters. He primarily writes at RedeemingGod.com, where he seeks to help liberate people from the shackles of religion. His site also provides an online discipleship group where thousands of like-minded people discuss life and theology and encourage each other to follow Jesus into the world.

If you appreciated the content of this book, would you consider recommending it to your friends and leaving a review online? Thanks!

JOIN JEREMY MYERS AND LEARN MORE

Take Bible and theology courses by joining Jeremy at
RedeemingGod.com/join/
Receive updates about free books, discounted books, and new books by joining Jeremy at
RedeemingGod.com/read-books/

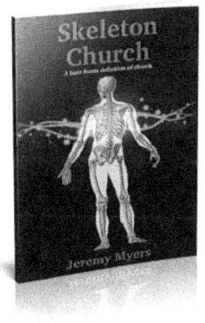

SKELETON CHURCH: A BARE-BONES DEFINITION OF CHURCH (PREFACE TO THE CLOSE YOUR CHURCH FOR GOOD BOOK SERIES)

The church has a skeleton which is identical in all types of churches. Unity and peace can develop in Christianity if we recognize this skeleton as the simple, bare-bones definition of church. But when we focus on the outer trappings—the skin, hair, and eye color, the clothes, the muscle tone, and other outward appearances—division and strife form within the church.

Let us return to the skeleton church and grow in unity once again.

REVIEWS

I worried about buying another book that aimed at reducing things to a simple minimum, but the associations of the author along with the price gave me reason to hope and means to see. I really liked this book. First, because it wasn't identical to what other simple church people are saying. He adds unique elements that are worth reading. Second, the size is small enough to read, think, and pray about without getting lost. –Abel Barba

In *Skeleton Church*, Jeremy Myers makes us rethink church. For Myers, the church isn't a style of worship, a row of pews, or even a building. Instead, the church is the people of God, which provides the basic skeletal structure of the church. The muscles, parts, and flesh of the church are how we carry Jesus' mission into our own neighborhoods in our own unique ways. This eBook will make you see the church differently. –Travis Mamone

This book gets back to the basics of the New Testament church—who we are as Christians and what our perspective should be in the world we live in today. Jeremy cuts away all the institutional layers of a church and gets to the heart of our purpose as Christians in the world we live in and how to affect the people around us with God heart and view in mind. Not a physical church in mind. It was a great book and I have read it twice now. –Vaughn Bender

The Skeleton Church … Oh. My. Word. Why aren't more people reading this!? It was well-written, explained everything beautifully, and it was one of the best explanations of how God intended for church to be. Not to mention an easy read! The author took it all apart, the church, and showed us how it should be. He made it real. If you are searching to find something or someone to show you what God intended for the church, this is the book you need to read. –Ericka

PUT SERVICE BACK INTO THE CHURCH SERVICE (VOLUME 2 IN THE CLOSE YOUR CHURCH FOR GOOD BOOK SERIES)

Churches around the world are trying to revitalize their church services. There is almost nothing they will not try. Some embark on multi-million dollar building campaigns while others sell their buildings to plant home churches. Some hire celebrity pastors to attract crowds of people, while others hire no clergy so that there can be open sharing in the service.

Yet despite everything churches have tried, few focus much time, money, or energy on the one thing that churches are supposed to be doing: loving and serving others like Jesus.

Put Service Back into the Church Service challenges readers to follow a few simple principles and put a few ideas into practice which will help churches of all types and sizes make serving others the primary emphasis of a church service.

REVIEWS

Jeremy challenges church addicts, those addicted to an unending parade of church buildings, church services, Bible studies, church programs and more to follow Jesus into our communities, communities filled with lonely, hurting people and BE the church, loving the people in our world with the love of Jesus. Do we need another training program, another seminar, another church building, a remodeled church building, more staff, updated music, or does our world need us, the followers of Jesus, to BE the church in the world? The book is well-written, challenging and a book that really can make a difference not only in our churches, but also and especially in our neighborhoods and communities. –Charles Epworth

I just finished *Put Service Back Into Church Service* by Jeremy Myers, and as with his others books I have read on the church, it was very challenging. For those who love Jesus, but are questioning the function of the traditional brick and mortar church, and their role in it, this is a must read. It may be a bit unsettling to the reader who is still entrenched in traditional "church," but it will make you think, and possibly re-evaluate your role in the church. Get this book, and all others on the church by Jeremy. –Ward Kelly

DYING TO RELIGION AND EMPIRE (VOLUME 3 IN THE CLOSE YOUR CHURCH FOR GOOD BOOK SERIES)

Could Christianity exist without religious rites or legal rights? In *Dying to Religion and Empire*, I not only answer this question with an emphatic "Yes!" but argue that if the church is going to thrive in the coming decades, we must give up our religious rites and legal rights.

Regarding religious rites, I call upon the church to abandon the quasi-magical traditions of water baptism and the Lord's Supper and transform or redeem these practices so that they reflect the symbolic meaning and intent which they had in New Testament times.

Furthermore, the church has become far too dependent upon certain legal rights for our continued existence. Ideas such as the right to life, liberty, and the pursuit of happiness are not conducive to living as the people of God who are called to follow Jesus into servanthood and death. Also, reliance upon the freedom of speech, the freedom of assembly, and other such freedoms as established by the Bill of Rights have made the church a servant of the state rather than a servant of God and the gospel. Such freedoms must be forsaken if we are going to live within the rule and reign of God on earth.

This book not only challenges religious and political liberals but conservatives as well. It is a call to leave behind the comfortable religion we know, and follow Jesus into the uncertain and wild ways of radical discipleship. To rise and live in the reality of God's Kingdom, we must first die to religion and empire.

REVIEWS

Jeremy is one of the freshest, freest authors out there— and you need to hear what he has to say. This book is startling and new in thought and conclusion. Are the "sacraments" inviolate? Why? Do you worship at a secular altar? Conservative? Liberal? Be prepared to open your eyes. Mr. Myers will not let you keep sleeping!

Jeremy Myers is one or the most thought provoking authors that I read, this book has really helped me to look outside the box and start thinking how can I make more sense of my relationship with Christ and how can I show others in a way that impacts them the way that Jesus' disciples impacted their world. Great book, great author. –Brett Hotchkiss

THE DEATH AND RESURRECTION OF THE CHURCH (VOLUME 1 IN THE CLOSE YOUR CHURCH FOR GOOD BOOK SERIES)

In a day when many are looking for ways to revitalize the church, Jeremy Myers argues that the church should die … so that it can rise again.

This is not only because of the universal principle that death precedes resurrection, but also because the church has adopted certain Satanic values and goals and the only way to break free from our enslavement to these values is to die.

But death will not be the end of the church, just as death was not the end of Jesus. If the church follows Jesus into death, and even to the hellish places on earth, it is only then that the church will rise again to new life and vibrancy in the Kingdom of God.

REVIEWS

I have often thought on the church and how its acceptance of corporate methods and assimilation of cultural media mores taints its mission but Jeremy Myers eloquently captures in words the true crux of the matter—that the church is not a social club for do-gooders but to disseminate the good news to all the nooks and crannies in the world and particularly and primarily those bastions in the reign of evil. That the "gates of Hell" Jesus pronounces indicate that the church is in an offensive, not defensive, posture as gates are defensive structures.

I must confess that in reading I was inclined to be in agreement as many of the same thinkers that Myers riffs upon have influenced me also—Walter Wink, Robert Farrar Capon, Greg Boyd, NT Wright, etc. So as I read, I frequently nodded my head in agreement. –GN Trifanaff

The book is well written, easy to understand, organized and consistent thoughts. It rightfully makes the reader at least think about things as … is "the way we have always done it" necessarily the Biblical or Christ-like way, or is it in fact very sinful?! I would recommend the book for pastors and church officers; those who have the most moving-and-shaking clout to implement changes, or keep things the same. –Joel M. Wilson

Absolutely phenomenal. Unless we let go of everything Adamic in our nature, we cannot embrace anything Christlike. For the church to die, we the individual temples must dig our graves. It is a must read for all who take issues about the body of Christ seriously. – Mordecai Petersburg

CHURCH IS MORE THAN BODIES, BUCKS, & BRICKS (VOLUME 4 IN THE CLOSE YOUR CHURCH FOR GOOD BOOK SERIES)

Many people define church as a place and time where people gather, a way for ministry money to be given and spent, and a building in which people regularly meet on Sunday mornings.

In this book, author and blogger Jeremy Myers shows that church is more than bodies, bucks, and bricks.

Church is the people of God who follow Jesus into the world, and we can be the church no matter how many people we are with, no matter the size of our church budget, and regardless of whether we have a church building or not.

By abandoning our emphasis on more people, bigger budgets, and newer buildings, we may actually liberate the church to better follow Jesus into the world.

REVIEWS

This book does more than just identify issues that have been bothering me about church as we know it, but it goes into history and explains how we got here. In this way it is similar to Viola's *Pagan Christianity*, but I found it a much more enjoyable read. Jeremy goes into more detail on the three issues he covers as well as giving a lot of practical advice on how to remedy these situations. –Portent

Since I returned from Africa 20 years ago I have struggled with going to church back in the States. This book helped me not feel guilty and has helped me process this struggle. It is challenging and overflows with practical suggestions. He loves the church despite its imperfections and suggests ways to break the bondage we find ourselves in. –Truealian

Jeremy Meyers always writes a challenging book ... It seems the American church (as a whole) is very comfortable with the way things are ... The challenge is to get out of the brick and mortar buildings and stagnant programs and minister to the needy in person with funds in hand to meet their needs especially to the widows and orphans as we are directed in the scriptures. –GGTexas

WHAT IS PRAYER? HOW TO PRAY TO GOD THE WAY YOU TALK TO A FRIEND

Stop worrying about how to pray, and just start praying!

This book reveals one simple truth: That you already know how to pray!

Once you discover that you know how to pray as revealed in this book, you will also discover that you already know what to pray for and how to see more answers to your prayers.

Read this book and find the freedom and power in your prayer life you have always longed for.

REVIEWS

I LOVE THIS BOOK! J. D. Myers has done such a great job of putting into clear words all the things about prayer that have been developing in my thoughts for years. If you wonder what praying means, if you wonder what praying should be like, or even if you wonder why on earth people should even pray, READ THIS. This is, so far, my favorite Jeremy Myers book. Not too deep, not too theological, not even too serious—though the subject matter is serious and is dealt with seriously. The tone of the writing is perfect, and the advice is genuine and extremely worthwhile. EXCELLENT BOOK. –B. Shuford

The book appears to be too simple but as you progress Jeremy covers many aspects of prayer in a way that is like a breath of fresh air. The book ends up being a natural encouragement to talking to God as a friend. I definitely recommend this book as the reader will definitely benefit from it. Not just intellectually but practically as well. Prayer will change from a chore or obligation to a pleasurable interaction with God. My heart was so filled with joy while reading this book. Jeremy you've reminded me once more that as you walk with Jesus and spend time in His presence, He talks to you and reveals Himself through the Scriptures. –Pete Nellmapius

When you finish this short book, you will know two things: 1) How easy it is to pray, and 2) How dangerous it is to pray! Prayer changes things, I used to hear. I heard in Jeremy's book, prayer changes me. I especially appreciated a page where Jeremy discusses how often we are the answers to our own prayers. I saw a "vision" of someone I am now praying for, and the Lord looking at him and looking at me, as if to say, "Well, I've put you in his life, haven't I?" A beautiful book. –Carol Roberts

WHAT ARE THE SPIRITUAL GIFTS? DISCOVER YOUR SPIRITUAL GIFTS AND HOW TO USE THEM

Let's cut through all the nonsense about spiritual gifts.

Here is a down-to-earth discussion about what the spiritual gifts are, how to discover your spiritual gifts, and how to use them in the real world.

This book answers such questions as:

-Why did God give spiritual gifts?
-What are the spiritual gifts?
-How can I know my spiritual gifts?
-Are some spiritual gifts better than others?
-What are the dangers of the spiritual gifts?
-Have some spiritual gifts ceased?
-What about the spiritual gift of tongues?
-How can I embrace and use my spiritual gifts?

This book also includes a 125-question Spiritual Gift Inventory test.

REVIEWS

J. D. Myers' title *What are the Spiritual Gifts?* is perfect and delivers in identifying spiritual gifts mentioned in the Bible and how to personally discover your gifts to help others. Those who grew up going to church are very familiar with the topic of spiritual gifts. I would encourage those who didn't grow up in the church to read as well if wishing God's help to make a difference in the lives of others through your talents, interests, skills, and abilities.

Those who grew up going to church want to understand more about gifts such as tongues, prophecy, etc. The book does a great job of discussing whether some gifts no longer exist and how we can understand such gifts. –Mike Edwards

Jeremy Myers pulls out all the distractions that keep us from understanding our spiritual gifts given to us from a loving God. –David DeMille

Why do we think spiritual gifts are a mystery? According to Mr. Myers, we shouldn't. In a simple presentation, he offers his view of the Spiritual Gifts, and some of the characteristics for each of them (with strengths and pitfalls). The book also suggests five simple ways of discerning your gift, including a test in the end. While a test can be useful, much more useful are the other ways, like asking yourself what you think other Christians should do more … –The Pilgrimm

WHAT IS FAITH? HOW TO KNOW THAT YOU BELIEVE

You might know what you believe … but do you know *that* you believe?

While many Christians know that they are supposed to believe, they don't know if they actually do believe.

Stop wondering if you have false faith, spurious faith, temporary faith, intellectual faith, or head faith instead of heart faith. All such terms are unhelpful and unbiblical, and cause many Christians to wonder if they have truly believed.

By reading this book, you will not only discover how faith works, but also how to know that you believe.

This book also answers some of your most pressing questions about faith, such as the relationship between faith and works, whether or not God gives the gift of faith, and how it is possible to be certain about your faith. This book also provides explanations for several key Bible passages about faith.

REVIEWS

Once again, Jeremy Myers brings clarity to a topic that many are confused about. Faith is such a difficult subject for some. Do I have enough faith? I have doubts, how does that affect my faith? What is child-like faith? Do I have little faith, small faith or great faith? Many Christians put faith in their faith. Jeremy does a wonderful job of explaining these concepts and more in this book. Having read, and listened to, many of Jeremy's books and podcasts, I can attest to his in-depth knowledge and proficient writing style. Whether you agree with all his points or not, you will come away with more knowledge and understanding after reading this book. This is a book that I would recommend all new Christians read and be used in discipleship classes. –Michael Wilson

I was privileged to receive an advanced copy and am happy to report that the book was enormously helpful. Having a firm foundation of knowing that you are fully loved and accepted by God is essential to spiritual growth, and in our day the greatest impediment to having this firm foundation is wondering, "Have I really believed?" Jeremy helps the reader answer this question. To any Christian who is unsure of your foundation, this book is for you! – K. E. Young

WHAT IS HELL? THE TRUTH ABOUT HELL AND HOW TO AVOID IT

Have you ever wondered if you are going to hell?

Many people are terrified about going to hell when they die. And for good reason. If hell is a fiery torture chamber where lost souls scream in agony for all eternity, everybody should be worried about meeting such a terrible fate.

But is this really what the Bible teaches about hell?

In *What is Hell?*, author J. D. Myers answers your most pressing questions about hell. After summarizing the three common views about hell, this book presents a fourth view. Myers defends this alternative view by showing how the concept of hell evolved over time, and then considers eight terms from Scripture that have traditionally been equated with hell.

As you read, you will learn the truth about hell. You will discover what hell is, where hell is, how you can avoid going to hell, and how you can rescue people who are in hell.

The book includes an Appendix which explains most of the key biblical texts that have traditionally been used to defend the doctrine of hell.

Read this book to be delivered from both the fear and fire of hell.

REVIEWS

My eyes have been opened and my understanding has changed for the better. I believe this book is a must-read for most Christians. The reason for the death of Jesus has also become so much clearer to me from reading this book. It just makes more sense now. This book will be used by me as a reference in the future so I will read it again. –Pete Nellmapius

This may be Jeremy's best book yet! What is more important than defending God's character? Jeremy shows in a scholarly but readable way that the traditional understanding of Hell does not actually exist. The Great News is that you don't have to defend or imagine God tortures people for beliefs while living for a short time on earth. – Mike Edwards - Writing at: What-God-May-Really-Be-Like

I've enjoyed every book of Mr. Myers until this one. But this one I LOVED! The book goes through great lengths in explaining how the Kingdom of Heaven that Jesus came to bring unto our world is opposed to the Kingdom of Hell that rules the Earth. And how Hell has been under siege ever since. –ThePilgrimm

Jeremy Myers does an exceptional job explaining the critical passages of the bible that are typically used to teach that there is a hell waiting for all of us sinners. He always is exceptional in explaining the original text and making it easy to understand. This is a great book if you are trying to understand this topic and I feel you will come away with a much greater understanding. –Jim Maus

NOTHING BUT THE BLOOD OF JESUS: HOW THE SACRIFICE OF JESUS SAVES THE WORLD FROM SIN

Do you have difficulties reconciling God's behavior in the Old Testament with that of Jesus in the New?

Do you find yourself trying to rationalize God's violent demeanor in the Bible to unbelievers or even to yourself?

Does it seem disconcerting that God tells us not to kill others but He then takes part in some of the bloodiest wars and vindictive genocides in history?

The answer to all such questions is found in Jesus on the cross. By focusing your eyes on Jesus Christ and Him crucified, you come to understand that God was never angry at human sinners, and that no blood sacrifice was ever needed to purchase God's love, forgiveness, grace, and mercy.

In *Nothing but the Blood of Jesus*, J. D. Myers shows how the death of Jesus on the cross reveals the truth about the five concepts of sin, law, sacrifice, scapegoating, and bloodshed. After carefully defining each, this book shows how these definitions provide clarity on numerous biblical texts.

REVIEWS

Building on his previous book, "The Atonement of God," the work of René Girard and a solid grounding in the Scriptures, Jeremy Myers shares fresh and challenging insights with us about sin, law, sacrifice, scapegoating and blood. This book reveals to us how truly precious the blood of Jesus is and the way of escaping the cycle of blame, rivalry, scapegoating, sacrifice and violence that has plagued humanity since the time of Cain and Abel. *Nothing but the Blood of Jesus* is an important and timely literary contribution to a world desperately in need of the non-violent message of Jesus. –Wesley Rostoll

My heart was so filled with joy while reading this book. Jeremy you've reminded me once more that as you walk with Jesus and spend time in His presence, He talks to you and reveals Himself through the Scriptures. –Reader

THE ATONEMENT OF GOD: BUILDING YOUR THEOLOGY ON A CRUCIVISION OF GOD

After reading this book, you will never read the Bible the same way again.

By reading this book, you will learn to see God in a whole new light. You will also learn to see yourself in a whole new light, and learn to live life in a whole new way.

The book begins with a short explanation of the various views of the atonement, including an explanation and defense of the "Non-Violent View" of the atonement. This view argues that God did not need or demand the death of Jesus in order to forgive sins. In fact, God has never been angry with us at all, but has always loved and always forgiven.

Following this explanation of the atonement, J. D. Myers takes you on a journey through 10 areas of theology which are radically changed and transformed by the Non-Violent view of the atonement. Read this book, and let your life and theology look more and more like Jesus Christ!

REVIEWS

> Outstanding book! Thank you for helping me understand "Crucivision" and the "Non-Violent Atonement." Together, they help it all make sense and fit so well into my personal thinking about God. I

am encouraged to be truly free to love and forgive, because God has always loved and forgiven without condition, because Christ exemplified this grace on the Cross, and because the Holy Spirit is in the midst of all life, continuing to show the way through people like you. –Samuel R. Mayer

This book gives another view of the doctrines we have been taught all of our lives. And this actually makes more sense than what we have heard. I myself have had some of these thoughts but couldn't quite make the sense of it all by myself. J.D. Myers helped me answer some questions and settle some confusion for my doctrinal views. This is truly a refreshing read. Jesus really is the demonstration of who God is and God is much easier to understand than being so mean and vindictive in the Old Testament. The tension between the wrath of God and His justice and the love of God are eased when reading this understanding of the atonement. Read with an open mind and enjoy! –Clare N. Bez

THE RE-JUSTIFICATION OF GOD: A STUDY OF ROMANS 9:10-24

Romans 9 has been a theological battleground for centuries. Scholars from all perspectives have debated whether Paul is teaching corporate or individual election, whether or not God truly hates Esau, and how to understand the hardening of Pharaoh's heart. Both sides have accused the other of misrepresenting God.

In this book, J. D. Myers presents a mediating position. Gleaning from both Calvinistic and Arminian insights into Romans 9, J. D. Myers presents a beautiful portrait of God as described by the pen of the Apostle Paul.

Here is a way to read Romans 9 which allows God to remain sovereign and free, but also allows our theology to avoid the deterministic tendencies which have entrapped certain systems of the past.

Read this book and—maybe for the first time—learn to see God the way Paul saw Him.

REVIEWS

> Fantastic read! Jeremy Myers has a gift for seeing things from outside of the box and making it easy to understand for the rest of us. The Re -Justification of God provides a fresh and insightful look into Romans 9:10-24 by interpreting it within the context of chap-

ters 9-11 and then fitting it into the framework of Paul's entire epistle as well. Jeremy manages to provide a solid theological exegesis on a widely misunderstood portion of scripture without it sounding to academic. Most importantly, it provides us with a better view and understanding of who God is. If I had a list of ten books that I thought every Christian should read, this one would be on the list.
—Wesley Rostoll

I loved this book! It made me cry and fall in love with God all over again. Romans is one of my favorite books, but now my eyes have been opened to what Paul was really saying. I knew in my heart that God was the good guy, but J. D. Myers provided the analysis to prove the text. … I can with great confidence read the difficult chapters of Romans, and my furrowed brow is eased. Thank you, J. D. Myers. I love God, even more and am so grateful that his is so longsuffering in his perfect love! Well done. —Treinhart

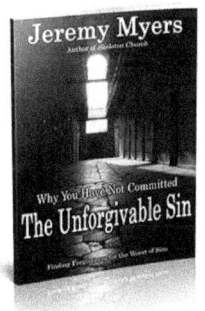

WHY YOU HAVE NOT COM-MITTED THE UNFORGIVABLE SIN: FINDING FORGIVENESS FOR THE WORST OF SINS

Are you afraid that you have committed the unforgivable sin?

In this book, you will learn what this sin is and why you have not committed it. After surveying the various views about blasphemy against the Holy Spirit and examining Matthew 12:31-32, you will learn what the sin is and how it is committed.

As a result of reading this book, you will gain freedom from the fear of committing the worst of all sins, and learn how much God loves you!

REVIEWS

> This book addressed things I have struggled and felt pandered to for years, and helped to bring wholeness to my heart again. – Natalie Fleming

> A great read, on a controversial subject; biblical, historical and contextually treated to give the greatest understanding. May be the best on this subject (and there is very few) ever written. – Tony Vance

> You must read this book. Forgiveness is necessary to see your blessings. So if you purchase this book, [you will have] no regrets. – Virtuous Woman

> Jeremy Myers covers this most difficult topic thoroughly and with

great compassion. –J. Holland

Wonderful explication of the unpardonable sin. God loves you more than you know. May Jesus Christ be with you always. – Robert M Sawin III

Excellent book! Highly recommend for anyone who has anxiety and fear about having committed the unforgivable sin. –William Tom

As someone who is constantly worried that they have disappointed or offended God, this book was, quite literally, a "Godsend." I thought I had committed this sin as I swore against the Holy Spirit in my mind. It only started after reading the verse about it in the Bible. The swear words against Him came into my mind over and over and I couldn't seem to stop no matter how much I prayed. I was convinced I was going to hell and cried constantly. I was extremely worried and depressed. This book has allowed me to breathe again, to have hope again. Thank you, Jeremy. I will read and re-read. I believe this book was definitely God inspired. I only wish I had found it sooner. –Sue

ADVENTURES IN FISHING (FOR MEN)

Adventures in Fishing (for Men) is a satirical look at evangelism and church growth strategies.

Using fictional accounts from his attempts to become a world-famous fisherman, Jeremy Myers shows how many of the evangelism and church growth strategies of today do little to actually reach the world for Jesus Christ.

Adventures in Fishing (for Men) pokes fun at some of the popular evangelistic techniques and strategies endorsed and practiced by many Christians in today's churches. The stories in this book show in humorous detail how little we understand the culture that surrounds us or how to properly reach people with the gospel of Jesus Christ. The story also shows how much time, energy, and money goes into evangelism preparation and training with the end result being that churches rarely accomplish any actual evangelism.

REVIEWS

I found *Adventures in Fishing (For Men)* quite funny! Jeremy Myers does a great job shining the light on some of the more common practices in Evangelism today. His allegory gently points to the foolishness that is found within a system that takes the preaching of the gospel and tries to reduce it to a simplified formula. A formula that takes what should be an organic, Spirit led experience and turns it into a gospel that is nutritionally benign.

If you have ever EE'd someone you may find Myers' book offensive, but if you have come to the place where you realize that Evangelism isn't a matter of a script and checklists, then you might benefit from this light-hearted peek at Evangelism today. –Jennifer L. Davis

Adventures in Fishing (for Men) is good book in understanding evangelism to be more than just being a set of methods or to do list to follow. –Ashok Daniel

CHRISTMAS REDEMPTION: WHY CHRISTIANS SHOULD CELEBRATE A PAGAN HOLIDAY

Christmas Redemption looks at some of the symbolism and traditions of Christmas, including gifts, the Christmas tree, and even Santa Claus and shows how all of these can be celebrated and enjoyed by Christians as a true and accurate reflection of the gospel.

Though Christmas used to be a pagan holiday, it has been redeemed by Jesus.

If you have been told that Christmas is a pagan holiday and is based on the Roman festival of Saturnalia, or if you have been told that putting up a Christmas tree is idolatrous, or if you have been told that Santa Claus is Satanic and teaches children to be greedy, then you must read this book! In it, you will learn that all of these Christmas traditions have been redeemed by Jesus and are good and healthy ways of celebrating the truth of the gospel and the grace of Jesus Christ.

REVIEWS

Too many times we as Christians want to condemn nearly everything around us and in so doing become much like the Pharisees and religious leaders that Jesus encountered. I recommend this book to everyone who has concerns of how and why we celebrate Christmas. I recommend it to those who do not have any qualms in celebrating but may not know the history of Christmas. I recommend this book to everyone, no matter who or where you are, no matter your background or beliefs, no matter whether you are young or old. –David H.

Very informative book dealing with the roots of our modern Christmas traditions. The Biblical teaching on redemption is excellent! Highly recommended. –Tamara

This is a wonderful book full of hope and joy. The book explains where Christmas traditions originated and how they have been changed and been adapted over the years. The hope that the grace that is hidden in the celebrations will turn more hearts to the Lord's call is very evident. Jeremy Myers has given us a lovely gift this Christmas. His insights will lift our hearts and remain with us a long time. –Janet Cardoza

I love how the author uses multiple sources to back up his opinions. He doesn't just use bible verses, he goes back into the history of the topics (pagan rituals, Santa, etc.) as well. Great book! –Jenna G.

JOIN JEREMY MYERS AND LEARN MORE

Take Bible and theology courses by joining Jeremy at
RedeemingGod.com/join/

Receive updates about free books, discounted books,
and new books by joining Jeremy at
RedeemingGod.com/read-books/

www.ingramcontent.com/pod-product-compliance
Lightning Source LLC
Chambersburg PA
CBHW071952110526
44592CB00012B/1062